FAIRBAIRN
AND RELATIONAL THEORY

FAIRBAIRN
AND RELATIONAL THEORY

Edited by

Frederico Pereira & David E. Scharff

KARNAC

LONDON   NEW YORK

First published in 2002 by
H. Karnac (Books) Ltd.
6 Pembroke Buildings, London NW10 6RE

A subsidiary of Other Press LLC, New York

British Library Cataloguing in Publication Data

A C.I.P. for this book is available from the British Library

 ISBN 1 85575 273 5

10 9 8 7 6 5 4 3 2 1

Edited, designed, and produced by Communication Crafts

Printed in Great Britain

www.karnacbooks.com

In memory of Stephen Mitchell

*His prolific and thoughtful work has paved the way for the
acceptance of many of the ideas pioneered by Ronald Fairbairn.
His untimely death in December 2000 has deprived us of
his continuing friendship and of the fruits of further contributions
of a wonderful psychoanalytic pioneer*

CONTENTS

ACKNOWLEDGEMENTS

The editors would like to thank the contributors to this volume for their generosity and cooperation in participating in the Lisbon conference and in the preparation of the volume. In addition, we are grateful to Leena Häkkinen of Karnac and Michael Moskowitz of Other Press for the confidence they have shown in publishing the book. Klara King copy-edited the manuscript with great skill and clarity. Mary Thomas and Anna Innes helped in Washington, D.C., while Prof. Dr Carlos Simões and Sara de Carvalho worked on the conference and the book in Lisbon. We are grateful also to *Petrogal, Caixa Geral de Depósitos e Tranquilidade*, which sponsored the Conference.

ABOUT THE EDITORS AND CONTRIBUTORS

ELLINOR FAIRBAIRN BIRTLES has a B.A. in History of Ideas and is co-editor of *From Instinct to Self: Selected Papers of W. R. D. Fairbairn.*

JAMES S. GROTSTEIN, M.D., is a Clinical Professor of Psychiatry at UCLA School of Medicine; a Training and Supervising Analyst at the Los Angeles Psychoanalytic Society/Institute and at the Psychoanalytic Center of California, Los Angeles; a psychoanalyst in private practice in West Los Angeles.

J. ALAN HARROW is a Psychoanalytic Psychotherapist and former Director of the Scottish Institute of Human Relations.

OTTO F. KERNBERG is Professor of Psychiatry, Weill-Cornell Medical College; Director, Personality Disorders Institute, New York Presbyterian Hospital, Westchester Division; Training and Supervising Analyst, Columbia University, Center for Psychoanalytic Training and Research.

ANTÓNIO COIMBRA DE MATOS is a Training Analyst and President of the Educational Committee, Portuguese Psychoanalytic Society; former Director of the Child Mental Health Center, Lisbon; Professor at the Higher Institute of Applied Psychology, Lisbon.

STEPHEN A. MITCHELL [1946–2000], Ph.D., was the founding editor of *Psychoanalytic Dialogues*. He was a Training and Supervising Analyst at the William Alanson White Institute, New York, and a supervisor and faculty member at the New York University Postdoctoral Program in Psychotherapy and Psychoanalysis.

FREDERICO PEREIRA is a Training Analyst; President and member of the Training Committee of the Portuguese Psychoanalytic Society; Director of the Higher Institute of Applied Psychology, Lisbon; a member of the Working Party on Psychoanalytic Education, European Federation of Psychoanalysis.

EMÍLIO SALGUEIRO is a Child and Adolescent Psychiatrist in private practice; Training Analyst of the Sociedade Portuguesa de Psicanálise; Associate Professor of the Instituto Superior de Psicologia Aplicada de Lisboa.

DAVID E. SCHARFF is Co-Director of the International Institute of Object Relations Therapy, Chevy Chase, Maryland; Clinical Professor of Psychiatry at Georgetown University and at the Uniformed Services University of the Health Sciences; a Teaching Analyst, Washington Psychoanalytic Institute.

ANNE TAIT is a Consultant Liaison Psychiatrist in the Regional Infectious Diseases Unit, Edinburgh, and a member of the Scottish Institute of Human Relations and of the Scottish Association of Psychoanalytical Psychotherapists.

MARY TWYMAN, M.A. (Oxon) was educated at St. Hugh's College, Oxford, and at the London School of Economics. She is a member of the British Psychoanalytical Society, where she teaches a course on The Independent Analysts of the British Society, including Fairbairn, and is an Honorary Lecturer at the Psychoanalysis Unit, University College London.

HENRI VERMOREL, Psychiatrist and Psychoanalyst, is a Training Analyst at the Paris Psychoanalytic Society; Doctor in Clinical Psychology; a former teacher at the University of Savoie (Chambéry).

FAIRBAIRN
AND RELATIONAL THEORY

Introduction

David E. Scharff & Frederico Pereira

I

In 1989, Fairbairn's biographer, John D. Sutherland, wrote:

> [Fairbairn] was the first to propose in a systematic manner the Copernican change of founding the psychoanalytic theory of human personality on the experiences within social relationships instead of on the discharge of instinctual tensions originating solely in the individual. In short, he replaced the closed-system standpoint of nineteenth-century science with the open-systems that were evolved by the middle of the present century to account for the development of living organisms, in which the contribution of the environment has to be considered at all times. [Sutherland, 1989, p. 162]

Fairbairn produced a paradigm shift in the theory and the practice of psychoanalysis. His extensive grounding in philosophy (E. F. Birtles, chapter 3, this volume; Fairbairn, 1994a, 1994b) contributed to his capacity to arrive at an independent view of psychoanalysis: his mind was not closed by slavish adherence to orthodoxy, despite his profound respect for Freud and Melanie Klein. Living in

1

Edinburgh, Fairbairn might have experienced geographic isolation from London and other centres of psychoanalysis, especially since he worked in a local climate of academic antagonism to psycho-analysis. What might have been a handicap became, instead, an important and creative source of heterodoxy.

In this cultural and geographic situation, Fairbairn created an object relations theory of the personality that is still the basis for modern relational theories and that has contributed substantially to the modifications of analytic technique that go beyond "classi-cal" interpretation, and have contributed to a new and enriched understanding of transference and countertransference and to our modern notions of growth in psychoanalysis.

Philosophically, Fairbairn's new theory constituted an implicit critique of Freud's Platonism, of the idealization of discrete parts or functions of human capacity considered in isolation which therefore led to Freud's acceptance of mind–body dualism and a view of man as being in fundamental conflict both with his own body and with society. Fairbairn embraced the Aristotelian line of discourse, and especially the ideas of Hegel—a line of thought attentive to the importance of the relatedness between the indi-vidual and the environment.

> [I]n Hegel's account of psychology, the innate capacities for language, symbolization and rational thought are dependent for their development on an adequate environment . The Dia-lectic exchange between the Subject and the Other results in a relationship, or synthesis, which forms the basis for man's ca-pacity for language and thought. Because subject–object rela-tionships encompass a progressive epistemological element, meaning and value, not gratification, provide Fairbairn with primary motivation. [Birtles, 1998, p. 37]

Fairbairn's use of this philosophical train of thought over the years led to his theoretical model as well as to an articulation with mod-ern paradigms in philosophy and science—a rapprochement dem-onstrated in this volume in chapter 3 on postmodernist views by Fairbairn's daughter, Ellinor Fairbairn Birtles, and chapter 11 on chaos theory by David Scharff.

But Fairbairn's thinking is about psychoanalytic theory and practice, where he contributes broadly in the areas of develop-ment, relationships, the building of psychic structure through in-

ternalization, schizoid phenomena, the organization of endopsychic structure, and the growth of the self—an area developed more
explicitly in the work of Guntrip and Sutherland (Harrow, chapter
10, this volume). His work leads to and is contemporaneous with
broad shifts in therapeutic process adumbrated in his landmark
paper on practice, "On the Nature and Aims of Psychoanalytical
Treatment" (1958).

In the area of development, Fairbairn's statement that "there is
an ego from birth" (1963a) constituted a radical critique of Freud's
concept of primary narcissism because the statement posits that,
from the beginning, the infant is related and open to influence from
primary caretakers. From the beginning, the child as a whole person seeks other whole persons and only moves to close itself off
from external influence as a result of inadequate responsiveness
from the other: "the child comes to feel that love relationships with
external objects in general are bad, or at least precarious. The net
result is that the child tends to transfer his relations with objects to
the realm of inner reality" (Fairbairn, 1940, p. 18).

The idea of the child's openness to the world from the beginning has been confirmed by psychoanalytic developmental research (Stern, 1985). The child's principal interest is to meet an
other, and as the self psychologists and, lately, the neurobiologists
have shown, to develop a relationship in which the other is in
attunement with the child (Schore, 1994).

Fairbairn asserts that libido is primarily object seeking, not primarily pleasure seeking. He wrote:

> Although Freud's whole system of thought was concerned
> with object-relationships, he adhered theoretically to the prin-
> ciple that libido is primarily concerned with pleasure-seeking,
> i.e. with relief of its own tension. This means that for him libido
> is theoretically directionless, although some of his statements
> undoubtedly imply the contrary. By contrast, I adhere to the
> principle that libido is primarily object-seeking, and that the
> tension which demands relief is the tension of object-seeking
> tendencies. This means that for me libido has direction. [1946,
> p. 149]

Of course, it is possible to attempt a synthesis between Fairbairn
and Freud's drive theories, as Otto Kernberg does when he maintains a Freudian position about drives but sees them as psychologi-

cal motivation with an affective component (Kernberg, 1980; chapter 1, this volume; Kernberg & Scharff, 1998).

The Fairbairnian child seeks mutuality with objects. When the object inevitably fails or in some measure rejects the child, that deprivation organizes both the child's suffering and the first defences against suffering. In our own words, we can say that the failures of mutuality, of the adult being present to the child, prompts the internalization of the object as bad. This concept of internalization is, in fact, one of Fairbairn's most important contributions to understanding the construction of the internal world. Recent observational research (Stern, 1985) has led to a revision of Fairbairn's idea that the child only internalizes experience with the rejecting parental object. We now see that children internalize all experience, and it is the splitting into good and bad that represents the first sorting of affective experience (Scharff, 1994).

Nevertheless, we can still see that when the parents are emotionally absent, toxic, intrusive, or psychologically disorganized, the process of internalization of bad objects taken in from the outside world occurs in order to create and to preserve an illusion of the goodness of the external parents. In the face of rejection or persecution by the external objects, the child then often performs another psychic manoeuvre described by Fairbairn: the child unconsciously decides that the parents are not bad; it the child itself who is bad. It is better to be bad and live with good, than to be good and live with the evil, wrote Fairbairn (1943). Through internalizing these bad objects and preserving the good objects outside, his *unconditional badness* is transformed in *conditional badness*. Now, if he can only satisfy the external "good" object, things will improve. This notion constitutes the *moral defence*, one of Fairbairn's most important contributions (see de Matos, chapter 4, this volume).

Fairbairn's developmental schema centres around the individual's transition from infantile to mature dependence. The use of what he termed *transitional techniques* is designed to deal with internal object relations during this slow growth, to protect the developing ego during its long period of attenuated dependence. These techniques include phobic, hysterical, obsessional, and paranoid organizations, which he saw not as syndromes but as techniques of dealing with internal object relations. In the same vein Fairbairn wrote that erotogenic zones are not loci that determine characteristics of the development of the libido, but channels for the expression of libidinal or aggressive impulses directed towards objects (1941).

Fairbairn was the first to say that what is internalized is not *an object* but an *object relation* or, better yet, a series of object relations—that is to say, the child experiences a series of relationships with people who are important to the child and then internalizes that experience through identification in order to build "endopsychic structure", Fairbairn's term for psychic structure. He viewed the mind as organized by splits into several sub-systems, each of these composed by the relationship between a self component and an object component: the central ego has its ideal object, the libidinal ego relates to the exciting object; and the internal saboteur (later called antilibidinal ego) relates to the rejecting object. But it was Fairbairn's genius to see that each of these organizations does not exist in isolation but, rather, bears a dynamic relation to others and to the whole of the endopsychic situation (Fairbairn, 1944). The reader puzzled by this short-hand summary should look at a more complete explanation of these elements in chapter 1, by Kernberg, and chapter 11, by Scharff, in this volume.

Fairbairn's work on dreams remains of great theoretical and clinical interest. His original description of *endopsychic structure* (1944) and his analysis of hysterical states (1954a) are illustrated by the analysis dreams. Through this vehicle, he invites us to view the mind not as a juxtaposition of structures without energy, or energies without structures, but as a *theatre of the mind* inhabited by energic structures. For Fairbairn, dreams represent and illustrate endopsychic structure and are, in fact, entitled to be regarded as the paradigm of all endopsychic situations—essentially, "shorts" of inner reality rather than representations of wish-fulfilments (1944).

II

This book brings together papers given at an international congress on the psychoanalytic work of W. R. D. Fairbairn, held in Lisbon on 28–31 October 1999, with papers given by presenters from Europe and the United States and with a large and enthusiastic attendance from European analysts and psychotherapists. There had been other congresses during the 1990s to celebrate and expand the work of Fairbairn, beginning with one celebrating the centennial of Fairbairn's birth, held in Edinburgh, Scotland, in 1989, and an American conference in New York City in 1996. These explored Fairbairn's contribution and its continuing relevance and helped to call attention to the way his work had silently influenced the mainstream of psychoanalysis around the world, often without acknowledgement from those who drew on his work without quite knowing where the ideas had come from. Awareness of the importance of Fairbairn's work continued to spread with the reissue of *Psychoanalytic Studies of the Personality* (1952a) in 1992 and through the publication in 1994 of many of his little-known papers in two volumes entitled *From Instinct to Self: Selected Papers of W. R. D. Fairbairn,* and edited by David Scharff and Fairbairn's daughter, Ellinor Fairbairn Birtles. There has been the biography by J. D. Sutherland, *Fairbairn's Journey into the Interior* (1989), and, in 1994, James Grotstein and Donald Rinsley edited *Fairbairn and the Origins of Object Relations*. Finally, Neil Skolnick and David Scharff edited a collection from the 1996 Fairbairn Congress, *Fairbairn Then and Now*, published in 1998.

The International Congress in Lisbon in 1999 made it clear that recognition of Fairbairn's importance was also growing in Europe and around the world. On this occasion, a highly participatory audience came to hear the fundamentals of Fairbairn's contribution and to consider diverse opinions about how to read his work, how to apply it to current concerns, how to integrate it with dominant theoretical approaches, and how to extend the potential of his ideas. In particular, there was an emphasis on the application of object relations to art and literature, and a number of papers examining how Fairbairn's ideas fit with and contrasted to other theorists.

The Lisbon conference demonstrated the growing recognition of Fairbairn's importance in Europe; it has been followed by publication for the first time of collections of his writings in French and German. It has been gratifying to us to see the enthusiasm with which his ideas are being embraced and the growing acknowledgement of his importance in the movement of psychoanalysis towards relational ideas in the last part of the twentieth century.

III

The chapters in this volume demonstrate the richness of Fairbairn's heritage. Beginning with Otto Kernberg's eloquent and encyclopaedic explication of Fairbairn's divers contributions (chapter 1), we begin a sojourn that demonstrates their richness. Mary Twyman compares Freud and Fairbairn (chapter 2), while Ellinor Fairbairn Birtles, a student of the history of ideas, demonstrates the capacity of Fairbairn's ideas to include a postmodernist approach (chapter 3). In part II, we explore three applications of Fairbairn. First is a study of depression—an area not specifically studied by Fairbairn himself (chapter 4). Vermorel's study of hysteria is undertaken from the standpoint of French psychoanalysis, showing the interesting way in which Fairbairn's ideas can augment a French Freudian point of view of this classical area of psychoanalytic theory (chapter 5). Finally, Tait describes her experience of learning Fairbairn during training and of applying object relations to the field of liaison psychiatry (chapter 6). Her description of employing object relations theory to understand the process of psychiatric consultation to those with physical illness is an original application of Fairbairn's work.

There have not been many studies in the modern literature applying Fairbairn's ideas to dreams or to aesthetics. This is a curious omission, given Fairbairn's original and important studies in both areas. This volume makes, therefore, a unique contribution in including in part III two chapters that combine an interest in these two areas, both from Portuguese contributors (chapters 7 and 8).

The final part offers investigations of new areas of theory. James Grotstein compares Steiner's idea of psychic retreats to Fairbairn's earlier theory of internal objects and concludes that Fairbairn's ideas cover the same territory in a more parsimonious and effective way (chapter 9). Alan Harrow, who works in Edinburgh, as did Fairbairn, examines the contributions of Fairbairn and his student, Sutherland, on the concept of the self (chapter 10). David Scharff looks at the way object relations theory adumbrates chaos theory, and that the combination of the two offers a new paradigm for psychoanalysis (chapter 11). The volume closes with a wonderful chapter by Stephen Mitchell, one of the founders of the Relational School of psychoanalysis. His chapter, on agency in Fairbairn's writing, was a highlight of the conference and was a fine example of Mitchell's probing analysis of theoretical questions (chapter 12). Mitchell's tragic and untimely death in December of 2000 saddened us as we completed initial work on this volume, and it is with respect for his colleagueship and sadness at his passing that we have dedicated this volume to him, keeping in mind his leadership in expanding the field of relational ideas in psychoanalysis and his profound respect for Fairbairn.

Fairbairn's work did as much as anyone to bring psychoanalysis into the realm of modern scientific and philosophical thinking. One can, of course, disagree with Fairbairn on matters of theory or technique. One can look elsewhere for models of mind. We can no more expect of Fairbairn than we could of Freud that any single contributor can have the last word. But we believe that his foresighted theory and his prescient formulation of the clinical problems and paradoxes facing psychotherapists have influenced the course of modern psychoanalysis and psychotherapy far beyond the scope of recognition he has received. Only in the last decade of the twentieth century did Fairbairn begin to garner the reputation warranted by the brilliance of his work, the clarity of his thinking, and the foresight of his ideas. This volume documents the best in recent thinking about the application of Fairbairn's work to the rapidly expanding world of analytic ideas and to the widening area of their application.

PART I

THE ORIGINS AND RELEVANCE
OF FAIRBAIRN'S CONTRIBUTION

CHAPTER ONE

A contemporary exploration of the contributions of W. R. D. Fairbairn

Otto F. Kernberg

The central importance that object relations theory has acquired in contemporary psychoanalytic thinking naturally draws our attention to the contributions of W. Ronald Fairbairn (1954b). Fairbairn first proposed an object relations theory as a basic structural model for the normal as well as pathological development of the psychic apparatus—a model that relates psychoanalytic theory in practical yet sophisticated ways to psychoanalytic practice along a broad spectrum of psychopathology. It is fair to say that Fairbairn has been the most radical proponent of an object relations theory model. This model, in my view, together with that developed independently by Edith Jacobson (1964), constitutes the most important basis for an integrated contemporary psychoanalytic frame. The introduction into Fairbairn's model of John Sutherland's (1963, 1965) concept of affects as the basic link between self and object representations has significantly enriched as well as made more explicit a central aspect of Fairbairn's theories. I consider my own proposed definition of object relations theories—namely, any psychoanalytic model based upon the internalization of dyadic units of self and object representations linked by a particular affect state as basic building blocks of the tripartite structure—a definition that is inspired by Fairbairn's original work (Kernberg, 1984, 1992).

While Fairbairn's most important contributions were made in the 1940s and 1950s, it would seem fair to say that significant attention to his work only emerged in this country and throughout much of the international psychoanalytic community outside Great Britain in the 1980s and 1990s. Although Fairbairn's ideas were extremely influential in the approach of the British Independent Group (formerly the "Middle Group"), appreciation of his work was more impeded by the intellectual and ideological barriers separating the ego psychological and the British Schools than was the case with Balint, Winnicott, and Melanie Klein. On hindsight, it is striking that the extraordinary parallelism of the contributions to psychoanalytic object relations theory of Ronald Fairbairn in Scotland and Edith Jacobson in the United States was not perceived by the psychoanalytic community at the time of their original publication.

In my view, Fairbairn's contributions to object relations theory constitute a fundamental bridge between the psychoanalytic theory of early development and the crystallization of psychic structures on the one hand, and a sophisticated contemporary theory of psychoanalytic technique spanning the entire spectrum from the psychoanalytic psychotherapy of psychosis to standard psychoanalysis of neurotic personality organization on the other.

I have attempted to summarize briefly Fairbairn's contributions in earlier work (Kernberg, 1980, chapter 4), and I will limit myself here to outlining and exploring what I consider his main contributions to contemporary psychoanalytic theory and technique.

A major contribution is summarized in Fairbairn's (1963b) statement that libido is object-seeking, implying that libidinal drive and object investment cannot be considered as separate. The search for libidinal pleasure coincides with the search for gratifying relations with the primary object, and, from a developmental perspective, the pleasure principle and the reality principle start out as being one. While thus reformulating Freud's theory of the libidinal drive, Fairbairn rejected the concept of an aggressive drive, regarding aggression as a secondary development derived from the frustration of libidinal needs.

From a structural viewpoint, however, Fairbairn considered the internalization of a frustrating, "bad" object as an essential mechanism to maintain the relationship with an object both needed and frustrating, experienced as both good and bad, so that the development of aggressively invested internalized objects parallels that of internalized objects invested with libido. Thus, from a clinical standpoint, Fairbairn considered aggression as unavoidable and, in fact, as contributing in a central way to the internalization of object relations and as motivating the development of the splitting of the internalized object into a libidinal object, an anti-libidinal object, and an ideal object. The latter represents the gratifying, accepted aspects of the object, shorn of the object's libidinally exciting and "anti-libidinally" frustrating aggressive aspects. The splitting of the originally internalized total object gives rise to a corresponding division of the originally pristine ego into the libidinal ego, the "anti-libidinal" ego, and the central ego—the latter corresponding to the aspect of the ego relating to the accepted, ideal object. Thus both libido and aggression are indissolubly linked to their investments in libidinal and antilibidinal internalized objects and their corresponding ego aspects. These dyadic libidinal and aggressive structures constitute the "building blocks" of the psychic apparatus: they are dynamic structures, not simply fantasies.

If we change Fairbairn's terms from "ego aspects" to "self aspects" (an eminently reasonable translation of the meaning he attributed to the split aspects of the ego), and the term "internal objects" into "object representations", we are left with the original formulation that the internalization of object relations occurs in the form of dyadic internalization of object representations and self representations. Thus, libidinal internalized object relations imply the simultaneous and parallel investment of a libidinal object representation and a libidinal self representation, while aggressive internalized object relations are constituted by the corresponding aggressively invested object and self representations.

Fairbairn was the first psychoanalytic theoretician to formulate the understanding that all internalizations are internalizations of an object relation, so that the process of identification is identification of the self not simply with an object, but with the relationship between self and object. The most important clinical consequence

of that discovery is the potential for reactivation of the past internalized object relation in the transference, with a re-projection of
the object representation onto the analyst while the patient enacts
the corresponding self representation, or the reciprocal projection
of the self representation while the patient enacts the corresponding object representation. This process, whose recognition is abso-
lutely essential to the psychoanalytic approach to patients with
borderline personality organization as well as to that of all patients
during severe regression in the transference, was first conceptualized by Fairbairn.

In my view, the most important addition to Fairbairn's formulation was John Sutherland's (1979) idea that the libidinal or
aggressive investment of the relationship between self and object
representation consisted of the libidinal or aggressive affect activated in their interaction. The drive was represented by a corresponding affect disposition, so that the essential unit of internalized object relations was a self representation linked with an object
representation by the corresponding affect.

Working completely independently within an ego psychological perspective strongly influenced by the work of Hartmann, Kris,
and Loewenstein, Edith Jacobson arrived at similar conclusions in
her seminal book on *The Self and the Object World* (1954). Bowlby's
work on attachment (1969) established the linkage of Fairbairn's
theory of the essential nature of libidinal object seeking with the
direct observation of infant behaviour and opened the road to the
study of attachment behaviour in mammals, particularly primates—a most powerful bridge between contemporary anthropology and psychoanalytic theory.

My own formulation of drives as the hierarchically supra-
ordinate integration of libidinal and aggressive affects pointed to
the centrality of the affects of rage, hatred, and envy within the
aggressive drive, and elation and sexual excitement on the libidinal side. This formulation linked psychoanalytic drive theory with
the psychobiology of affects and with the disposition to affective
investment of object relations as a primary psychic phenomenon.
From a developmental perspective, I have proposed that the internalization of object relations according to the models proposed by
Fairbairn and Jacobson gradually crystallizes into the tripartite
structure, while the integration of the corresponding libidinal and

aggressive affect dispositions embedded in this internalized object relations matrix originates the hierarchically supraordinate aggressive and libidinal drives (Kernberg, 1992).

Fairbairn's formulation of the "moral defence" in the formation of the superego, and the consequences of its exploration in the course of psychoanalytic treatment, is a major contribution. Fairbairn placed the ideal object in a dynamic relationship with the central ego and thus separated the persecutory aspects of early superego formation (the antilibidinal object and the corresponding, antilibidinal ego) from the ego ideal. His notion of the antilibidinal ego and its dynamically related antilibidinal self or "internal saboteur" conceptually correspond to the punishing, prohibitive aspects of Freud's (1923b) superego and to the early superego precursors that had been described by Melanie Klein (1935, 1940). In fact, Klein's observations regarding the earliest superego development clearly influenced Fairbairn's formulations, while his descriptions of early splits in the pristine ego and the schizoid position (1940) motivated Melanie Klein (1946) to change her formulation of the paranoid position into that of the paranoid-schizoid position.

Fairbairn proposed that the frustrating aspects of the primary object, split off in the form of the antilibidinal object, sequester one segment of the ego that maintains its attachment to the frustrating but needed antilibidinal object and, in fact, attempt to dominate the rest of the ego as agents, so to speak, of the antilibidinal object. The term "internal saboteur" coined by Fairbairn to signal that function of this sequestered, anti-libidinal part of the ego opens, for the first time in psychoanalytic literature, the understanding of a fundamental mechanism involved in superego functioning and masochistic pathology in the broadest sense.

Why does such a savage collusion develop between the punishing antilibidinal object and the submissive, punishment-seeking internal saboteur? And why is such enormous power invested in the internal saboteur as to affect the rest of the individual's ego functioning? Fairbairn responded to these questions with the observation of the parental objects perceived, at points of maximal frustration, as sadistic persecutors, and the infant's desperate need to orient himself in a world controlled by such persecution. Fairbairn suggested that it is preferable to be a sinner in the world of a cruel God than to live in the world ruled by the Devil. In other words, the sadistic transformation of the needed object (be it because of the actual sadism of the parental objects or the projected aggressive affects derived from their frustrating effects on the infant, or a combination of both) makes it essential for the infant to create an internal order to ensure survival under such circumstances. To rationalize in some primitive way the behaviour of the sadistic object and to attempt to submit to it as a way of restoring a safe dependency on the sadistic yet needed object are the motives enacted by the internal saboteur. The "moral defence" consists in taking on the bad qualities of the needed object in order to preserve the dependent relationship with it: the patient becomes a "sinner" relating to a cruel but idealized moralistic object.

This formulation explains the nature of the sadistic control the primitive superego exerts over the ego, and the powerful masochistic tendencies related to early superego crystallization. Fairbairn pointed to the paradoxical consequences of psychoanalytic resolution of superego pressures and unconscious guilt. The dissolution of the advanced structure of the superego would activate the underlying, primitive antilibidinal object and ego in the transference, in the form of a re-projection of that "bad" object onto the analyst, and the activation in the patient of the internal saboteur to maintain and strengthen that particular relationship (Fairbairn, 1943). Simultaneously, the exciting libidinal relationship as well as the central ego-ideal object relationship would be completely split off and potentially endangered with destruction by the overwhelming, primitive, all-bad relationship in the transference.

This formulation applies particularly to patients with severe psychopathology, such as cases with a history of severe physical and sexual abuse, where the internalization of a relationship between the patient's perpetrating object and victimized self determines an unconscious dyadic identification with both victim and perpetrator that is enacted in the transference with rapid role reversals. The transference developments of these patients are dominated by the activation of sadomasochistic transferences, in which analyst and patient exchange the roles of victim and perpetrator under the effect of projective identification and related primitive defences operations (Kernberg, 1994).

Under optimal conditions, in less severe cases, the reactivation of primitive superego precursors typically manifests itself in the emergence of paranoid features in the transference at advanced stages of psychoanalytic treatment. In the worst cases, sadomasochistic transferences may dominate the treatment from early on, and, even more destructively, the internal saboteur—that is, the part of the patient's self identified with the sadistic object—may attempt to destroy the relationship with the analyst as an object in external reality by relentless efforts to undermine, corrupt, and castrate the good object and the relationship with it. As I have pointed out in earlier work (Kernberg, 1992), when psychopathic transferences are dominant, their analysis takes precedence over the analysis of paranoid defences; these, in turn, as Melanie Klein (1950) pointed out, require working through for depressive mechanisms to emerge dominantly in the advanced part of psychoanalytic treatment.

Reflecting on Fairbairn's contributions from the standpoint of contemporary scientific developments within psychoanalysis as well as in other related sciences, the essential nature of affective investment in early object relations as a basic motivational system in human beings seems evident. From the viewpoint of the interface between psychoanalysis and the biological sciences, I believe that the consideration of libidinally invested and aggressively invested early internalized object relations makes eminent sense. The extended dependency of the infant mammal on parental care has fostered the philogenetically recent biological system of affects as primary motivation and a system of communication, organizing the infant's total world experience and the caregiver's awareness of the infant's needs. Contemporary anthropological research on patterns of affiliation and sexual behaviour in mammals points to the basic biological mechanisms that protect the gene pool as a major motivation for males' aggressive competition for access to females and females' choice of the fittest males both for impregnation and for protection of the early mother–infant relationship. Darwinian fitness, at the level of primates, no longer refers to simple brutal force, but to the capacity for social affiliation and the ability to protect the early mother–infant relationship. In the animal kingdom, the fundamental instincts refer to feeding, to fight and flight as part of the aggressive competition among males, defending of territory, and shared protection of the young, as well as ruthless killing of predators, rivals, and even the infants produced by rivals, and to mating, the primary activity geared to perpetuate and expand the gene pool.

At the level of the human species, Freud's seminal discoveries signalling the replacement of biological instincts by psychological drives as intrapsychic motivational systems that organize the dynamic Unconscious or the id culminate in the formulation of libido as the sexual drive and the death drive as the aggressive drive. That both drive systems are intrinsically and indissolubly linked to internalized object relations was already implicit in Freud's (1923b) proposal that the core of the ego is constituted by abandoned object relations, and it was further elaborated by the conceptions of Fairbairn, Melanie Klein, and Jacobson.

The primitive defensive mechanisms centring around splitting described by Fairbairn and Melanie Klein organized the dynamic Unconscious into idealized and persecutory internalized object relations, the gradual development and integration of which determines, at the same time, the crystallization of the tripartite structure. That libido and the aggressive drive develop in parallel on the basis of the respective integration of libidinal and aggressive affects was already foreshadowed by Freud's discovery of the intrinsic relationship between sexual and early affiliative affects in his analysis of developmental stages of the libido. The structural models of Fairbairn, Klein, and Jacobson made it possible to relate the mechanisms of condensation and displacement—that is, the basic mobility of affective charges—to the respective crystallization of libidinal, aggressive, and combined internalized object relations.

Freud's (1915d) statement that the only thing we know about drives are affects and representations can now be translated into the statement that drives are manifested in the affective investment of self and object representations. That drives develop in parallel to the structural integration of their corresponding internalized object relations has been formulated explicitly in the theoretical approaches of Laplanche (1987) and myself (Kernberg, 1992). A contemporary psychoanalytic view of drives, as perhaps most significantly contributed by Melanie Klein (1952a, 1957) and Laplanche, conceives of them as affectively charged unconscious fantasies that involve desired and feared relations between the self and internalized objects, and I have described the combination of self representation and object representation under the frame of a dominant peak affect state as the basic unit of unconscious fantasy (Kernberg, 1992).

In my view, the gradual integration of the "all good", idealized, pleasurable affective experiences with mother with the erotic implication of the unconscious meanings injected in the form of mother's "enigmatic" messages (Laplanche, 1987) will constitute libido as a drive, in the same way as the integration of all painful, terrifying, rageful affective experiences with the unconscious meanings injected in the respective interactions will constitute the death drive. Fairbairn, paradoxically, while reserving the concept of drive only for libido and not for aggression, described, at the same time, the corresponding structural integration of aggression as a major motivational system.

I believe that to consider libido as primary and aggression as secondary denies both the evolutionary evidence stemming from biology and anthropology and the fact that biological dispositions to erotic activation that require actual object relationships to become effective parallels the biological disposition to aggressive responses that also require particular object-related stimuli to become effective. Thus, both libido and aggression are either "secondary" to the activation of object relations under varying affectively dominated circumstances, or else both are "primary" in terms of a biological disposition on the basis of which the psychological drives will develop, "leaning on" the corresponding biological functions, as Laplanche has proposed.

I believe that contemporary affect theory constitutes a bridge between biological structures and intrapsychic structures, while, at the same time, in my view, affect theory cannot replace a drive theory. Primitive affects are inborn psychophysiological structures, and, regardless which classification of affects one accepts, they reflect multiple dispositions in the relations to any particular object that are less important than the deeply repressed, constant, stable unconscious relations to the parental objects. And affects, shorn of the object relations in the context of which they enter the psychic apparatus, would not be able to reflect, by themselves, the nature of unconscious fantasy, of motivating desire. Unconscious desire leans on primitive, affectively invested object relations, and I agree with Laplanche in the fundamental difference between biological functions and unconscious fantasy based upon such biological functions. The term "anaclitic" as used in English does not have the same quality as the direct translation of Freud's German "*Anlehnung*" into "*étayage*", in French, and "*apuntalamiento*", in Spanish.

At the same time, drives and object relations constitute, in my view, intrinsic, indissolubly linked psychic structures. An object relations theory devoid of the theory of drives tends to evolve, as I see it, into a theory of interpersonal functioning that may stress the unconscious aspects of intersubjectivity but is usually attracted by sociological models of development, in which the actual aspect of past interactions directly models the unconscious world of the present transference developments. This leads to a neglect of the psychoanalytic exploration regarding unconscious mental structures. This development, in my experience, tends to accentuate superficial aspects of unconscious functioning, the role of adaptation and reality, and to minimize the awareness of the uncanny aspects of primitive hatred and the primitive nature of early erotic and sadomasochistic unconscious fantasy. Usually an object relations theory devoid of the theory of drives tends to underemphasize aggression and to de-emphasize eroticism as well, in contrast to a stress on pregenital, pre-oedipal, dyadic relations as the origin of the dynamic Unconscious.

On the other hand, the emphasis on a traditional drive theory that does not explore the implications of object relations theory and affect theory for our conception of drives eventually tends to relegate drives to a mythical structure, such as the equation of the Unconscious with the structure of a natural language, or an assumption of primary, innate development of the drives that may propose the inheritance of philogenetically determined primary fantasies. And, finally, a replacement of drive theory by an affect theory relegates motivation easily to the nature of biological structures, underemphasizing the importance of unconscious fantasy and the psychological nature of human desires.

Fairbairn's proposal that all transference developments imply the reactivation of a dyadic relation between self representation and object representation has profoundly influenced psychoana-

© 1996

lytic technique. The contemporary tendency to focus on those aspects of a patient's material that are affectively dominant, and the analysis of the relationship between self and object representations involved in the cognitive implications of that particular affective enactment, have replaced the formulation of supposedly "pure" drive manifestations, or even the analysis of affect as if it ever were independent from representations of self and object.

By the same token, the analysis of rapid role reversals between enacted and projected self and object representations in borderline conditions has helped to clarify the nature of what used to be perceived as chaotic manifestations in the transference (Clarkin, Yeomans, & Kernberg, 1999). Here the technical applications of the analysis of primitive object relations and defences of the Kleinian school have been of central importance. Fairbairn's own applications of this model to the analysis of dreams, his concept of multiple representations of the self as well as of significant objects in the imagery of the dream, is a central contribution to dream analysis. The traditional ego psychological concept of the dynamic of defence-impulse analysis has definitely shifted into the concept of a dynamic conflict between defensively activated and impulsively activated internalized object relations.

Fairbairn's (1940) description in depth of the dynamics of the schizoid personality stands out as an unmatched contribution to clinical psychiatry and psychoanalysis. He starts with his description of the split-off nature of the psychic apparatus that results from the internalization of ideal, exciting, and rejecting aspects of the object and the consequent splitting of the ego into a central, conscious ego relating to an ideal object, a repressed libidinal ego relating to the exciting or libidinal object, and a repressed anti-libidinal ego relating to the rejecting or anti-libidinal object. Fairbairn describes this original state of affairs as a basic schizoid state. If the aggressive elements of the personality are dominant, this original disposition may consolidate into a schizoid personality in which this original state persists. The schizoid personality's rigid isolation and his "ideal" relation to the therapist (corresponding to the conscious dominance of the central ego in relation to an ideal object) protect the patient against his unconscious conflicts. Together with introversion and detachment, the patient's attitude of superiority and control, his omnipotence of thought and intellec-

tual speculations express his unconscious conflicts around depending and the defences against it, around giving and not giving, the
fear of expressions of love, and of hating and being hated by the
frustrating objects. All these conflicts are expressed in the patient's
fantasy world. The consistent analysis of the patient's fragmentation of his affective experience, and of his defensive aloofness and
hidden superiority in the relationship with the analyst, gradually
permits the emergence of the deeper conflicts around dependency,
the negative therapeutic reaction linked to the activation of the
relationship with a bad object, the transformation of guilt over his
own demandingness into paranoid fears. The resolution of these
conflicts eventually leads to the very depth where the original
libidinal relationship to the object may be activated and fully experienced in consciousness. One might say that while the rapid reversal of self and object representations in the transference and the
expression of unconscious conflicts mostly in the form of transference acting-out are typical of the infantile and borderline patient,
the expression of these same role reversals and enactments in the
schizoid patient's fantasy world accounts for the apparently detached and subdued quality of his transferences.

The application of Fairbairn's structural model to the analysis
of such intimate dyadic relationships as marriage has permitted
the fundamental contribution of Henry Dicks (1967) to the analysis
of marital conflicts—in my view the most important psychoanalytic contribution to that field. Dicks, in applying Fairbairn's object
relations concepts, pointed to three levels of mutual adaptation of a
marital couple: namely, that of their conscious expectations of self
and other in terms of a life to be constructed jointly, that of their
autonomous and yet adaptive relationship to the surrounding culture and social network, and, very fundamentally, that of their
dominant unconscious, unresolved conflictual relationship to their
significant parental objects. Dicks described how, by means of projective identification, the marital couple tends to mutually induce
the dominant unresolved object relationship from the past in their
interactions, thus determining the dialectic between an unconscious collusion of the couple on the one hand, and its sharply
contrasting conscious counterpart on the other. These three levels
of interaction, Dicks suggested, determine the overall dynamics of

the marital couple, and this formulation has crucially influenced the field of marital therapy to the present time.

I have already referred to the fundamental importance of Fairbairn's conception of the moral defence in analysing the activation of the relationship with bad objects in advanced stages of the treatment, as well as his general formulation of the development of intense sadomasochistic transferences during severe regressions. Here Fairbairn's formulation of the re-enactment of the relationship with a bad object as a consequence of the resolution of the moral defence and as a crucial aspect of the working through of the deepest layers of the mind may be enriched with our contemporary knowledge of the regressive transferences of borderline patients. I propose that this re-enactment of the relationship with a bad object may be characterized by a consistent identification of the patient with that object, while the rejected, traumatized, mistreated self is projected onto the therapist. This, in fact, may be one of the most extreme manifestations of what André Green (1993) has described as the "deobjectalizing" function of the death drive, namely—the relentless, unforgiving, unwavering attack on the relationship with a potentially good object, where even the secret hope that the object may resist this onslaught and prove after all to be a good one is no longer available, and, to the contrary, would only trigger further envious and destructive onslaughts. This, the most severe manifestation of the negative therapeutic reaction, expressed as a paradoxical, "deobjectalizing" relationship with a potentially good object onto which the traumatized self has been projected, may be the deepest equivalent of suicide as an ultimate temptation.

There is one area in which Fairbairn's clinical contributions evince, in my view, an important limitation, a limitation shared, however, with much of the technical psychoanalytic literature other than French psychoanalysis. I am referring to the position of the psychoanalyst as an "outsider" to the primitive dyadic relationships activated in the transference, the analyst's "third position". The analyst's reflective remaining outside the transference–countertransference bind, his interpretation of the meaning of the distortion of the initially provided treatment frame by the transference–countertransference regression constitutes this "third position", a term introduced in French psychoanalysis.

The split into an observing and an acting part of the ego originally described by Richard Sterba (1934) represents the activation of the patient's self-reflective function derived from the internalization of the reflective function of the caregiver—not simply from mother's empathy with the infant's own experience. I have proposed, in earlier work (Kernberg, 2000), that we need a three-person psychology, not a one-person or a two-person psychology, the third person being the analyst in his specific role, in contrast to all other interpersonal relationships of the patient, including the particular transference–countertransference bind that is being explored in the psychoanalytic situation.

There exists, of course, the danger that the analyst, in misusing or abusing his specific function of remaining outside the transference–countertransference bind, may develop an attitude of arbitrariness, of authoritarianism, or indoctrination of the patient. I believe, however, that it is naive to attempt to protect the patient against this danger by eliminating the realistic, functional authority of the analyst in the treatment situation. The analyst's third position—interpreting the nature of the transference–countertransference relationship from an "external" perspective—may symbolically replicate the role of the oedipal father in disrupting the pre-oedipal, symbiotic relationship between infant and mother, thus originating the archaic oedipal triangulation (Chasseguet-Smirgel, 1986). The symbolic condensation, at points of severe transference regression, of primitive symbiotic, and, simultaneously, archaic oedipal situations represents an important linkage between earliest development and the vicissitudes of the Oedipus conflict, between pregenital strivings and genital eroticism.

The analyst as an "excluded third person" also constitutes, of course, a "real" good object, and the reality of that constructive relationship with the analyst—in contrast to the activation of regressive conflicts in the transference–countertransference bind—was considered by Fairbairn an important and implicit important therapeutic agent. Fairbairn thus implicitly constructed a "triangularization" in the psychoanalytic relationship, without, however, linking it theoretically to the archaic oedipal situation.

It needs to be stressed, however, that to the end of his life Fairbairn maintained a strict psychoanalytic technique (Fairbairn, 1958), and that his work should not be misinterpreted as implying that he would support a viewpoint according to which the reality of the analyst's attitude is as important a therapeutic factor as interpretation. On the contrary, I believe that it would be consistent with Fairbairn's technical approach to say that the reality of a good relationship is a non-specific factor of human growth present in all human relationships, blocked by psychopathology and distorted in the transference–countertransference developments. It is interpretation, and interpretation alone, that makes it possible to resolve that blockage in the patient's psychopathology and permits the patient, in the context of the analytic relationship as well as in all others, to resume the normal growth potential of all good object relations.

Moreover, this general perspective—the analyst's function as a "third excluded other"—is an important source of his reflection and, eventually, of the self reflectiveness of the patient, a powerful stimulus for the development of introspection, insight, and autonomy of the patient, including autonomy in the search for further understanding of the deeper layers of the dynamic Unconscious.

While Fairbairn rightly, I believe, stressed the possibility of a replacement of genuine object relations by an escape into polymorphous perverse infantile sexual strivings, and importantly contributed to the analysis of unconscious internalized object relations symbolically expressed in polymorphous perverse behaviour, he tended to underemphasize the erotic dimension in the psychoanalytic encounter. Patients with a borderline personality organization are particularly prone to experience the interpretive role of the analyst as a violent disruption of the symbiotic link between patient and analyst, and they strenuously resist it, precisely—among other reasons—to avoid the traumatizing effects of the discovery of the relationship of the parental couple, the differences between sexes and generations, the envy of the parental couple, the shock of the primal scene, and the most primitive level of frustration and anxiety in the form of fear of annihilation related to the establishment of archaic triangulation.

Laplanche (1992) has pointed to the crucial function of mother in activating the erotic aspects of her relationship with the infant by means of "enigmatic" messages, the erotic implications of which can only be elaborated "après coup" the infant's unconscious fantasy, at a later stage of development. Braunschweig and Fain (1971,

1975) pointed to the "teasing" aspect of mother's alternating between the erotic investment of her child and her withdrawal of this erotic investment from the child to her relationship with his father. The implication of these observations, and also of the psychoanalytic exploration of the nature of erotic excitement, is that erotic excitement is intimately linked to such stimulation and frustration and contains, therefore, both libidinal and aggressive elements. In other words, in the activation of regressive polymorphous perverse relationships there may be not only a denial of the dependent nature of an object relationship, but also an enactment of a very complex and primitive erotic one, the sexual aspects of which have not only defensive functions but also contain a potential enrichment and strengthening of libidinal relationships. I believe it is fair to say that this element of polymorphous perverse erotic developments in the transference was not sufficiently considered by Fairbairn.

Or rather, in describing the unavoidably frustrating aspects of the good object that led to the original splitting of the ego or self, one might add to Fairbairn's formulation that, embedded in the frustrating aspects of the object, there is also a most fundamentally libidinal one: the original erotization of the infant's body and his relationship to mother.

In conclusion, Fairbairn emerges as one of the major theoreticians of psychoanalysis. His fundamental thrust, linking psychic drive to internalized object relations, has moved psychoanalysis into a new dimension. That linkage, complemented by Sutherland's introduction of the role of affects, facilitates potential bridge-building between psychoanalysis and the psychophysiology of affects and the neuropsychology of the development of representations of self and others. Fairbairn's formulations facilitate the understanding of unconscious motivation not only at the level of the individual, but also at the level of the couple, the group, and the institution. The activation of multiple, unconscious representations of self and others in the dream world of the individual as well as in the reality of unstructured social groups links the dynamics of dream formation and unconscious intrapsychic conflicts with those of regressive groups described by Bion (1961), Turquet (1975), and Anzieu (1981).

In criticizing Fairbairn's rejection of the primary nature of aggression, it needs to be kept in mind that, at the time of his contributions, the contemporary differentiation between intrapsychic drives in psychoanalytic theory and the modern concept of instincts in biology had not yet been formulated. And, from a practical viewpoint, Fairbairn's central consideration of the structuring of aggression into internalized object relations is clearly commensurate with a contemporary Freudian formulation of the dual drive theory. Having re-encountered Fairbairn's contributions and found them eminently useful within contemporary psychoanalytic theory and practice, it is the task of a new generation of psychoanalysts to further apply this theory to our understanding and treatment of severe psychopathology of the individual, couples, and groups.

CHAPTER TWO

Freud and Fairbairn: continuities and discontinuities

Mary Twyman

Charles Rycroft, in his paper "The Function of Words" (1968a), writes the following:

> One special function of words is their permissive function. The formulation and communication of a previously unconscious idea involves the overcoming of internal resistances . . . in defiance of an internal object. This is why the expression by the analysand of a previously unadmitted idea is preceded by anxiety or an increase of defences against anxiety . . . followed by a sense of release when the idea is finally communication. *This is also why the formulation of original ideas, even those of a scientific and impersonal nature, requires moral courage. The analysand and the original thinker or artist both have to face the fear of being neither understood nor approved.* [p. 71]

One can read these words as a *cri du coeur* from Rycroft, an analyst of a rigorously independent mind, as at this time he was formulating original ideas about the nature of symbolism in psychoanalytic thinking. However, it applies equally to the body of work Fairbairn produced, and it reminds us of the courageous task he undertook when he broke the continuity with Freud in major areas of his thinking.

There was not much support—indeed, an absence of approval—in quarters where he might have expected a measure of understanding. A review of *Psychoanalytic Studies of the Personality* by D. W. Winnicott and M. Masud R. Khan (Winnicott, 1989: review dated 1953) was critical, even disparaging.

To start with libido: Freud's concept of libido is a vastly different one from Fairbairn's: libidinal development as sexuality is replaced by libidinal development as including the whole field of development as sequential states of dependence. Where tension relief is secondary, a safety valve, it marks a strategy in the struggle to repair a failure in the aim of relating to an object. Where thumb-sucking for Freud represented a repetition of a sexual gratification, for Fairbairn the baby was providing himself with an object in the face of the absence of the breast and its significance for relating. Where Abraham's stages had provided Freud with the notion of the signposts to libidinal pleasure, for Fairbairn they furnished signposts to the object. Orality found a place in Fairbairn's scheme—after all, the breast was a functioning biological object. Anality did not—Freud's sequence was not followed here. For Fairbairn, infantile dependence contained Abraham's later oral stage; Abraham's final genital stage encompassed mature dependence. But between these Fairbairn instituted a *transitional* stage, one more fully dynamic in its emphasis on the interplay of object-seeking and -relating. It is, of course, a term perhaps more widely recognized in connection with Winnicott's work, with his concept of transitional objects and transitional phenomena, but Fairbairn was using it ten years earlier. Fairbairn defines his sense of the term as "characterised by an increasing tendency to abandon the attitude of infantile dependence and an increasing tendency to adopt the attitude of mature dependence" (Fairbairn, 1952a).

Primary identification is clarified by Fairbairn in terms of the non-differentiation of subject from object, and so development involves the increasing differentiation of the subject from his objects. Rycroft, in the opening of his essay "Symbolism and Its Relationship to the Primary and Secondary Processes" (1968b), commented on the trend in modem thought, outside as well as inside psychoanalysis, which constituted a movement away from analysing into things and towards analysing into *processes*. It is, I think, Fairbairn's outstanding achievement to have made a constant attempt to formulate a development model based on the processes involved in the internalization of object relations and to establish a theory of object relations that aims to replace Freud's traditional metapsychology and, especially, to set aside instinct theory. A further discontinuity with Freud's thinking is evidenced in Fairbairn's approach to the Oedipus situation. While Klein tried to keep continuity with Freud, retaining the centrality of the oedipal complex, but shifting it to a much earlier date, Fairbairn took a very different approach, declaring that the Oedipus situation is not basic but a derivative of a situation that dynamically has priority over it, logically because of the primacy of the mother/infant situation, but also in temporal terms. This prior situation issues directly out of the earlier relationship, in which Fairbairn does not admit of the father as a significant object as yet. However, going into further detail in this area, we find the following: "the technique underlying aggression employed to subdue libido is a process which finds a common place in Freud's conception of 'repression' and my own conception of 'indirect repression'" (Fairbairn, 1968, p. 116). Here we have some signs of continuity. However, his views on the origin of the technique differ. In paraphrase, Freud's views on the libidinal incestuous wishes towards the parent of the opposite sex and the aggressive (parenticidal) wishes towards the parent of the same sex constitute the setting of the Oedipus complex. Fairbairn views the technique as originating in the infant's efforts to reduce the expression of libido and aggression towards the mother, the infant's only significant object, and the object upon whom he is totally dependent. This is a major discontinuity from Freud.

For Freud, the Oedipus situation is an ultimate cause; for Fairbairn, this is a position with which he cannot agree. The ultimate cause for Fairbairn is now the phenomenon of infantile dependence. The Oedipus situation is seen "not so much in the light of a causal phenomenon, as in the light of an end product" (1944). Fairbairn dispenses with the ultimate cause position because of the need to formulate something to account for strategies the infant adopts to cope with the *ambivalent situation* it experiences in the course of its total dependence. These strategies pre-date the Oedipus situation, and it is not until the basic endopsychic situation has been accomplished, that the infant encounters the Oedipus situation. Fairbairn then sees it, not as a fundamental explanatory concept, but as a phenomenon to be explained in terms of the (now pre-existing) endopsychic structures. Here we have a major discontinuity.

I can touch only briefly on other areas where the issues of continuity and discontinuity between Freud and Fairbairn occur. To do otherwise would be to attempt to recapitulate much of the work done by such writers as James Grotstein, Otto Kernberg, Richard L. Rubens, Judith Hughes, and others who have contributed to the detailed study of his work. Richard Rubens's work, "Fairbairn's Theory of Depression" (1998), brings us firmly into a fascinating area of difference, for instance. Observing that Fairbairn has little to say about depression and noting that its origin is located in the (Abraham) later oral stage, which he accepted, Rubens lands the depressive's predicament, as outlined by Fairbairn, squarely on the problem of preserving the object from being destroyed by the subject's hatred. This, of course, for Fairbairn is a stronger position psychically than that occupied by the schizoid, whose more serious predicament involves the threat to his object from his loving feelings. As the primary state of all human psychopathology, Fairbairn sees this state as basic, fundamental, and of greater importance. It seems that the drive emphasis in Freud's theory of depression may account for its relative absence from Fairbairn's theory, and he was critical of Freud's emphasis on the problem—or the situation—of melancholic depression. There is an interesting discussion to be had on the equivalent, or otherwise, of Freud's descriptions in "Mourning and Melancholia" (1917e [1915], pp. 243–258) and the schizoid's state of futility in Fairbairn. In Fairbairn's opinion, Freud was more object-related in his thinking, closer to the real experience of people in relationship, when he was engaged in formulating the structure of the superego. But in my view Fairbairn seems to bypass the integral importance of depression and its structuring and developmental function in psychic growth. His theory, depending as it does on the primacy of split-off sub-systems within the self, has sacrificed something extremely important. But this may be a very "English" view.

In discussion with American colleagues recently, the emphasis given to considerations of depressive phenomena and their vicissitudes was commented on as being something that marked a particularly "English" bias in our clinical accounts.

It may be, however, that Fairbairn implicitly subsumes depressive experience in his sense of futility. Rubens sees "depression as constituting a very general mechanism of conservation of the endopsychic situation and stasis in the closed system of experiencing the world" . . . "depression is a technique for avoiding, or at least denying the existence of change" . . . "the desire to deny change and thereby to deny the experience of loss, is one of the deepest of human resistances" (1998, p. 224). As such, it appears as a strongly active obstacle to progress in the analytic situation. One has the impression, working with a patient in the course of a long analysis where such resistance is at work, that a very active process is engaged. This differs perhaps from Fairbairn's sense of futility, where energy for the struggle to reconnect with the object may be minimal. Where the technique of depression, as Rubens defines it, is at work, there is a sense that a relationship with an object, external or internal, is in existence, and, problematic as it is, experience of it in either its presence or its absence can be taken account of. It has to be related to, even as it is being denied and the patient is trying to exclude it from the analytic space. We do have to take account of the distinction Fairbairn makes between patients ". . . who are often called 'depressed' in clinical practice" and those he felt should be "more properly described as suffering from a sense of futility" (1944, p. 91). Such a state of futility is characterized by a state ". . . where the ego is reduced to a state of impotence . . . and is quite incapable of expressing itself" (1944, p. 91).

Rubens, rightly in my view, draws our attention to the difficulty Fairbairn creates when he fails to notice the continuity existing between some of the levels at which both depression and a sense of futility are having their origins, and makes those competing concepts. It is then quite a shock to read the following: "As my experience goes . . . individuals of the depressive type do not constitute any appreciable part of the analyst's clientele."

Clinical vignette

A man of 41 comes for a second analysis. He lives alone and has never been married. His sexual relationships, when they exist, are heterosexual, and there have been a series of these, two of some considerable duration, and in each a child was conceived and then aborted. Over the two and a half years of analysis a life of very considerable restriction is revealed: a conscientious worker at his profession, with a few friends, but with a life lived in an over-all atmosphere of substantial constraint, imposed by no one but himself.

The patient brings the first dream of the analysis.

He is in prison with a female companion. They are being escorted by security guards, who at some point leave them. They then go on alone—they make their way across an open space where the prisoners are—he is aware this is unusual—it becomes clear that he works there.

His associations focus on the open space, reminding him of a school he has taught in once. He was an assistant and never had a full class of his own. He/they doubted his capacities. However, he thinks he did good work there, and he wonders if it might be about doing good work in the analysis. I interpret that he does feel imprisoned in his world, stuck in his life as we had talked of recently, that the prisoners represent aspects of himself that were restricted, that the guards might have a dual meaning (the referring analyst who has sent him to me and then left him with the female companion in the dream); and also the defensive patterns he might have to leave behind as he goes on with me in the open space of the analysis. He may doubt his and my capacities for this endeavour, though he recognizes that an analytic space exists, but neither of us is to forget that we are in the prison of his unconscious structures.

After two and a half years, what do I know about this man? And, perhaps more importantly, what does he know about himself? He has been secretly—perhaps less so now—engaged in limiting my effectiveness with him. He can tell me I speak thoughts that should never be spoken; my interpretations can be "accurate"—his best commendation—but that I am radical in what I say. Radical can be dangerous, disruptive, like a revolutionary, or someone who tries to get to the root of things. I introduce complexity into the emotional field that he is trying to keep simple. Things I say elicit responses from him, feelings of envy, dependence, gratitude, curiosity, feelings he would rather bypass. He wants to *keep things simple*. These plain phrases give us a currency in the analysis. He says: "You can have too much of a good thing—even relating." I introduce the phrase "psychic minimalism" to describe his technique for limiting himself and trying to limit my agency in the analysis. With time, the compelling fantasy of reducing emotional need to a minimum has less of a hold on him.

These clinical details are rather stark. For the sake of brevity, much has been excluded. But the clinical situation raises interesting questions. Is this man depressed? Is he suffering from a sense of futility? He complains of neither, but most of us faced with this picture would be struck by the monumental defensive structures that guard against the awareness of the deeply impoverished life that he leads. My sense recently is that a profound sadness is present from time to time, accompanying a realization that there is more in the world than he has allowed himself to know of, and that there is more in him than he has allowed himself to encounter. And that analysis is the arena in which such an encounter might take place. Recently he said that he thought he understood something: that the analysis might be something he could contribute to, that it needed more of him. This statement, which stunned me, perhaps because I had assumed he had always known this, caused me to realize afresh the profound extent of his passivity and indeed the manifestation of his defences against an awareness of a sense of futility. To be able to experience depression, or a sense of futility, the individual has to know that something has failed in object-relating. I think with this patient that level has not yet been reached.

I want to come, finally, to some of the wider aspects of both Freud's and Fairbairn's contributions. Both were men of vision and originality. One built upon the foundations of the other, and to invoke Winnicott's dictum, made use of the object, both offering destruction, but also respecting its survival—both substantive contributions to the foundation and development of psychoanalytic

theory and clinical practice. In addition, both had interests in the
wider culture, thinking and writing on art, literature, and the fields
of social and political structures.[1]

It is, of course, not possible to recruit Freud entirely to the camp
of object relations, and yet his important statement in "On Narcissism" (1914c, p. 69): "A human being has originally two sexual
objects—himself and the woman who nurses him" lays the foundation in theory for its development. On the wider front of social
relationships, in *Group Psychology and the Analysis of the Ego* (1921c,
p. 69), he declares: "In the individual's mental life, someone else is
invariably involved, as a model, as an object, as a helper, as an
opponent, and so from the very first individual psychology in this
extended but entirely justifiable sense of the words, is at the same
time, social psychology as well."

And lastly, for Fairbairn it seems incontrovertible that the major problem for the individual was of love not responded to. In a
letter to Jung, Freud (1974, p. 154) wrote: "Psycho-analysis is in
essence a cure through love."

CHAPTER THREE

Why is Fairbairn relevant today—a modernist/postmodernist view

Ellinor Fairbairn Birtles

Why *is* Fairbairn relevant today?—it is because he reorientated psychoanalysis upon an active interrelational view of the "human condition" derived from Aristotle and Hegel. From this, he developed a living systems psychic model, commensurate with European philosophy and science, and in which he systematically addressed the issues raised by modern science and philosophy—modernism and postmodernism. For these reasons, Fairbairn's concepts should be assessed within the wider context of twentieth-century European thought.

Fairbairn expressly says, "In the twentieth century atomic physics has revolutionized the scientific conception of the physical universe and has introduced the conception of dynamic structure; and the views which I have outlined represent an attempt to reformulate psychoanalytical theory in terms of this conception" (1949, p. 176).

My theme is that it is through an acknowledgement of a radical shift in consciousness that we can understand modernity and postmodernity. How did this shift in consciousness occur? I look at the progenitors of this change, which is best understood as a state of "uncertainty" engendered by the absence of firm grounds for any universal "knowledge" or "truth". I follow this with a short account of the origins of modernity. I shall discuss Fairbairn's contributions to psychoanalytic thought and demonstrate how his ideas are consolidated by those of contemporary theorists in different disciplines.

Fairbairn's reorientation of psychoanalytic theory is based on an individual who can accommodate altered perspectives, or what Vargish and Mook in *Inside Modernism: Relativity Theory, Cubism, Narrative* (1999) call an "epistemic trauma". They use this term to describe the change in consciousness that resulted from "the dissociation of realist methods of representation [in science, art and literature] from their religious underpinnings" (p. 42). They continue: "The nineteenth century saw the gradual shift of realistic space and time away from their origin as absolute space and time in the mind of God" (p. 42). This dissociation from validation "in the mind of God" had enormous repercussions. Here, Vargish and Mook (p. 22) note that Einstein's theory of relativity was initially perceived by scientists as alienating. They argue that this, "lies in its apparent proposal to alter fundamental constituents of consciousness itself: space (the medium of images) and time (in which language functions)". This they contend is a "phenomenon of Modernism". Thus "time and space are not what we assumed them to be" (p. 22).

Fairbairn understood that it is the whole context within which we exist that determines our thoughts, meanings, and beliefs. So Fairbairn specifically addressed this shift in consciousness, which we call modernism and postmodernism. Properly speaking, postmodernism is a negative aspect of modernism.

Time and space in Einstein are no longer absolute: they become space–time, a four-dimensional continuum. A space–time continuum means that there are no separate entities called space and time. Space has collapsed. Kuhn (1970) explores the effect of this paradigm change from the Newtonian to the Einsteinian world, the primary effect of which is unintelligibility. This occurs because the same terms are used to describe changed definitions. If we see time as absolute—psychic events are singular. If we look at the space in which I interact with you as constant, then reality is an area of serial occurrences, rather than a series of interrelational occurrences within which it is the differences between them that define the event. Freudian theory remains with the singular event as the root of psychopathology, but his persistent unconscious sees the "past" as the unacknowledged motivation for present action. Fairbairn incorporates the series of interrelational occurrences as the basis of his endopsychic structure.

We have moved from a position in which we can consciously assert, in Vargish and Mook's (1999) words, that "absolute duration was the true medium of our consciousness, the time in which we actually live" (p. 24), to a situation where it is "the physical contexts" that determine our perceptions. It is now the relationship between the subjective observer and the observed object that will determine our view of the event. In Einstein's experiment it was the man's position *vis-à-vis* the train that defined his perception of it. Einstein validated the status of individual subjectivity. In Fairbairn it is the incorporation of dynamic structure into psychology that consolidates the status of individual subjectivity.

The progenitors of changes in consciousness

Our century has been an "era of suspicion" orchestrated by the impact of three thinkers: Marx, Nietzsche, and Freud. Nothing is quite what it was. Marx exposed the hypocrisy of society and politics; Nietzsche exposed the hypocrisy of double standards and religious practice; and Freud exposed human self-deception and unacknowledged motivation.

Marx exposed the superficial view of society and politics as a deceptive image cloaking the operation of power. In the process he developed a theory of individual alienation, which operated psychologically and subtly induced social conformity. In his early "Economic and Philosophical Manuscripts" (1844), Marx says that consciousness is socially constructed. In his words: "[I]t is the alienation of self-consciousness which establishes thingness" (p. 387). Marx's view is directly derived from Hegel's argument that self-consciousness is mankind's defining characteristic. Self-consciousness involves the process of self-reflection, so it is an intrinsic state of ego-splitting. This validates Fairbairn's notion that ego-splitting is an inevitable fact of life.

Nietzsche, through irony, exposed the cowardice of conformity, for his "superman" is no fascist imposing his views upon others, but a man who understands and overcomes the dichotomy between individual integrity and conformity, thus gaining freedom. Moreover, in "God is dead", Nietzsche (1882–83) identifies two phenomena: (1) we pretend that we believe in God, but we behave as though He is dead; (2) the recognition that God could no longer act as the guarantor of "truth". Nietzsche (1887) wrote: "We of the present day are only just beginning to form the chain of a very powerful feeling, link for link—we hardly know what we are doing" (1887, p. 268). Thus he anticipated "the epistemic trauma" described by Vargish and Mook (1999). Fairbairn (1941) addresses these issues in his theory of infantile and mature dependence, in which infantile dependence is a state of "primary identification with the object" (Fairbairn, 1952b, p. 41). In the unmediated infantile mode uncertainty induces anxiety—ambiguity cannot be contained. The mature mode involves "relationships with differentiated objects"—ambiguity can be embraced.

Freud's theory of the dynamic unconscious challenged standard assumptions about "time" itself. The Freudian unconscious allied to transference theory provided a cogent theoretical confirmation of an altered view of time. So, as Lechte (1994, p. 1) says, "The past can no longer be understood in its own terms because now the past is to be understood in terms of the concerns of the present." Taken literally, this implies that time can only be defined by the subjective individual. In *Time and Free Will* Bergson (1889) described experienced time as "duration"—a process that defines reality subjectively but remains impervious to the operation of instinct. Time, as defined by Freud, is the result of instinctual activity in the subject. As such, it cannot be separated from instinct. Thus Freudian theory cannot accommodate a total dislocation of consciousness. Freudian psychopathology is empirical because it relies upon a first cause, the elision of "truth" and "knowledge". So, we cannot agree with Lechte's contention that Freud's dynamic unconscious *alone* was able to initiate a total shift in consciousness; it only caused a semi-disjunction. Hence Freudian theory cannot account for "epistemic trauma" described by Vargish and Mook.

In Fairbairn's theory the past is also active in the present in inner reality, but it is held within a relationship coloured by affective experience. His endopsychic structure incorporates Einstein's view that structure and energy are inseparable. In Fairbairn energy and structure are inseparable from the relational positions adopted by his ego/object structures. Fairbairn's theory of endopsychic structure can then describe a "physical context".

I identified space as a vital component of the disjunctive change in consciousness. Here, dreaming in Freud and Fairbairn clarifies the difference between the basic assumptions of the two theories. In Freud, dream content is interpreted in terms of linguistic disjunction, double meanings, and assumed instinctual desires. Dreaming is seen as a primitive or irrational process. So space is constant, and time is duration. The meaning of the dream objects assumes authority via their etymological roots. Certainty is established, and ambiguity is vanquished. But language is always changing, so it cannot remain authoritative.

Fairbairn sees dreams as film "shorts" (1952a, p. 99): a dramatic enactment of internal space–time relationships within which change is accommodated. Interpretations are made through the understanding of the structure of the relationships between the subjects and the objects contained in the dream. Roles can be exchanged (1952a, pp. 8–9), which indicates an active internal reality that accommodates space–time and ambiguity. This is possible because the whole inner world of endopsychic relationships is involved. Dreaming is neither primitive nor irrational; on the contrary, it is a process of exploration of inner states.

Modernism and postmodernism

Late nineteenth- and twentieth-century European philosophy, whatever its form, is a response to Kant and Hegel. Commonly, the terms "modernism" and "postmodernism" have referred to art, architecture, and literature. Whatever, its classification, European philosophy focused upon the study of differential relationships and their effects on human beings and their institutions. The primary aim of modern philosophy has been to establish the relationship between the subject and the object, the substance of Fairbairn's work. I see modernism in terms of the change in consciousness that this study entailed. Philosophically, postmodernism is the deconstruction of the differential relationships that form the structure of the institutions or disciplines.

"Modernity" was initially seen as the emergence from the cage of truth by for example, Dostoevsky, who in *The Double* (1846; the second part of *Notes from Underground*, 1864) metaphorically examines the implications of the escape from the cage of dogma through his account of Golyadkin's descent into chaos. This occurs when he allows his alter ego to take over his activities as a form of personal indulgence, with no regard for the effect his actions may have on others. This attitude denies personal responsibility.

An additional face of modernity is that of the uninvolved "observer of modern life". Baudelaire saw the artist Daumier as such a man—a man for whom any aspect, public or private facet or object of life can become the object of art and comment. This perceived elevation of the ordinary and the private to objects of "Art" was another radical assault upon received consciousness. We can see here that Modernism thus encompasses a positive and a negative or deconstructive dichotomy.

Modernity also refers to industrialization or technological change, which alters the relationship between the human subject and its object, resulting in a dislocation of the previous relationship. Benjamin addressed these issues in 1934 and 1936. Benjamin (1934) sees the *position* of the worker with respect to his *actual* work as defining the *function* of his work. The factory worker is dissociated from the product of his work and thus has lost his autonomy. Benjamin finds that artists or writers also lose autonomy if they make their work conform to a specific ideology. Benjamin saw the woodcut as the first example of mechanically reproducible art. So, when a Gutenberg press became available to Dürer through his uncle, "the printer" of Nuremberg, Dürer was able to increase his income. For Dürer, the woodcut had the potential for greater reproducibility than did the copperplate. But Benjamin argues that "The uniqueness of a work of art is inseparable from its being embedded in the fabric of tradition" (1936, p. 220). While Dürer, himself, retained his personal autonomy, today, when the original work of art is superseded by, say, a photograph, which itself becomes another "original", which in its turn is reproduced, the dissociation of the work of art from the originator, or artist, is virtually total. The work is now divorced from its tradition, dislocated from its place in history, and its relationship with the artist in space and time has been severed.

Kant is seen by Greenberg (1965) as the father of modernism, for, in *The Critique of Pure Reason*, "logic" itself is the critical tool. In Greenberg's words, "Modernism criticises from the inside through the procedures themselves of that which is being criticised" (p. 6). Moreover, he says: "Scientific method alone asks that a situation be resolved in exactly the same kind of terms as that in which it is presented—a problem in physiology is solved in terms of physiology, not in those of psychology; to be solved in terms of psychology, it has to be presented in, or translated into, these terms first" (1965, p. 8). This requirement imposes either a reordering and subsequent reinterpretation of physiology into psychological terms, or the containment of the ambiguity between them.

In *Legislators and Interpreters*, Bauman sees that "the concepts of modernity and post-modernity stand for two sharply different contexts in which the "intellectual role" is performed; and two distinct strategies which develop in response to them" (1987, p. 3). Here he sees the modernist strategy as "legislative", or authoritative, and the post-modernist as "interpretive". In the modernist view, the world is seen as an "orderly totality"—moving towards universality. The notion of universality and the inevitability of progress are the modern remnants of the Enlightenment.

Turning to postmodernism, Bauman writes,

The typically post-modern view of the world is, . . . one of an unlimited number of models of order, each one generated by a relatively autonomous set of practices. Order does not precede practices and hence cannot serve as an outside measure of their validity. Each of the many models makes sense solely in terms of the practices which validate it, and in which "Systems of knowledge can only be evaluated from 'inside' their respective traditions". [1987, p. 4]

This leads Bauman to define "knowledge" as "embeddedness" in its particular tradition. For Bauman the intellectual role of the "interpreter"

consists of translating statements, made within one . . . tradition, so that they can be understood within the system of knowledge based on another tradition. Instead of being orientated towards selecting the best social order, this strategy is aimed at facilitating communication between autonomous (sovereign) participants. It is concerned to prevent the distortion of meaning in the process of communication. [1987, p. 5]

Postmodernism can be seen as a modern variety of scepticism. As Bauman argued, it is anti-authoritarian and deconstructive. It can best be described as an attitude of mind in which protest becomes the pursuit of "interest" and thus a form of anarchy. Stirner, in the *Ego and His Own* (1845), suggests that the individual can choose to associate with specific groups for a period of time until his, or her, self-interest has been achieved. Thus freedom is reformulated as a question of personal interest.

Discussing MacIntyre (1985), Beveridge and Turnbull write: "'The dominant moral theory in contemporary thought is emotivism; it is emotivism which informs everyday attitudes . . .'—as MacIntyre says '. . . people now think, talk and act as if emotivism were true. . . . Emotivism has become embedded in our culture' (MacIntyre, 1985, p. 22)" (Beveridge & Turnbull, 1989, p. 101). So individual morality takes the form of "persuading others to adopt the same attitudes", Beveridge and Turnbull continue, "'this is good' means that I approve of it; please do so too" (1989, p. 101). It is the denigration of genuine feeling into an active mode of emotivism, which itself is detached from a genuine appreciation of reality. In Fairbairn's terms the individual is operating at an infantile level in which the incorporating attitude towards objects has become a fixed characteristic (1952a, p. 18).

Hegel and endopsychic structure

The importance of Fairbairn's reliance upon Hegelian psychology cannot be overestimated. In Hegel's theory, human maturation is dependent upon a satisfactory environment. Maturation is a process of "coming to be" held within the limitations of human biology and an interactive environment.

Hegel was the first thinker to provide a coherent account of how meaning and value, belief and emotion are associated with the objects in our minds. Hegel (1817, p. 243) described an unconscious process through which affect is associated with "facts" or "contents" in the mind. This association, which may be a single affective response or a complex of affects with the "fact" (the mental image), becomes a *"special object"*. Thus inner objects are composed of "fact" (the image of the object) and the affect, or affects, attached to it. In Fairbairn, the mother, as the "fact" or "content" of a "special object", is seen in three affective modes: alluring, rejecting, and acceptable or "good". These are the *"forms"* assumed by the "contents". Each form in conjunction with the "fact" (the mother) then gives rise to the "exciting", "rejecting", and "ideal" objects. Because the mother is defined by three separate affective experiences, she becomes three separate mothers. The three separate mothers then embody a separate relationship with the child.

The first two aspects of the mother (as an object) are associated with an ego structure to form a sector of Fairbairn's endopsychic structure, which is comprised by the dyadic relationships between the split-off parts of the ego attached to the exciting and rejecting objects, respectively. Both dyads must be understood as the *unsatisfying* or *"bad"* aspects of the earliest relationship as it was experienced and assessed by the infant. As both these relationships have been identified as unsatisfying, these two dyadic structures are repressed to form the dynamic of the closed part of the inner world. The adequately satisfying aspects of the infant/mother relationship become the "ideal object". It is "ideal" because it is shorn of the unsatisfying aspects of the mother. The ideal object is in direct relationship with the central ego and is thus accessible to change and modification in accordance with external "reality". Reality here is seen as that which is "other" and consists of the environment within which the self exists, as well as the other selves with whom the individual interacts. For Fairbairn, reality is that which exists its own right, and the mother comes into this category. The extent to which the infant–mother relationship is satisfying will determine the capacity of the self for adaptation to change. The endopsychic structure is then a dialectic environmental response to an object.

Discussing the evaluation of "good" and "bad" in terms of "the friends/enemies opposition", Bauman in *Modernity and Ambivalence* argues that this opposition "sets apart truth from falsity, good from evil, beauty from ugliness. It also differentiates between proper and improper, right and wrong, tasteful and unbecoming. It makes the world readable and instructive" (1991, p. 54). Later, Bauman writes: "Following Simmel, we may say that friendship and enmity, and only they are forms of *sociation*; indeed, they are the archetypal forms of all sociation, and together constitute its two-pronged matrix. [Moreover] . . . Being a friend and being an enemy, are the two modalities in which the *Other* may be recognised as another *subject*" (p. 54; italics in original).

For Fairbairn and Bauman it is relationships that determine meaning and value, while Fairbairn's oppositional dyads of "inner reality" could well be described as determining "the archetypal forms of all sociation", especially as Bauman specifically describes "a two-pronged matrix".

In his work Bauman relies upon a theory of object relations and confirms Fairbairn's contentions. So, in line with modernist thought, Fairbairn's model of endopsychic structure, based upon differential relationships, provides a matrix for subsequent relationships.

Being in the world

Heidegger sees the human infant as being "thrown into the world"—each individual is precipitated into a specific space–time. A specific time and space involves everything that impinges upon the child. How can the child cope with the enigma of being thrown into the world? Following a discussion about instinct as the capacity for unlearned behaviour and the human infant's incapacity for purposive behaviour, but who is yet "fitted" for survival, in *Persons in Relation*, Macmurray writes: "He is, in fact, 'adapted', to speak paradoxically, to being unadapted, to a complete dependence upon an adult human being. He is born into a love-relationship which is inherently personal" (1961, p. 48). But to survive he must maintain his dependent relationship with the carer. Fairbairn writes: "The capacity to apprehend relationships between situations or objects and the constituent elements of both is . . . the highest function of adaptation to reality" (1930, p. 142). It is to this capacity for adaptation that Fairbairn ascribes our ability to understand and maintain relationships.

Heidegger cites language as an example of this adaptability. For although the capacity for language is inherent, the actual language of the family is not. Not only is the language specific to the culture, but it is also so in a particular stage of its development. Language structures thought and imposes parameters of its own.

In *Modernity and Ambivalence*, Bauman sees language as the capacity to name and classify. He says: "to classify means to set apart, to segregate" (1991, p. 1). The process of classification results in the identification of similar and dissimilar entities. This is followed by the process of realizing (making real) the entities, "by linking differential patterns of action to different classes of entities. . . . To classify, in other words, is to give the world a *structure*: to manipulate its probabilities; to make some events more likely than some others; to behave as if events were not random, or to limit or eliminate randomness of events" (1991, p. 1).

Thus for Bauman language promotes the illusion of order that allows us to predict events, but "Ambivalence confounds calculation of events and confuses the relevance of memorized action patterns" (1991, p. 2). Here Bauman is suggesting that the capacity for language itself is a condition of "splitting". Moreover, he implies that the incapacity to accommodate ambivalence can cause confused reactive responses. This is very much Fairbairn's own position.

Discussing language in semantic terms, Bauman defines ambivalence as "the possibility of assigning an object or an event to more than one category. . . . It arises from one of the main functions of language: that of naming and classifying. . . . Ambivalence is therefore the *alter ego* of language, and its permanent companion—indeed its normal condition" (1991, p. 1; italics in original).

In 1930 Fairbairn discussed "silence" and the benefits of linguistic expression in the psychoanalytic session; he says:

> language is a conceptual function and the patient's attempt
> to express his thoughts in words involves some degree of conceptual mastery of the ideational material. Here it may be remarked that some of the periods of silence which occur in the course of analytic treatment appear to be due not so much to the patient's resistance as to his inability to express his

thoughts in words. This difficulty is, of course, more marked when the patient's reaction is at the perceptual than when it is at the ideational level. It is of the utmost importance, however, that the patient should be required to make a maximum effort to express his thought and feelings in words; for whatever success he meets in doing this is so far a victory for the conceptual functions. The interpretations offered by the analyst, on appropriate occasions, aid the conceptual function by enabling the patient to grasp more fully the relations existing between his various ideational processes. [1930, p. 144]

A state of self-consciousness acknowledges that "I" can observe "me". It carries with it the concept of "recognition". We can consciously assert that we exist in the form of a self because we are recognized as a self by another person. Being known and being communicated with is essential to confirm a certainty of one's "self" and its identity. To be active and free in the world, reciprocal relationships are a necessary condition. It is from this position that the development of human potential becomes viable. The philosopher Ortega wrote: "To be free means to be lacking a constitutive identity, . . . to be able to be other than what one was, . . . The only attribute of the fixed, stable being in the free being is this constitutive instability" (Ortega, 1941, p. 11, cited in Kaufmann, 1975, p. 156). Here Ortega has defined freedom as the capacity for change—to leave one position and move on to another. In Fairbairn's endopsychic structure, we have a living systems model that is designed to accommodate such change.

Fairbairn's theory of mature dependence: the containment of ambivalence

Because Fairbairn relies upon Aristotle's definition of "man" as a "social" and "political" animal, a condition of dependence is inevitable in Fairbairn's theory. Macmurray confirms Fairbairn's view in these words: "It is that he cannot, even theoretically, live an isolated existence; that he is not an independent individual. He lives a common life as one term in a personal relation. Only in the process of development does he learn to achieve a relative independence, and that only by appropriating the techniques of a rational social tradition" (1961, p. 50).

For Fairbairn, the inner world and the endopsychic structure arose in a condition of complete dependence. Initially the mother promotes affective responses in the infant. These patterns of response are then categorized by the infant and solidified as affective states of loving and hating to form the preambivalent object. Eventually, the dichotomy is too intense for the infant to accommodate, and the preambivalent object is divided and repressed in combination with split-off parts of the ego to form the ego/object dyads. Thus loving and hating are separated but remain active in the inner world. However, Fairbairn introduced two categories of dependence: infantile dependence, the psychic attitude of which is "taking" and "incorporating", as opposed to the mature attitude of "giving" and "non-incorporation". In "Arms and the Child" (1937) Fairbairn wrote: "It is as natural for the young child to be dependent as it is desirable for the adult to be independent; and, if the young child does not get the assurance of the love and support which he demands, the result is that his craving for it is increased, instead of diminished, and he is confirmed in a dependent attitude" (1937, p. 330).

Mature dependence is attained when the individual is able to contain the ambivalence of loving and hating. This occurs when the mother is accepted and interacted with as a reality-based individual with strengths, weaknesses, and sexuality (1952a, pp. 38–43). This implies an attitude of responsibility towards others. Bauman writes: "My link with the stranger is revealed as *responsibility*, not just indifferent neutrality or even cognitive acceptance of the similarity of condition . . . It is revealed, . . . as a commonality of destiny, not mere resemblance of fate. Shared fate would do with mutual *tolerance*; joint destiny requires *solidarity*" (1991, p. 236; italics in original). This statement introduces a moral aspect into the containment of ambivalence. The whole ethos of Fairbairn's work contains within it an underlying acceptance of personal responsibility for others. When the inner world of the adult is excessively closed, its operating mode is infantile. We can conclude with Fairbairn that excessive ego-splitting and a high degree of rejection of internal objects is equivalent to the refusal to acknowledge our personal obligations within society.

Identifications: the social construction of reality

During the 1930s Fairbairn wrote a number of papers on child development and education on which I draw here. The child's early relationships with its parents take the form of a series of "identifications". The initial identification will be with the mother. However, for Fairbairn, *the dynamic of identification is a need* (Fairbairn, 1994a, p. 116; italics in original). The extent of the child's need introduces ambivalence into this primary relationship. Similar identification with the father occurs, though it is complicated by two factors: (1) the child judges the father's relationship with the mother, in respect of the extent to which the mother's attention is diverted from the child to the father, as confirmation that she prefers the father; (2) this is further complicated by the "power and authority" that the father exhibits towards both the mother and the child. "[T]hus, Fairbairn says, "the young child's attitude to both parents is characterised by ambivalence" (Fairbairn, 1994b, p. 358). The result of the ambivalence, in each parental relationship, is that some of the original warmth incorporated within the primary identification is transferred to the father and vice versa. Power and authority exhibited by each parent in respect of each other and the child becomes a factor in further identifications. The child may make stronger identifications with the parent of the same sex or the opposite sex. Fairbairn (1955) sums it up: "identification is a *specific* process which is *affective* rather than cognitive, and is essentially *active*" (1994a, p. 116; italics in original). Thus multiple identifications during maturation form a matrix from which interpersonal relationships are developed throughout life. Here it is important to realize that Fairbairn's living systems model has the intrinsic flexibility to accommodate multiple object relationships. The human personality is then a social construct within which object relationships are, for Fairbairn, the road to meaning, value and belief.[1]

Berger and Luckmann argue that "Apprehension does not result from autonomous creations of meaning by isolated individuals, but begins with the individual "taking over" the world in

---

[1] These quotes and exegesis are from "Psychoanalysis and the Teacher" (1931b, pp. 358–359); "The Superego" (1929b, pp. 87–91); "In Defence of Object Relations Theory" (1955, pp. 115–117).

which others already live" (1967, p. 150). Thus I come to understand not only another individual's subjectivity, " . . . but also the world in which he lives, and that world becomes my own" (p. 150). This then is the process of identification and its solidification to become an intrinsic aspect of the child's own subjective reality. Berger and Luckmann continue: "The significant others who mediate the world to him modify it in the process of mediating it" (p. 151). The content of this selective process depends upon the mores of the society and personal biography of the transmitter.

Truth and knowledge

We started off with Fairbairn's reformulation of psychoanalytic theory from a cultural situation in which "knowledge" was seen to be problematic—and where there appeared to be no accepted authority through which "truth" could be established. The dissolution of absolute space and time to form a space–time continuum caused the "epistemic trauma" of uncertainty and ambivalence. Fairbairn responded to this situation by developing a psychoanalytic theory within which ambiguity is contained. Subjective experience is necessarily limited; nonetheless, it has veracity. In the process of self-reflection we can mitigate entrenched positions and understand our own historicity. Speaking of scientific "truth", Fairbairn remarks: science is "essentially an intellectual tool and nothing more . . . scientific truth, so far from providing an . . . accurate picture of reality as it exists, is *simply explanatory truth* [moreover] . . . *science is an intellectual construct*" (1994a, p. 78; italics in original).

So, for Fairbairn, science and culture are both mental constructs. As such, there is no reason to separate them on the grounds of the superior status of scientific explanation as "truth" or "knowledge". Fairbairn sees subjective and scientific knowledge of equivalent validity, with the proviso that the application of appropriate scientific method can confirm or deny the claims of practice.

In *Reason and Emotion* Macmurray wrote: "For science things exist in terms of something else. Reality is that which exists in and for itself, the individual. Knowledge is the grasp of reality, the contemplation of the individual in its own proper being. This is precisely what art gives us and science does not" (1935, p. 92).

Hegelian psychology formed the intellectual bedrock for Macmurray and Fairbairn. It is, therefore, directly from Hegel's concepts of recognition, negation (which subsumes self-consciousness), and a dialectic environment that both Macmurray and Fairbairn forged their theories. "Knowledge" is a subjective condition which, in Macmurray's work, is obtained through the "self" acting as an agent (Macmurray, 1957)—an active participant within an interactive environment and in communication with other human selves.

To clarify Macmurray's position (1957, pp. 100–103), "knowledge" is a subjective condition that is dependent upon an active self or "agent". Macmurray writes: "a self which does not act cannot exist" (p. 100). We could say that if we only think, we are inoperative, unable to intervene in the external world; we could not be even recognized as a subject by another subject. Macmurray argues that "knowledge arises in action"—"We can only think about what we already know" (p. 101). For Macmurray, this is "primary knowledge" or "experience". While this personal knowledge, or "experience" is valid, such knowledge has its limitations. It cannot take full account of the reactions of the external world or of another self upon and between which the self as agent acts. Both Macmurray and Fairbairn maintain that such subjective knowledge is not necessarily irrational. On the contrary, it is essentially rational. This is Fairbairn's argument for ego splitting as a rational response on the part of the infant. Macmurray argues that, "thought [alone] cannot provide a criterion of truth, but at most a criterion of the correctness of the process of thinking" (1957, p. 102). Here, Einstein adds his voice: "Pure logical thinking can give us no knowledge whatsoever of the world of experience; all knowledge about reality begins with experience and terminates with it" (1933, p. 144).

On the question of agency, Macmurray maintains: *"The Self can be agent only by being also subject"* (1957, p. 101; italics in original).

To act and to know that I am acting are two aspects of one experience; ... There cannot be action without knowledge. Yet

action is logically prior to knowledge for there can be no
knowledge without an actual activity which supports it; but
there can be actual activity without knowledge. Such activity
however is not action but only movement; or at most reaction
to stimulus; not a deliberate effort to modify the Other.
[Macmurray, 1957, pp. 102–103]

We can see here that Macmurray has confirmed Fairbairn's model
of an active participant with personal agency, which operates
within an interactive environment in direct interpersonal communication with other human selves. Macmurray has validated the
claims of subjective experience as knowledge. Philosophically Fairbairn concurs, but with the understanding that in adverse environmental or genetic circumstances, which themselves cause excessive
splitting, psychopathological attitudes are likely to emerge. In such
cases the validity of subjective knowledge is compromised. Subjective knowledge is the best we have, but "truth" remains conditional.

We remain in the uncomfortable postmodern situation in
which, on the one hand, subjective knowledge is conditional, and
on the other, science is unable to provide us with universal "knowledge" or "a priori" truth. Macmurray (1961) described science as
"the world of information which is anybody's" as opposed to
"knowledge which is always somebody's" (in Conford, 1972,
p. 18).

When we fully accept this ambivalent position, we can draw
upon both information and personal knowledge to accommodate
"uncertainty" as a necessary limitation to human omnipotence.
As Bauman and Fairbairn suggested, interpretation is the key to
understanding and mutual respect. Psychoanalysis is an interpretive discipline; as such, it should be able to fulfil its potentially
mediative role, not only in the microcosm of the intersubjective
psychoanalytic session, but in the macrocosm of the socio-cultural
arena in which we all live, act, and have our being. I see Fairbairn's
theoretical contribution as providing a secure philosophical foundation for the further development of psychoanalytic thinking
in the wider field of societal, intercultural, and interconflictual
relations.

PART II

FAIRBAIRN'S THEORY APPLIED

CHAPTER FOUR

The problem of melancholia in the work of Fairbairn

António Coimbra de Matos

A little more sun—and there would be blazing heat,
A little more blue—and there would be a heavenly sky.
To reach it, I lacked a decisive strike . . .

Mário de Sá-Carneiro, 1913

The problem of melancholy passes like a shadow through the work of Ronald Fairbairn. Indeed, it is a psychopathology that he does not greatly explore, and that almost only appears as a counterpoint to schizophrenia.

Fairbairn begins by distinguishing the schizoid position—which he describes and to which he attaches more importance—from the depressive position, as conceptualized by Melanie Klein. He dismantles the paranoid position already described by Klein, and he describes paranoia as being merely a defensive technique used to deal with bad objects that have been internalized (together with obsessive, hysterical, and phobic techniques) from the transitional period between infantile dependence and mature interdependence; furthermore, the paranoid position takes priority over the depressive position. The nucleus of all psychopathology is, for him, the schizoid phenomenon—the splitting of the self—conceiving this (the self) as a dynamic structure, as a structure with energy: the self has an objective—its libido seeks an object.

The relationship between the self and the object is the axis of his conceptual system, of his theory of personality: indeed, Fairbairn is a theorist, and one of the most illustrious at that, on *object relationships*.

The *nature of the object*, its relationship to the self as it is *lived* and experienced, does not escape perspicacious clinical investigation by the author. Thus the duplicity of the object—its "ambivalent" nature, sometimes good, sometimes bad, satisfactory or unsatisfactory, gratifying or frustrating, accepting or rejecting, and, lastly, in Fairbairn's theory, accepted or rejected because of being rejecting or exciting—will influence (although this affirmation is implied[1]) the splitting of the self, which itself follows the splitting of the object.

The primordial conflict occurs between the tying and the untying, the investment and non-investment of the object (the non-investment of reality—understood, above all, as the object world—had already been described by Freud, 1911c [1910], in his psychoanalytic study of the autobiography of Schreber, as being the primary process or defence mechanism leading to psychosis), or, as Fairbairn points out, between loving and not loving the object, suckling or not suckling at the breast. This is the state of pre-ambivalence of the self, trapped in a *conflict of original ambi-tendency*—seeking and rejecting the self. In the primary schizoid conflict, this aggressiveness is absent (if we accept the rejection/ avoidance of the object as disproving aggressiveness); there would therefore be no ambivalence but now only ambi-tendency. In effect, in the treatment of autistic children, when hate emerges in the transference, it is a sign that positive evolution is in progress. The unconnected self withdraws itself from reality, and the distracted attitude of the schizoid patient, said to be one of introversion,

---

[1] In fact, Fairbairnian conception does not completely surpass the concept of a dynamic self that qualifies the object, without reaching the level of a theory of dynamic self-object inter-relationship—in other words, of a mutual and mutually intentional relationship that is attuned [Daniel Stern's affective attunement (Stern, 1985)] or non-attuned.

therefore emerges. We could say that the self is more than split—it is dismantled (Meltzer, 1980) and disorganized, subject as it was to the effects of passive and multiple "splitting" through a lack of object tying. This self in fragments is only linked to vestiges of the good introjected object.

Schizoid functioning is contemporaneous with the first oral sub-stage described by Karl Abraham (1911), and at any time during life the individual may regress into or make use of this function.

In contrast, melancholic conflict is a conflict of ambivalence between love and hate, suckling or biting the breast: contemporary with the second oral sub-stage, which is cannibalistic and sadistic. However, Fairbairn does not accept the theory of instincts, and that of the death instinct even less. For him, aggressiveness is *a reaction to frustration* ("It is the experience of libidinal frustration which leads to aggression"—Fairbairn, 1944). Here, the value and the significance of the object emerge once more and more firmly.

In melancholia, the bad object is interiorized and repressed; the (aggressive) conflict with the object—in other words, the relationship of the bad object—is therefore internalized. The preponderance of this internal bad-object relationship characterizes depressive or melancholic functioning. The sado-masochist relationship, and especially the masochistic relationship, of the internal bad object, buried within what I call the *pit of demons*, consumes the self from within and is insidiously reflected in external behaviour; but when defence by repression fails, the return of the repressed bad objects is accompanied by fury and/or terror (in dreams or in insomnia), with a negative therapeutic reaction, aggressive transference, or even panic attacks and auto- or hetero-aggressive disruptive behaviour, *verbi gratia* suicide, homicide, and destructive activity.

Fairbairn also shows us another defensive mechanism—which we ourselves describe as being fundamental in depression—which he calls "moral defence", "defence through guilt", or "superego defence": in his own words, "the child takes upon himself the burden of badness which appears to reside in his objects" (Fairbairn, 1952a, p. 65). We call this process—which is pathological and pathogenic—*malignant introjection* or *introjection of the evil of the object* (Matos, 1997a).

We may now conclude that in melancholia the destiny of the object is twofold: (1) in part, it is introjected orbitally, making up the internalized bad object; (2) in part, it is introjected as a nucleus, incorporating the evil extracted from the object into the very substance of the ego. This transformation of the identity of the individual by introjecting the malign aspect of the object is or forms a full trait of the melancholic personality—loaded, by the individual himself, with guilt.

The moral defence—employed to save the face of the object, to make it good—is one of the mechanisms that most destroys self-esteem—*the removal of guilt from another by blaming oneself.*

Nevertheless, the pathological, excessive, and illogical guilt evident in the depressive is not rooted in this alone; it also results from two other origins:

1. The first origin of irrational guilt arises from the guilt induced by the aggressor, implanted by the latter in the victim (as Ferenczi, 1933, has already observed in his work on "language confusion", we can see the concept of "identification with the aggressor" as an "identification with the guilt of the aggressor"). The phenomenon is more strictly defined as the process of assimilating the assigned guilt, which falls under the more general process of identification with the assigned identity— the looking-glass self or *imagoic-imagetic identification* (Matos, 1996) with the imago and/or image that the other assigns to oneself. It is a primitive process for constructing an identity, but for this very reason it is very impressive. It is guilt arising from the guilt-assigned projection of the object or, rather, from the projective pathological and evacuative identification of the object—which the self introjects (projective counteridentification: taking on a role, having the identity that the other has assigned to him). The depressive personality or the personality predisposed to depression, the depression itself, is a disease of introjection (the diametric opposite of paranoia).

2. The other origin of irrational guilt is based on a rationalization to explain the affective loss, the loss of love for the object, that is the first and final cause of the depressive reaction: "the object abandoned me because I am bad," thinks the patient.

And thus the aggressiveness is inverted towards the individual, sparing the object. It is a movement that once again is pathological and pathogenic, morbid and causing morbidity for the *inflection of aggressiveness*.

* * *

The internal dynamism of melancholia does not end here, however. Other factors enter the picture; other mechanisms are used.

Fairbairn, at one point in his life and work (1944—*Endo-Psychic Structure in Terms of Object Relationships*), describes a child's experiences of humiliation and shame at the hands of its mother who rejects its love (humiliation with regard to the loathing of its love, shame of the manifestation of a need that is disregarded and minimized). These actions, which are of a narcissistic nature, make the child feel inferior.

The feelings of inferiority translate into narcissistic depletion or discharge and consequent low self-esteem—a rupture of the self-esteem that has, since Freud (in melancholia, there is a loss in the self) and more explicitly since Bibring (narcissistic ruin of the depressed), been considered to be an important sign of depression. However, Fairbairn prefers to consider this "loss of libido", as he calls it, as a cause of the feeling of uselessness that is typical of the schizoid character. In our opinion, the feeling of uselessness results from a more drastic and stronger narcissistic discharge, which is the basis for psychotic collapse, with a depersonalization and disintegration of the mind—indeed, primary self-esteem is the cement for the cohesion of the self and the feeling of identity.

In melancholia there is certainly a loss of the good object; however, there is also a loss of the part of the self, which disappears with the good object, given the narcissistic relationship (or the primary identification, as Fairbairn calls it, following in the footsteps of Freud). Furthermore, there is also a loss (and how!) of the good object in schizophrenia. The difference, according to us, is in the degree.

In schizophrenia there is also a breakdown of identity, given the predominance of the relationship of identification once the relationship is lost. In depression, on the other hand, where there is already some autonomy and framework of identity, the loss of the relationship with the object merely entails a vacillation of the identity, resorting to an identity with a social role as an artificial replacement.

Whatever the case, to return to what has previously been said, what cannot be overcome is the fact that, in depression (or melancholia), the idealized object, which is lost in reality because it is unlovable, is conserved inside; in schizophrenia, on the other hand, the good internal object is almost not formed or is snuffed out. There is an enormous void left by the good object, and this feeling of emptiness is a characteristic of the schizoid personality—and, by extension and through similarity, it is always present in psychotic and borderline personalities.

In melancholia, the idealized object fills an important space in the mind. And this internal object is the target for an unconscious powerful libidinal investment. Even Freud said, in a letter to Abraham (5 May 1915), that the main problem of melancholia was the "unconscious investment of the object" (Freud & Abraham, 2002). Safeguarded and adored in what I call the *sanctuary of the idols*, a kind of private inner sanctum, the *idealized lost object* captures the majority of the libido of the self, which is thus derived in an internal circuit and which is lacking for the investment in reality. This is the depressive withdrawal into a world with a certain inner happiness, withdrawal into the chancel. Psychotic withdrawal is into the cold and into the void, in the chilling silence of the graveyard. Once again, there are transitions of pathologies and variations in degree—nevertheless, for the most part it is close to or below zero.

Within the parameter of libidinal investment (which relates to the object and is narcissistic), as occurs, as we have described, for the parameter of aggressiveness and guilt, the hyper-investment/idealization of the object of love is accompanied by the non-investment/devaluation of the self. It is the process I describe as *ideality lost in the idealization of the object*, which couples and intertwines with the *process of blaming the self* (Matos, 1982). These two dynamic, intricately linked processes together sustain the occurrence of melancholia.

* * *

Ronald Fairbairn, perhaps because of his experience of war psychology—although certainly not just because of this (remember his work with abused children)—pertinently develops the theme of separation anxiety. This anguish, as almost always occurs with reference to the schizoid model, with several incursions into the psychopathy of hysteria, is also observed in the light of the phenomenon of splitting the self (Fairbairn, 1954c).

Separation anxiety is conditioned by immature or infantile dependence: on the mother, the breast, and the familiar and protective environment (the object as security object, so to speak); immediately, obviously, and consequently by the persistence of the emotional ties to the internalized primitive objects, both real and symbolic, and their extensions resulting from their formal/functional proximity, continuity, and similarity (i.e. operations of the primary process of thought or symmetrical logic).

In schizoid, infantile dependence—anaclatism (as well as primary identification—belonging, narcissistic fulfilment/repletion)—is considerable; although it is frequently disguised. For this reason, the threat of severing the link results in separation anxiety (which is almost pathognomonic in the borderline personality).

However, dependence upon the object is also to be found in the depressive personality, although in a different mould. Indeed, the depressive is highly dependent upon his object; he is truly addicted to it. Nevertheless, he depends more upon the love of the object than upon the object itself. The need to be loved is overriding, constant, and almost insatiable. The person wants to be the only and special target of the object's love. From this perspective, the depressive promises a canine loyalty, in order to ensure forever the love of the object, although for the most part he behaves like a disloyal cat because he is afraid and does not want to be dependent. Jealousy, therefore, always rears its head. The threat of loss or the loss of the object's love does not cause separation anxiety or insecurity but, rather, depressive anxiety or depression (despondency). This is the difference between *helplessness* (abandonment) and *hopelessness* (loss of hope).

The difference, then, is that one—the schizoid—depends upon the object, whereas the other—the depressive—depends upon the object's love.

Jealousy, as mentioned above, reveals a trait of narcissistic weakness, which brings the depressive closer to the schizoid—although without confusing the two: the depressive's narcissistic

62 FAIRBAIRN'S THEORY APPLIED

insufficiency is less and manifests itself through inferiority; in the schizoid this insufficiency is profound and translates into a lack of cohesion of the self. In addition to this, the depressive is less separated: the self as a whole is more unified, the split parts are smaller, and the central self—in Fairbairn's nomenclature—is greater, denser, and there is more cohesion; the accepted object—still using Fairbairn's nomenclature—which is totally and predominantly good, is of an appreciable size, and the self establishes a closer, more appropriate and harmonious relationship with it.

In summary: *depressive functioning* is based on the other side of the barrier, in the neurotic section of the personality, whereas *schizoid functioning* is based in the psychotic part of the personality, where pathological splitting and projective identification are dominant. Furthermore, the depressive is more object-oriented, he loves his objects; the schizoid is narcissistic—above all, he loves himself (Matos, 1980).

The depressive, as we have already stated, is dependent upon the love of the object; the schizoid is dependent upon the object. The former suffers from depressive anxiety, a fear of losing the object's affection—when he loses it, depression ensues. The latter suffers from separation anxiety, a fear of losing the object—when he loses it, a state of non-compensation prevails (panic attack, delirious breathing, mental confusion, depersonalization, and so on). One becomes depressed, the other collapses.

* * *

Depression is the loss of the object *while it is an object of love* (Matos, 1985b). For this reason, the person does not become sad; neither does he mourn. He becomes dejected and angry, diminished and guilty; he persists in the representation of the object.

And there is more: the depressive lives in an internal world that is saturated with objects, both good and bad; some that are idolized, to which the person pays homage; and others that are malevolent, which require effort in order to be buried. He inhabits a world saturated by the investment of good objects and by the counter-investment of bad objects; or, if you like, he lives occupied with object repair and control of aggression. There is no libido available for new investments, there is no space left for creation.

How can he forget the lost object if a part of the self and the unfinished project were lost along with it? How can he abandon a *relationship that fell short of desire and fantasy?*—Only by recovering the failed project, by resuming the suspended relationship. These are difficult, apparently impossible, tasks given the little hope that remains and the great unhappiness.

How can the lost object be replaced when the self is so weakened and devalued? Or how can the lost object be reinstated when rage stands in the way of this process? It is the *depressive impasse*: neither a different object nor the same object.

And what of the injustice of which the individual was a victim? Perhaps a path can be opened through this aspect. And we find the path of change, but it is *internal change*: a change in attitudes, a change in procedures—changing the styles of relationships, the type of relationship with the object. To list these styles:

1. leaving the depressive and depression-inducing movement in which the person gives more than he receives (in affective currency);

2. more narcissistic repair and less object repair, in order to balance the investment of the self and the investment of the object;

3. object non-idealization and narcissistic improvement—in other words, *recovery of the ideal lost in the idealization of the object*;

4. deflection of the inflected aggressiveness;

5. blaming of the aggressor (abandoner) and removal of blame from the victim (abandoned);

6. progressive alteration of the dominance of the *loci* for regulating self-esteem, in the sense of deactivating to a certain extent the external *locus* in favour of reinforcing the internal *locus*, which is the equivalent of diminishing the dependent narcissism (in the eyes of the other) and developing self-sufficient or self-governed narcissism; the result will be better and more stable self-esteem;

7. in reinforcing self-esteem, giving priority to experiences of success over experiences of gratification and appreciation—in

other words, self-acknowledgement becomes a better criterion than recognition by others; the *idiomorphic identification* is superimposed on the *panallotriomorphic identification;*

8. the principle of responsibility replaces the moral principle (people are responsible rather than guilty); on the other hand, the moral will increasingly be an endogenous moral, resulting from empathy and from feelings of compassion, which is an autonomous moral; the exogenous moral—dictated by others and by the superego (imposed rules), this heteronomous moral—will collapse;

9. guilt and shame—the caustic and corrosive results of depression (in their aspects related to culpability and inferiority, masochistic and narcissistic)—are replaced by *respect* for others and by personal *dignity;*

10. a progressive growth of contact with reality, which goes together with an expansion of the mind.

* * *

Fairbairn sets out a theory of *internalized object relationships*: parts of the self that have been split and repressed in dynamic relationship with parts of the object or objects that have been split and introjected. This is how he conceives psychopathology: as a result of splitting and introjection. The processes of projection (or *exteriorization*, as he calls it) are secondary—techniques to deal with the *rejected and internalized* objects; in other words, there is a precession and precedence of the introjection (*internalization,* to use Fairbairn's term). He does not dwell on projective identification, even in his latest works—although we may perhaps consider it to be implicit in his dream theory, which includes figures composed of the self and of the object, *but* which are interpreted as being the result of introjective fusion (of *nuclear introjection,* in Wisdom's sense) and not of the *projective identification onto the internal object.*

The object seems to be too much in his thinking and beliefs, in his axioms, even though, in contradiction, he encounters difficulties in attributing it energy, needs, desires, and intentions, or granting it the status of a person, of another self, the alter ego. Curiously, he qualifies the internalized object as a dynamic structure, but one that has a borrowed or contaminated energy, originating from the split portion of the self in relation to it.

Therefore, the lucid and radiant Fairbairnian conceptualization, seems to be more adapted to the explanation of depressive pathology, and particularly of borderline pathology—with the internal presence of two split relationships, which alternate in their external or behavioural expression: the bad object relationship and the good object relationship (or in his conception, the rejecting object relationship and exciting object relationship, coupled, respectively, with the libidinal self and the internal saboteur—the anti-libidinal sado-masochistic self).

In depression, which we understand to be a psychopathological organization of a higher degree than the borderline organization, there is only a splitting of the self—it is a bi-facial self (in the manner of Janus), with one vision that is blind and full of rage for the bad object, and one that is enchanted and supplicating towards the ideal object. The object is also not split—strictly speaking, it is an *amphoteric object* .[2] In other words, in the same way as the self, it is bi-facial or divalent (neither ambivalent, as in neurosis, nor univalent, as in psychosis): when it is lacking, it is idealized; when it is present, particularly when its presence is continuous, it is bad and intolerable.

In schizoid functioning, the splitting of the self—again in our opinion—does not predominantly result in repression (which retains a certain degree of integration) but, rather, in projective identification and dispersion, discharge and non-identification (projective), disintegration and loss of the self—a path leading to the feeling of emptiness and uselessness and to unnamed terror. The split object has an extraterritorial destiny: the ideal object and the bad object are projected *outside the privileged relationship*, which becomes lessened; they are gods and monsters that are present in the aspects surrounding the self. Conglomerated with these are particles of the self that are overloaded with aggression and raw and primitive libido—constituting Bion's bizarre objects.

---

[2] Which unites two opposing qualities without merging them; sometimes it acts or reacts as if good, and other times as if bad (in chemistry, as a base or as an acid).

The close internal world, the city of the schizoid, is peopled—if one can call it that—with crumbs of good and of devastation: a graveyard with flowers, split, certainly, but also empty, given the massive projective evacuative identification, useless, solitary, and sterile, with no object and no direction—lost.

And the melancholic? He lives in a state of nostalgia for the lost object of love—a unique, indispensable, irreplaceable object, but one that is, at the same time, impossible, because it is lost in reality (it exists only in the inner world—and so it is a semi-lost object, illusorily possessed). It is also impossible because it is damaging— unlovable, captivating (of non-sacrificial love), guilty, and devaluating, *narcissistic*—and therefore induces a severe lack of narcissism. The individual's dilemma results from the ambiguity of the object experienced and lived, *conceived as an ideal* and *felt as malevolent*.

*   *   *

What stands out in Fairbairn's work is that personality is constructed in the relationship and that it is the object relationship that determines the libidinal attitude and aggressive reaction.

It is more difficult to follow him when he says that "psychology may be summarized as a study of the relationships the individual has with his objects" and that "psychopathology can be more specifically summarized as a study of the relationship of the self with its internalized objects". I prefer to affirm that health and mental growth are the result of the healthy and development-oriented relationship with healthy and expansive, enthusiastic objects, and illness results from the constrained relationship with pathological and pathogenic objects, some of which are external and others internalized, the latter being the most significant, whether in terms of good or bad.

But Fairbairn refers to the relationships between the central self and the internal saboteur and libidinal self, and the relationships between these and the rejected and internalized objects (which are the rejecting object and the exciting object), which limit object internalization by the rejected objects through their evil or over-excitement.

Nevertheless, Fairbairn also affirms, on other occasions or in other tracts of his work, that the *accepted object* is interiorized as a kind of good superego, which he prefers to equate with the ego ideal. Thus, the good and accepted object is also, as far as Fairbairn is concerned, internalized.

The problem, then—to follow his schema for the structure of personality—lies in the "quantity" of central self and accepted object in mutual interrelationship: that is, of the portion of the object relationship that is freer of a dynamic of rejection and excitement, as well as of guilt, shame, and fear; which is the same as the extent of the expansive relationship *covering the real and the passage from one state to another*. The internalization/interiorization of the relationship/object persists throughout the individual's life, transforming the inner world, which, in turn, transforms, through projective communicative identification—adding knowledge and substance, encouraging growth—the external world, the real object, the object world. We are therefore witness to a true *transformational process*, which is both transforming and transformative, in which *both* self and object transform and become transformed. They change while growing (Matos, 1997b).

This is the principle of development and psychoanalytic cure. Analysis is a transformational process (which achieves in the "laboratory" what life did not achieve), and the analyst is a *transformational object*—or the analysis is not an analysis: the one being analysed would end up more ill than at the start, and the one performing the analysis would become more stupid. In the analytic relationship, repetition is reduced and the *new relationship* develops.

* * *

Returning specifically to melancholy in the work of Fairbairn, the following are pillars of his comprehension of melancholic psychopathology:

1. acknowledgement of the weight and significance of *hate* (to be understood as a sustainable and sustained aggression, which assumes that there is some consistency of the self, which is not the case with the schizoid, in whom aggressive explosions prevail; just as it assumes that the relationship with the object is relatively solid, while in fact the schizoid has a tenuous and fragile relationship);

2. the investment of *the mother as a whole*: in the schizoid, libidinal

investment is essentially concentrated in the object, which in part represents the breast;

3.   the consideration of *affective frustration* [in 1911, Karl Abraham—in *Urverstimmung*, a work that is not cited by Fairbairn—had already observed the importance, at the origin of melancholia, of experiences of disappointment, having also described original depression in the same work];

4.   the observation and description of what we call *nuclear introjection of malignity*—which we consider to be the central process in melancholic construction;

5.   the notion of the internal saboteur as a split portion of the self, libidinally connected to the rejecting object (but this is a relationship that Fairbairn does not explore sufficiently in order to outline melancholic psychopathy), which is a good example of what we describe as a *cyst resulting from the internalized sado-masochistic relationship* of the melancholic;

6.   infantile attachment or emotional dependence upon objects from infancy, as well as *adolescent conflict of ambi-tendency* between progression and regression (releasing/failing to release the objects of the past), which were both observed by Fairbairn in war neuroses, are characteristics of the depressive personality and reinforce the difficulty of severing the ties with the past;

7.   inflection of aggressiveness upon the self.

* * *

It is harder to understand, in the light of Fairbairn's psychopathology, the depressive's nostalgia, this longing without there being an object: something is missing, but the depressive does not know what it is; there is an absence of something that is faceless and shapeless. It is The Black Sun, *"Le Soleil Noir"*, of the French poet Gérard de Nerval, or perhaps more accurately the *blackness of the sun*—the sun that has become a shadow. What the depressive lacks—something that he knows exists and that he once had it—is, in our opinion, his mother's love, which was lost prematurely.

This is yet another difference between psychosis and depression: the psychotic is the poor man who has always been poor (he never had any maternal love or enough of it), the depressive is the rich man (averagely rich) who has become poor.

At a point very early on in life, the depressive has experienced affective abandonment. There may be several reasons for maternal non-investment—a mother in mourning, a new target for the mother's love (another child, for example), a narcissistic mother who does not tolerate the child's progressive affirmation—all this, obviously, within the vision of the vulnerable and hypersensitive infant.

And who knows if the analytic cure is also—although not only—a cure through love? Winnicott knew this—see the splendid work by Harry Guntrip, *My Two Analyses: With Fairbairn and Winnicott* (Guntrip, 1975), and it is of no importance that Guntrip has a schizoid defect.

The internal relationship between the libidinal self and the exciting object of Fairbairn's endopsychic system effectively explains the exaltation of the borderline pathology and hysterical passion, as he himself observes. The model is less appropriate for depressive nostalgia. In depression, it is the *object conceived* by the idealizing libido that is the narcissistic source and, above all, the purpose; it is based on an immature self-seeking and on needing the admiration of the object—of the aesthetic object that it needs to provoke— so that it may, over and above all else, be acknowledged and defined, identified. It is the Baby Jesus lacking the loving look from his parents—indeed, as Abraham had already noted in 1911, depression is more severe if the disappointment stems from both the mother and the father. The fantasy of the "divine child" in the scene of the "narcissistic trio"—to use the expression coined by Francis Pasche (1969)—was not fulfilled.

The problem of melancholia in Fairbairn's work is thus an open question, an unfinished exploration. Interpreting the nostalgic relationship as a consequence of an obsessive technique of retention would be insufficient, and, in any case, it does not figure in the author's work, although such an interpretation may be admitted as being in line with his thinking.

Fairbairn does, however, make comments that, at this juncture, are worthy of reflection: "the internalization of bad objects represents an attempt on the part of the child to make the objects in his environment 'good'" (1951, p. 164), and, describing moral defence in 1943: "one of his motives in becoming bad is to make his objects 'good'. . . . By this means he seeks to purge them of their badness" (p. 65). The issue of depressive nostalgia is, indeed, *a purified object*.

Nevertheless, this is too little. It lacks the essential acknowledgement of the *great investment in an object that is frustrating because of its incompleteness and insufficiency*. This not only explains the origin of melancholic desperation, but also the motive for the attachment to such an object. It is a beautiful but incomplete object; it tantalizes the subject. It is also an insufficient but grandiose object, it attracts investment. It is a false and narcissistic object. The idol has feet of clay and the intelligence of a flea.

The person suffering from melancholy lacks enthusiasm (enthusiasm means "God within me"), because he does not have God within him, but a likeness. And this is basically his problem.

What can be done, then?

The precedence and priority of the countertransference is the secret of art. I only analyse whom I appreciate, and I only cure whom I support. And so I choose my subjects for analysis.

The intrinsic quality of the analyst is his *introjectibility*. Only patients who take me along with them achieve analytical success, and this depends on my specific quality for a certain patient (whether, for example, he finds me likeable). For this reason, the patient should chose the analyst.

* * *

Remaining with Fairbairn, and in terms of the object relationship: the great problem encountered by the depressive is the *non-acceptance of the reality of the loss*. The depressive does not exactly deny reality or perceptive reality—this occurs in psychosis. The depressive *denies affective reality*—in other words, affective loss: it is the *non-acceptance of the affective loss*. It all takes place at the level of affect; it is an affective illness par excellence.

This is because the affective loss is more difficult to confirm through reason. And it is so painful that the patient chooses to ignore it. It is more painful still for the patient because of his great affective dependence—"emotional dependence", as Fairbairn would say. And it is yet more difficult to bear because of his narcissistic deficiency and because of his feelings of inferiority and incapability, which lead him to consider it impossible—or almost impossible—to replace the lost object, because he feels himself to be incapable of finding another or, rather, unable to conquer another.

Furthermore, the depressive finds it difficult to change object, but also to be *objective*: he finds it hard to progress from infantile love—pre-genital, protection-seeking love—to mature genital or adult love, a love of cooperation (as Fairbairn points out), a complementary and creative love. He does not achieve this new dialogue of love, because he feels small and inferior—it is his micro- or nano-mania. What is particularly affected is the person's image in terms of sex, gender, or sexual identity: it is a *secondary narcissistic fault or phallic–narcissistic fault*, which follows the primary narcissistic fault or Balint's *basic fault* (Balint, 1968).

Who is not familiar with adolescent depression? Who does not know about depression in middle age? And what about the depression of the genital infantile stage itself, in which *rendering narcissistic the image in sexual terms* is first consolidated?

Therefore, depression is not as far removed from neurotic pathology as one might think.

A change of the objectives of the self is where the depressive fails—the permanent relationship of dependence, not of cooperation *for creation*. It is this qualitative leap that is intended by the development of the object relationship in the analytic process, with the aid of a calm, patient, fearless analyst who *interpretatively* lights the way—Margaret Mahler's (1968) lighthouse is, strictly speaking, the lucid, uninquiring, and creative analyst that Fairbairn has taught us to be. As far as he is concerned, psychoanalysis is not a doctrine but a science—open knowledge, an investigation to be conducted.

* * *

According to Fairbairn, resistance to change is the result of moral defence (or guilt) through which the patient avoids the loss of the parents' goodness—in other words, the internal object. It is, therefore, a defence *in order to conserve the love of the object*, but one that involves blocking hate, deflected into the self. The individual remains within an enclosed system, doubly enclosed—both within self-destruction and within *poverty*—since the individual affectively feeds off the object's leftover love. These are therefore leftovers that undergo hypertrophy through idealization. This is the other essential defence—the *idealization of the lost object*, of the past, of infancy, which translates into longing *for what never was but could have been* (as the Brazilian poet Manoel Bandeira said in his poem "Antologia"). The strong resistance to change, to the investment in the present, results from this defence: *historical illusion*. Furthermore it is a relationship that is lost, dead, from the past: the individual is living with an embalmed corpse, the transparent body of his illusion.

Nevertheless, resistance to change is not limited to this aspect alone. It is heightened because in the meantime—and significantly—the individual has starved and failed to invest in himself; he has neither absorbed nor produced protein, a basic substance for increasing personal worth. His narcissistic physical constitution is fragile and precarious and is too slight to throw itself, in a determined and daring manner, into conquering and taking possession of a new object or objects—to journey through the adventure of existence. The restoration of the adipose and de-calcified self—since the sun failed to shine in the individual's life—is the difficult task that falls to the analyst, if skill and art, as Camões used to say ("Os Lusíadas"—Canto I, Strophe 2, Verse 8), help him along the way.

The world of psychopathology, says Fairbairn, is one of internalized objects, the closed system; and the world of psychology is one of external objects (Fairbairn, 1958). Opening the patient up to this real, new, promising world—and reality is always new and promising—is what psychoanalysis terms *transference*, its main objective: transference of desire, from the *remaining libido* to the world that every day is renewed, transformed, and expanded and of which the analyst is finally and simply the ambassador—discreet but attractive because he loves truth.

CHAPTER FIVE

Metapsychology of hysteria: from Freud to Fairbairn and beyond

Henri Vermorel

W. Ronald Fairbairn is a modern clinician, and a profound and original theoretician, one of the principal post-Freudian psychoanalysts. His interest in the schizoid factors of the personality and the relationship of dependence upon an object led him to become interested in many forms of non-neurotic pathology. The light he shed on the subject also considerably renewed the psychoanalytic approach to neuroses and in particular to the neurosis of hysteria (Fairbairn, 1954c). As far as I am concerned, Fairbairn's ideas represent the most important psychoanalytic contribution on hysteria after Freud.

Freud and hysteria

From Studies on Hysteria *to the Dora case*

The theme of hysteria is historically central since it has accompanied the creation of psychoanalysis and has become, gradually in the works of Freud, the paradigm of the Oedipus complex and of the functioning of the psyche in general. Since his *Studies on Hys-*

teria (1895d), Freud believed that the hysteric suffers from *"reminiscences"* and attributed the origin of the illness to a sexual incident during infancy.

At the end of 1900, Freud started on one of his first analyses with an 18-year-old girl, Ida Bauer, who suffered from various symptoms of hysteria and who became immortalized under the name "Dora". Psychoanalysis was in its infancy, and the cure was terminated after three months. Notably, Freud only recognized the elements of transference in retrospect. Nevertheless, even though they were incomplete, the theoretical considerations based on this case are still valuable a century later and are worth briefly summarizing (Freud, 1905e [1901]).

Freud was particularly interested in clarifying the genesis of the multiple symptoms of his patient's conversion and in finding a meaning in them by defining *the hysterical identification* already tackled in *The Interpretation of Dreams* (Freud, 1900a). In Dora's case, her two parents were sexually differentiated, but Freud states that more often than not the choice of object gives way to feminine or masculine identifications, to people who are loved or not loved. These identifications are of an oedipal nature, but the genital level is only partially achieved, and so it reveals the lability, the multiplicity, the incompleteness, and the partial nature of these identifications. Thus each of the masculine or feminine objects is invested simultaneously as an object of desire and as an object of identification; what Dora wants is to remain a third figure in the desire of the two members of the couple while being sheltered by her identifications (Hollande, 1973), by playing one against the other through her role. Therefore in this partial failure to attain Oedipus, these identifications are infiltrated by the primary process, implying that the symptom of hysteria spans two levels.

As the specific mode of defending hysteria, repression became, for Freud, the cornerstone of psychoanalysis. Just like dreaming, according to him, the symptom is one of the roundabout means by which one expresses repressed sexual contents. Thus, hysterical conversion appears as a product of retrospective revision [*Nachträglichkeit*], as a displacement onto a part of the body of a repressed sexual fantasy: Freud interprets Dora's cough as an identification with her beloved father, who suffered from tuberculosis (it is noticeable that many of these identifications are of a negative nature).

Or the meaning Freud assigned to a limp—following a painful illness of the lower abdomen described as "appendicitis"—was that of a pregnancy fantasy, an assignment he made upon discovering that the symptom appeared nine months after the famous lake scene, during which Mr K had seduced Dora by kissing her, pressing her against him, and so on.

In his subsequent works, Freud more thoroughly explained the bisexual dimension of the symptom. Thus the hysterical crisis represents—in the manner of a pantomime—a coitus where the subject, simultaneously and in condensed form, takes on the role of male and female (Freud, 1908a).

The Dora case and its blurred areas

During Dora's cure, Freud had left a number of points in the dark, such as the analysis of his patient's depression and her losses of consciousness; even so, he failed to solve the mystery of the origin of the *"somatic compliance"*, an early term for the subsequent location of the symptom on a part of the body. All this is to understand Freud's difficulty, in this analysis, in locating the trauma—which he deemed to be the origin of hysteria—in Dora's early childhood. Admittedly in 1923 Freud (1923b), who 20 years before had described Dora's close relationship with Mrs K, attributed the termination of his analysis to his delay in interpreting the homosexuality of his patient; but even so, he does not mention the possible link between this pathology and Dora's first relations with her mother, who was presented as being affected by *"housewife's psychosis"*.

Furthermore, Freud was unable to specify the exact mechanism of identification, and a few years later he expressed his reservations *vis-à-vis* the concept of introjection developed by Ferenczi (1909).

From the mother as "first object" (1905e [1901]) to the "first seductress" (1940a [1938])

However, in his first works on hysteria, Freud had mentioned the notion of splitting. Hypnotists had for a long time been describing the phenomenon of *"double conscience"*, and during Charcot's era hysteria was associated with multiple personality which Freud mentions in his *Studies on Hysteria* (1895d), describing dissociation as "*a fundamental phenomenon*" in hysterical neurosis.

But it was only in 1920 that the author again approached the issue, while discussing Dostoevsky: "Hysteria is a result of the mental constitution itself, it is an expression of this very organic inherent power which blossoms in an artist's genius. But it is also the sign of an unresolved and particularly acute conflict which bursts through these inherent dispositions and ends up tearing the mental life into two camps" (Freud, 1966/1920, p. 361).

Very early on, Freud had predicted the importance of the first relations in the genesis of hysteria: he wrote to Fliess that "it is the nostalgia" (of the mother, the "first love", according to Goethe, whom he cites) "which first of all characterizes hysteria" (letter dated 27 October 1897—Freud, 1950a [1887–1902]). This primary relationship was to be dealt with more thoroughly in "A memory of Infancy by Leonardo da Vinci" (Freud, 1910c), but it was only during the 1930s that he stated that "this stage of the connection to the mother leads us to assume a particularly intimate relationship with the aetiology of hysteria" (Freud, 1931b). Ruth Mack Brunswick, in a work written with Freud during the last six years of his life although published only after his death, makes a new distinction between the triangular situation of the Oedipus complex and a "primitive Oedipus complex", linked to the mother as a first exclusive object and a "source of the most primitive and the most fundamental identification with the mother", from which comes "the considerable impact of the narcissistic wounds inflicted by the mother" (Mack Brunswick, 1940).

And in one of his last writings, Freud makes new statements on the baby's relationship with its mother's breast—the first erotic object, which precedes the person as a whole, "love leaning on the fulfilment of its need for nourishment" (Freud, 1940a [1938]). Thanks to the nourishment but also to the care bestowed by the mother, she becomes the "first seductress" of the child. But it is true that, despite these predictions, Freud's theoretical structure leaves room for a more profound conception of hysteria. For the subject with which we are concerned, one notices the new accent placed on the maternal seduction in order to structure narcissism, which

Paul-Claude Racamier has defined as a "narcissistic seduction", a relationship of "mutual seduction which is aimed at the all-powerful unison" (Racamier, 1992). This entails an investment of the bodily envelope and of the erotogenic zones. And it is within the vicissitudes of the narcissistic seduction—which is necessary for structuring the psyche—that research needs to be carried out on the initial stages of hysteria.

Fairbairn's capital contribution

It is on this point that Fairbairn makes a major contribution. Since he knew the German language and culture, he was familiar with Freud's writings, which enabled him to enter into relevant discussions. His works were backed up by a high-quality clinical practice and he put forth a solidly constructed and extremely coherent model, which he would develop further over the years. One might think that Fairbairn, like all the other great psychoanalytic thinkers after Freud, had to confront—with enforced vigour—the power of the ideas expounded by the founder of psychoanalysis, which certainly had its downfalls but which had the insight of a genius to open up new routes to knowledge which were not always easy to assimilate or to fight against. In this sense, Fairbairn's attempt to construct a joint psychoanalytic theory capable of being measured against Freud's theory is a success, since it sheds new light, especially on hysteria, and since his multi-layer system of thinking encourages reflection (Fairbairn, 1954c).

Basic endopsychic structure and hysteria

In Freudian metapsychology, the accent is placed on the drive towards the object, and, in support, the object participates in the creation of this drive; but, as authors such as André Green have stated, Freud lacks a certain metapsychology of the object. And yet Fairbairn precisely places the object at the centre of his works by proposing a theory of object relations that he even proposes should replace Freud's drive theory.

Fairbairn differs from Freud in placing the origin of hysteria within the realm of the first relationship with the mother. As far as Fairbairn is concerned, the ego is present right from the beginning, and in hysteria the accent is placed on the early splitting of the ego and its objects that coexist, with repression located at a much earlier level than the oedipal repression described by Freud in hysteria. What Freud only suspected, Fairbairn attempts to explain by his description of the "basic endopsychic structure".

The defence mechanism of hysteria results, according to Fairbairn, from "the introjection of an unsatisfying object", the source of direct repression and of splitting, which explains the suffering involved in hysteria. An indirect repression provokes a splitting of the unsatisfactory object into two parts: the exciting object and the rejecting object; and in hysteria the exciting object is excessively exciting and the rejecting object is excessively rejecting. The author uses the terms "libidinal ego" and "anti-libidinal ego" to name the parts of the ego in their respective relations with the exciting object and the rejecting object. The author ends up with the idea of an early triangulation—central ego–exciting object–rejecting object—which he distinguishes from the oedipal triangulation described by Freud—father–mother–subject. The accent placed on the splitting accounts for a major symptom of the hysteria, the *"belle indifférence"* of the patient with regard to the symptoms, which had until then remained unexplained.

Fairbairn shows that if one takes the analysis of the oedipal situation in hysteria far enough, one releases the presence of an *"internal exciting mother"* and *"an internal rejecting mother"*. And it is certainly true that the analysis of hysterics—both male and female—should reveal the premature disruptions of the mother–baby relationship. This is the origin of the initial trauma, the source of a fundamental disappointment. More often than not, this relates to a relationship in which the mother blows hot one moment and cold the next, all the while longing for a relationship quality that preserves a central ego in order to promote a certain degree of evolution towards the genital Oedipus—all highlighting the neurotic quality of this affection. Here, hysteria differs from the borderline states, and more so from the psychotic or perverse pathologies, where there is damage that is much greater for the ego.

Orality and sexuality in hysteria

Fairbairn also shows that in hysteria the libidinal ego is affected by a powerful oral component, by early maternal frustrations, and by ambivalence towards the first object. Its intensity explains that "whereas the sexuality of the hysteric is at bottom extremely oral, his (or her) basic orality is, so to speak, extremely genital" (Fairbairn, 1954a, p. 25), which is a condensation in concert with Freud's opinion of the hysteric as being on a permanent quest for the breast in erotic mode. Fairbairn attributes this to a premature excitation of sexuality in the hysteric, which freezes her in a state of immaturity. In effect, the adult hysteric reacts to frustration with a never-ending quest for the absent mother of her first moments, by pursuing her in a seductive fashion through objects of both sexes, from behind which the negative hallucination of her mother emerges; here, by means of the libidinal co-excitation mechanism, it is the absence that may become the most powerful source of excitation which is stronger than that of all the present objects. I feel that it is this paradoxical mechanism which, when pushed to the extreme, is in play within hysterical madness.

Discussion of Fairbairn's ideas

The two traumatic nuclei of hysteria

Fairbairn's contributions enabled significant advances to be made in understanding hysteria by emphasizing the first traumatic stage, and by creating an early triangulation, which is distinct from the oedipal triangulation, the place of which is nevertheless acknowledged by the author. As Fairbairn (1944) wrote: "I have departed from Freud in my evaluation of the Oedipus situation as an explanatory concept" (p. 120). Oedipal conflicts and their specificity also tend to be confused with those forming the basic structure; they are present in hysteria only in the form of a "variety of techniques employed to protect the ego against the effects of conflicts of an oral origin" (1941, p. 30).

And yet I feel it necessary to consider the existence in hysteria of two traumatic nuclei that are connected to the two oedipal stages.

The basic endopsychic structure described by Fairbairn relates to unbound energies (narcissistic wounds), which are the source of acting out and brutal ruptures, of rapid cathexis and withdrawal of cathexis, of losses of consciousness as well as of plunging into morose depressions and suicide attempts. The symptoms of conversion bear witness to bound energies (Lubtchansky, 1973), and it is in retrospective revision that the initial traumas of childhood (narcissistic wounds) take on sexual (genital) significance.

The self

In the basic endo-psychic structure, the early ego of which Fairbairn speaks is, rather, the self whose wounds lead to difficulty in constituting an oedipal ego. Narcissism and oedipal sexuality are in a diachronic relationship, the source of a tension that is liable to create antagonism. Fairbairn has a modern conception of the psyche in that he distinguishes the stages of the mother as an ambivalent object from the oedipal stages, which are addressed to the two sexual parents. He rightly states that infantile dependence emerges from the oedipal background; and it is certainly true that the castration complex arises from the powerlessness of the infant, but it is also—and this Fairbairn does not describe in detail—the consequence of a new conflict with regard to the sexual parents of giving up the infantile omnipotence of sexual ambivalence in order to be a man or a woman, but not both at the same time. If the Oedipus complex is linked to the difference between the sexes and the generations, and to castration, then the first traumatic nucleus arises from the incompleteness of support for the Self by maternal seduction, which results in difficulty during separation, and the anxiety that is linked to this; it is also a register of disappointment, depression, and helplessness.

It is the traumatic splitting of the Self that handicaps the journey towards Oedipus and causes its partial failure, which, in turn, encourages a regression towards the first traumatic nucleus. The coming and going between the two registers can be pinpointed in the course of analytic cures; but there also occurs a condensation of the two traumatic nuclei, and its intensity may pose formidable therapeutic problems. During treatment, it is important to repair

their dual existence while avoiding premature interpretation of
narcissistic wounds in terms of genital sexuality. This work should
be achieved beforehand through the anaclitic phase of the cure.

This is what Freud was confronted with in his analysis of
Dora: by prematurely making interpretations of a sexual nature,
experienced by her as seductions, he created a negative therapeutic
reaction, which contributed to his patient leaving his therapy.[1]
Moreover, he disregarded the fact that she was still an adolescent,
for whom fantasy and reality are more enmeshed, and that she had
a tendency to act out. This is what has been later shown through
analytic experiences with adolescents.

Introjection and splitting

Fairbairn's tendency to condense the two stages of Oedipus goes
hand in hand with an ego that is constituted from the outset. He
"can think of no motive for the introjection of an object which is
perfectly satisfying" (Fairbairn, 1999, p. 188 n). It is an opinion that
is difficult to sustain, and it contradicts Kleinian theories. I feel that
if the introjections of unsatisfying objects lead to the incomplete
identifications of hysteria, the introjections of satisfying objects are,
conversely, fully assimilated by the Self; they are the source of
oedipal identifications and enable the attainment of an ego that is
capable of separating itself from its mother.

Fairbairn rightly states that repression and splitting are of the
same nature, but he neglects to show the specificity of early repression—closer to suppression [Unterdrückung]—through its relationship to oedipal repression [Verdrängung], which is more developed
and which refers to genital contents. He does not specify, as those
after him have done, following Freud, that there are different types
of splitting, ranging from denial [Verleugnung] to foreclosure [Ver-
werfung]. It seems to me to be impossible to identify—as Fairbairn
did—the splitting of the hysteric with that of the schizophrenic; the
kaleidoscopic ego of hysteria is not the fragmented self of the
schizophrenic.

---

[1]It relates to a pitfall which may confront the analyst during each treatment
of a case of hysteria; it can only be overcome by taking into account that there
are two traumatic nuclei, which leads to a strategy adapted to the therapy.

Superego and basic endopsychic structure

Fairbairn challenges the Freudian theory but nevertheless devotes much attention to the superego as a "phenomenon". He identifies it first of all with the anti-libidinal self; he then considers that the Freudian superego is "really a complex structure comprising the ideal object or ego ideal, the antilibidinal ego and the rejecting (or antilibidinal) object" (Fairbairn, 1994a, p. 156). It remains for me to describe the genesis of a post-oedipal superego with a fantasy of murdering the father and of interiorizing parental tenderness, which is capable of humanizing the severity of the primitive super-ego, constituting the moral conscience. In the hysteric, the repressing force of the anti-libidinal ego cannot be tempered by tenderness, and so the resulting masochism and repetition compulsion express it through symptoms and behaviour.

Freud, the biologist–romantic of the mind

Fairbairn considers that Freud's psychoanalysis is based on a falsely scientific biologism. He criticizes Freud, like later authors such as Jean Laplanche who spoke of "the misleading biologizing of sexuality in Freud" (Laplanche, 1993). Although these theoreticians begin from different foundations, they share a view that by infiltrating purely biological models, Freud failed to afford his basic intuition its full mental value. This criticism can be understood since there is certainly an agreement, in the identity of Freud the creator, between his biological training and an inspiration of another nature, which I put down to the depth of his Goethean and romantic identity.

And here Fairbairn (who nevertheless was familiar with German culture), like a number of European psychoanalysts, misunderstood this dimension of Freud's work. Freud had certainly been a researcher in physiology at Brücke and had introduced a thoroughness inherited from experimental medicine in order to construct psychoanalysis. But he should not have been mistaken about its positivism, which is simply a masking veneer, hiding a profound source, the heritage of Goethe—Freud's favourite author—and of the German romantics, who had left important works to science and particularly to biology—works that were largely unknown outside Germany (Vermorel, Clancier, & Vermorel, 1995). And yet Freud's inspiration draws on all his essential concepts, such as the ego, unconsciousness, repression, and drive, in all that is specifically mental within them. And Freud's post-Darwinism is rather a resurgence of the philosophy of nature from the start of the nineteenth century (Ellenberger, 1970). More than just being scientific, Freudian biology is a fiction—a biology in the romantic mode of Fechner or Fliess.

The Freudian word *Reiz* [excitation] should be understood in its metaphoric connotation, emerging from romantic biology. The concept of drive (impulse) [*Trieb*] comes close to the highest point of this heritage of romantic philosophy and medicine, while also attempting to express the search for a compromise between nature and culture, between science and myth in the body's reach towards the object and the world. Freud drew a fundamental distinction between *Trieb*, the mental representative of an excitation coming from the body which arises from human specificity, and *Instinkt*, which applies to the instinct of animals. Fairbairn did not misunderstand this distinction when he translated *Trieb* as "impulse". But he repeatedly used the word "instinct" to talk about impulse, and he produced a different meaning following Strachey, who had translated *Trieb* and *Instinkt* as the same English word, "instinct", which had metapsychological consequences. When Fairbairn refers to "life instincts" and "death instincts", he tends to reduce the mental specificity to psychology.

Impulse and object

What Fairbairn criticized in Freud is that the latter declared the maturation of the impulse to be the search for pleasure even while it is aimed at the object. Fairbairn sees pleasure as a simple indicator of the relations with the object.[2] (For Freud, however, the object

---

[2] Characterizing Freudian metapsychology as hedonism, as Fairbairn did, seems to me to be a grave misunderstanding of the consequences. In reality it is a question of the pleasure–unpleasure principle, which in Freud's theories entail a place given over to sufferance, life being a combination of life drives and death drives. The original encounter between the mother and the baby

is not just guided by the impulse; it contributes to it by supporting the creation of the impulse.) The force and the novelty of the psychoanalyst from Edinburgh is inherent in the accent placed on internal objects, which maintain relations with the ego that are similar to the relations between the ego and an external person; it is a conceptualization that parallels that of Melanie Klein, created independently. As far as Fairbairn is concerned, impulses represent the dynamic aspect of the structures of the ego ; qualified by libidinal attitudes, they are reduced to techniques to control object relations (Fairbairn, 1952a, p. 41–46). He also proposes that the Freudian theory of drives should be replaced with a theory of object relations.

Faced with the preponderant role Fairbairn gives the object, the relationship between the impulse and the body is erased, and the erotogenic zones are "zones for the circulation of the libido" along "the path of least resistance" (1941). The ego therefore runs the risk of being reduced to a passive role before the object, which is contradicted by recent studies which reveal the infants' active search for the breast. The nipple is a primordial object, but the mouth takes part in the co-creation of the impulse. It was later Winnicott who stated that the original subject–object encounter was described as object found–created.

Fortunately, Fairbairn did not take his proposition to its conclusion of replacing the theory of impulses with a theory of object relations, since he places the conflict between the libidinal ego and the anti-libidinal ego at the heart of the basic endopsychic structure, which is a way of reintroducing the second Freudian theory of drives, challenged elsewhere.

What remains under discussion is the passage of the biological body to the mental body. Ethologists have shown that need arises from a genetic programme which entails, with attachment, the expectation of a father and a mother, and the mental structure can only be fulfilled in an encounter with the object: this model of reciprocal interaction, which makes the connection between nature and culture, is one of interactive epigenesis (Cosnier, Grosjean, &

---

gives rise to a hallucinatory satisfaction of desire, the source of mental life and notably of fantasy, which is absent from Fairbairn's theory; and in hysteria there is a pathological excess of precisely this fantasy life.

Lacoste, 1994), which ties in with Fairbairn's hypothesis of an in-born capacity for internalization of external objects.

By using introjection to describe an intrapsychic situation, the Edinburgh psychoanalyst brings about a dialectic that seems to me to be based more on intersubjectivity than on relational theory. The pitfall here would be to reduce psychoanalysis to the exchange of relations, or to a communication, or to return to an academic psychology, which certain ambiguous Fairbairnian formulations strive for, such as the formulation relating to the hysterical state, which begins with "the substitution of a bodily condition for a personal problem" (Fairbairn, 1994a, p. 29). Psychoanalysis arises from the intrapsychic, intersubjective, and transsubjective (transgenerational). It is a metapsychology, not a psychology reduced to "relations" in which the essential aspect of psychoanalysis would be renounced.

Violence and death drive

Fairbairn questions the bipolarity of life and death impulses, which he incorrectly calls "instincts". On the other hand, he rightly detects in Freud's ideas another theoretical current, which tends to consider hostility or aggressiveness as an inherent impulse. The debate over this issue is one that is taking place today; by following Fairbairn's theory of a libidinal ego being in opposition to an anti-libidinal ego, one could identify, along with Jean Bergeret, the activity of the libidinal Self with a basic violence that would be present throughout life—violence against another (analogous with cruelty of animals) without an object connotation and, as such, different from hate, from one level to the more object level (Bergeret, 1994). This vital inherent tendency would be opposed by the anti-libidinal Self resulting from anti-narcissism (Pasche, 1964). If the death impulse is a mental destruction against the subject, it is a product of anti-narcissism and not only, as Fairbairn and many other authors believed, of the reversal of the inherent violence onto the subject. Mental life would therefore find its source in this compounding of these mainly narcissistic opposed forces, and antagonism would then meet up with the oedipal sexual accession in life- and death-drive antagonism: a "sexual death drive", according to

Jean Laplanche (1992). Therefore, like Fairbairn, one can assign an important role to violence and aggressiveness through renouncing, like him, drive bipolarity.

The compounding of narcissism and anti-narcissism produces Freudian "erogenous masochism", a guardian of life (Rosenberg, 1991). And Fairbairn, who had correctly located hysterical sufferance in the premature splitting of the Self, enables us to understand that the (moral) masochism of this pathology results precisely from the intensity of this splitting and from the (destructive) anti-libidinal force of this premature superego, which, having received insufficient oedipal parental tenderness, cannot become a post-oedipal superego that protects and civilizes. This results in the hysteric's sacrifice of sexuality, as highlighted by Fairbairn.

The hysteric's repetition compulsion [*Wiederholungszwang*] is a destructive action, and it provokes the repetition of symptoms on changing scenes. But one cannot reduce this repetition to a pure death drive, since even in the intense forms of masochism one may see in this movement an attempt to overcome trauma. Jean Bégoin tells us that, like Pirandello's characters, hysterical symptoms "are in search of an author", which can sometimes be accomplished in life but is more likely in an analytic cure in which "they need to be received and interpreted" (Bégoin, 1987).

Hysterical symptoms and psychosomatic symptoms

Some of Fairbairn's hysterical patients suffered from physical illnesses: one (Olivia) from psoriasis, a qualified psychosomatic symptom; another (Jack) from sinusitis (Fairbairn, 1954c). This latter symptom was interpreted by the author as the result of anal retention from childhood and as the effect of imprisonment by the patient's mother. In Fairbairn's era, there was not yet a distinction between symptoms of hysterical conversion and psychosomatic symptoms. The former are the effect of repressed fantasies and the latter entail an organic disturbance, and their meaning cannot be immediately pinpointed. The lack of fantasies seen in psychosomatic pathology, "*La pensée opératoire*" (Marty & de M'Uzan, 1963), and the denial of affect in alexithymia are the polar opposite of the excess of fantasy and affect seen in the hysteric. They bear witness to the most traumatic wounds to the Self. But it is certainly true that at its limit, the distinction between the two categories of symptoms is not always easy to define; and there are elements of possible transition from one to the other, as Marty and colleagues showed in terms of Dora's symptoms, some of which belonged to both structures (Marty, Fain, de M'Uzan, & David, 1967). This may be the case with Jack's sinusitis, similar to the allergic component—this being the psychosomatic affection that is closest to hysteria. And Fairbairn's interpretation (1954a, p. 31) that ended the symptom ("he was dramatizing a state of imprisonment by his mother") may also be understood as a meaning given in retrospective revision by the development of the cure for a symptom which perhaps was not there at the start.

After Fairbairn

The majority of works on hysteria after Fairbairn deal with the nature of seduction and the relationship between narcissism and genital sexuality.

Paternal seduction in the genesis of hysteria

Ute Rupprecht-Schampera was inspired by Fairbairn's model of early triangulation to reintroduce the father into the premature seduction, thus making a major contribution to the metapsychology of hysteria. It is the difficulties of the premature mother–child relationship that hinder the accomplishment of the early triangulation, which leads to difficulty in the child separating herself from her mother. In response to the maternal disappointment and faced with this impasse, the child may turn to her father "by using oedipal triangulation to obtain pre-oedipal triangulation and thus separation from the mother" (Rupprecht-Schampera, 1995). It is therefore a premature appeal to the erotic father to fill the narcissistic void, to which the father may respond either through seduction or through abandonment. This would be the source of a second disappointment, this time linked to the father.

From this point of view, one might think that Freud was some-what misunderstood on the nature of the attachment—certainly real—of Dora to her father, thinking that the girl would naturally turn towards her father, while Dora's brother would turn to her mother. In truth, it is more as a result of disappointment with her mother that Dora turns to her father, preserving an idealization of her mother in order to protect herself from the menacing maternal object, and then repressing the resulting hatred of this disappointment, which leads to the comment: "Daddy is not honest". But she was also disappointed with her father because he seduced and abandoned her.

I would gladly see in this premature appeal to the genital father a modality of Racamier's "anti-Oedipus" (Racamier, 1989), a con-densed version of the ante-Oedipus, which, if it is traumatic, may be transformed into the anti-Oedipus, which hinders the active accession to Oedipus, as one can witness in the formulation of hysteria by Rupprecht-Schampera. Thus the primitive mother–child relationship is not a pure duo, and father's and the parents' sexuality are present right from the earliest times.

Sexual symbolism and the pre-symbolic dimension of narcissism

Inspired by Fairbairn and Melanie Klein, Wisdom tried to describe the symbolism of the symptom of conversion: it takes on the form of a penis containing a toothed vagina (oral eagerness) (Wisdom, 1961). This inherent symbolism can be compared to the form of a hollow penis (Chasseguet-Smirgel, 1989), a condensed version of the male symbol and the female symbol, which shows that narcis-sism contains genital sex in power. One may also consider this problem from the point of view of a representation of the non-separated mother–child interface or from the point of view of a *dual bodily pre-Self* (Anzieu, 1990).

Narcissistic seduction and primary hysteria

Racamier defined narcissistic seduction from the earliest times as the necessary cathexis, by the mother's Eros of the child's body.

The mother's erotic desire is inhibited with regard to the purpose: in other words, it is sublimated, and the presence of the father in the mother's desire is another aspect of the early triangulation. Another formulation of this problem is provided by Denise Braunschweig and Michel Fain with "primary hysteria" and the "lover's censure" (Braunschweig & Fain, 1975). Regressively linked to the baby, the mother invests it in a union that tends to exclude all external disturbances; but she soon rediscovers her feminine desire for her partner. Upon perceiving the withdrawal of investment that momentarily results, the baby feels a void (close, one may think, to primitive agony). For these authors, this is the *princeps* model of inhibitions and hysterical paralyses, whereas the excitation that results from the perception of the parent's coital act is one of hysterical crisis.

In Laplanche, one finds a criticism—parallel to Fairbairn's—of Freud's erogenous zones and Abraham's stages of libido, as well as the affirmation of the primacy of the object in the creation of the drive, but the exit proposed is different: Laplanche places the accent on the human specificity of the drive which is radically different from physiology; for him, the need arises from the self-preservation drives and it is through "leaning-on" that the drive is constituted. According to the theory of *generalized seduction*, from birth the baby is immersed in the enigma of its parents' sexuality: what it perceives of it—the "enigmatic meanings or messages"—form the original unconscious and constitute "the object—source of drive", internal objects of a type that enables the author to re-establish an interaction between drive and object (Laplanche, 1984b), which is lacking in Fairbairn's theories.

Narcissistic seduction and incest

It is the narcissistic investment through the necessary maternal seduction that provides the bodily foundation for the Self. It is the vicissitudes of this investment, to a greater or lesser extent, that take part in the creation of future starting points for the symptoms of conversion, which explains the nature of "somatic compliance".

Rupprecht-Schampera's model re-establishes the place of paternal seduction next to the mother's in the genesis of hysteria.

Racamier distinguished the incestuous fantasy (repressed and structuring) from *incestuality*—in other words, the transgressive acting out of this fantasy (Racamier, 1995). Certainly adults do sexually seduce children, but we also find, notably in hysteria, behaviours or words that are more discretely transgressive, but no less traumatic. Freud had described this in Dora's family circle, which, with her parents and the K couple, formed a true incestuous foursome, where seduction was combined with abandonment: the father gave his daughter to Mr K in exchange for his silence over the liaison with Mrs K, who once shared her room with Dora in a somewhat blurred intimacy that was not without its ulterior motives with regard to the liaison with Dora's father. Mr K had tried several times to press sexual seduction on this adolescent, whose father preferred to deny reality. Even Mrs Bauer, affected, according to Freud, with "housewife's psychosis"—which involves a rejection of sexuality—closed her eyes to this erotic merry-go-round, which as a whole translated into a denial of the difference between generations. Freud rightly considered Dora's disgust of sexuality as an essential sign of hysteria. However, in this adolescent a certain degree of sexual disgust towards adults may have been a normal manifestation of self-preservation *vis-à-vis* incest; and Dora, who had only herself to protect her, accentuated this defence, which became pathological.

Incestuousness in hysteria seems to be of the general rule, as if it were necessary for there to be maternal and paternal disappointments at the same time, as described by Ute Rupprecht-Schampera, and there is an incestuous family climate (seduction and abandonment in a denial of the difference of generations) in order to constitute this affection. I have mentioned Freud's delay in noticing the narcissistic dimension of Dora's symptoms, which led him to make premature sexual interpretations—a pitfall that any psychoanalyst may face. If Freud was rigorous elsewhere, had he not committed a major error in analysing his own daughter, Anna—a reality that had for a long time been covered up by silence or denial? One recalls Ferenczi, who, in analysing his mistress's daughter, had fallen in love with her and hesitated before marrying her mother, all under the complacent eyes of Freud, who was analysing one of them. And Melanie Klein analysed two of her children, publishing the case of one of them, and so on. This shows that although the fact that the *prohibition of incest* had been placed as the basis of analytic theory, there was a lack of time to release, under analysis, the place of seduction and of incestuousness and to implement an appropriate analytic framework.

Epilogue

This homage to the fertility of Fairbairn's ideas leads me to lengthy discussions on the structural conceptions of metapsychology. They are useful since they highlight the background of the countertransference of the psychoanalyst as a necessary landmark. But when the psychoanalyst is in consultation with his patient, it is a transference–countertransference encounter that takes place, without concern over structures, which one sees elsewhere in the therapy, varying in their presentation. And this is the specificity of analytic treatment.

Postscript: Freudian hysteria and self-analysis

On the subject of the Dora case, I have noted that Freud was not able to provide evidence of the mother's role in the origins in the genesis of hysteria, which goes hand-in-hand with the absence of analysis of his patient's depression and the episodes of loss of consciousness. This misunderstanding can be put down to the fact that Freud himself was subject to fainting fits. These notably occurred in the course of his relationship with Fliess, who, we know, was the support for his original self-analysis, which opened up into the creation of psychoanalysis (Freud, 1950a [1887–1902]). It was within this setting that Freud experienced a loss of consciousness in 1894, during a visit to Fliess, who was ill, at Munich's Park Hotel. He had another fit during his witnessing of a surgical intervention on his patient Emma Eckstein, whom he was treating for hysteria; but she was also in the care of Fliess, who was cauterizing her turbinate bones because of his nasal theory of sexuality. But during one of these operations, Fliess left 50 centimetres of gauze in one of

Emma's sinuses, which resulted in a later operation, during which the occurrence of a serious haemorrhage placed the patient's life in danger. Freud felt unwell and left the operating theatre.

During this era, Emma is typical of the role taken on by hysterics as Freud's double (they were both treated by Fliess). Through the intermediary of this person, he could place his own femininity at a distance, although in a letter to Emma he mentions her "primordial femininity" (Masson, 1984), in an elusive pre-conscious intuition of the maternal dimension of the origins of hysteria in his patient. Emma is present in the associations to the famous injection dream on Irma, a dream considered as being the foundation of psychoanalysis.

If Freud uses his self-analysis to update the first elements of the Oedipus complex, he leaves open the analysis of primary relations with his mother, although he points to the "nostalgia" of the "first love" (maternal) as a concern of hysteria (see above) and the role of Nannia, the maid from his childhood, as the "sexuality teacher" and "first seductress".

The transference onto Fliess had the dimension of a relationship with the brother as a paternal replacement, while the maternal transference, misunderstood at the time, refers to a traumatic event during early childhood. During the second year of life, Freud had to face the premature death of his young brother Julius, born a few months earlier. André Green treated this theme passionately as the "dead mother" (Green, 1983), frozen in bereavement for her baby, which, affecting those around her, momentarily freezes the mental life of the surviving baby. Freud's losses of consciousness can be seen as reliving in the transference this momentary mental paralysis. The baby, still linked anaclitically to its mother, feels "dropped". This results in a collapse of mental life, related to primitive agony, which is reproduced in future hysterical blackouts.

Unanalysed, this aspect of the relationship between Freud and Fliess certainly intervenes in their break-up and does not cease to haunt it, notably through brooding over the fateful dates of death that were one of Fliess's theoretical pet subjects. In 1904, at the strongest point of their break-up, Freud went to Athens for the first time. When he climbed the Acropolis (see Kanzer, 1969), he experienced in front of the Parthenon his famous "disturbance of memory" [Erinnerungsstörung]. Jones considered this to be a minor equivalent of his losses of consciousness, but this time associated to his creative development. Freud spent his whole life attempting to analyse this episode, which eluded him. He only succeeded in this self-analysis in his famous text of 1936 (Freud, 1936a). It is a letter to Romain Rolland, an *alter ego* who, in his self-analysis at the end of his life, he picked up where the previous one with Fliess had left off (Vermorel & Vermorel, 1993). This explanation is in parallel with the progressive emergence in Freud's works of the mother, considered not only as the "first object" but also as the "first seductress" (Freud, 1940a [1938]). This narcissistic wound is at the same time a source of its creation, since the "dead mother" finds its reverse side in the young mother, Amalia, who had over-invested the future genius. The fantasy of self-engendering—self-disengendering underlies the creative movement as the symptom of hysterical loss of consciousness.

CHAPTER SIX

Fairbairn's philosophic and pragmatic appeal

Anne Tait

Among the theorists on our psychoanalytic psychotherapy training reading list in Edinburgh, Fairbairn stood out for me, not only as a psychologically and philosophically satisfying theorist, but as a mentor in the process of learning that the training involved. He clearly acknowledged what he had learnt from his own theoretical mentors, particularly Freud and Klein, and also had the capacity to present different formulations and his revisions of these over time. His writings manifest his own "mature dependence" (Fairbairn, 1941, p. 34), including what Macmurray described as "sincerity in the mind" (Macmurray, 1935, p. 76).

Fairbairn expressed very clearly what he thought and believed, in a way that encourages rather than inhibits serious debate and further development. The following passages, in which he took the measure, practically, of his own work and that of psychoanalysis as a whole, are important in this regard.

In his paper published in the *International Journal of Psycho-Analysis* in 1958, "On the Nature and Aims of Psycho-Analytical Treatment", he wrote:

It may seem strange that hitherto I have made only the scanti-
est reference in print to the implications of my theoretical formulations for the practice of psychoanalytical treatment. From
this fact it might be inferred that, even in my own opinion, my
views are of merely theoretical interest and their implementa-
tion in practice would leave the technique of psychoanalysis
unaffected. Such an inference would be quite unwarranted—
the fact being that the practical implications of my views have
seemed so far reaching that they could only be put to the test
gradually and with the greatest circumspection if premature or
rash psychotherapeutic conclusions were to be avoided. [Fair-
bairn, 1958, p. 374]

Later, he touched on the obsessional and schizoid connotation of
scientific interest, as opposed to therapeutic aim, in psychoanalysis, and he admitted his own predominant scientific interest
in "promoting a more adequate formulation of psychoanalytical
theory . . . but", he emphasized, "this interest is accompanied by
the hope that such a reformulation will have the effect of rendering
the application of psycho-analytical theory a more therapeutic in-
strument" (Fairbairn, 1958, p. 376).

In "Freud, the Psycho-Analytical Method and Mental Health",
published in the *British Journal of Medical Psychology* a year earlier,
he suggested:

. . . it must be acknowledged that the most important contribution of psychoanalysis to the cause of mental health in the
future lies in the preventative, rather than the therapeutic field.
It is in the application of psychoanalytical principles to the
upbringing of children that the chief hope lies; for, of all
Freud's findings, none has been more surely established than
the finding that the ultimate source of all disturbances of mental health is to be found in the conditions of early childhood. It
is, therefore, to the enlightenment of the general public, and of
parents, doctors and educators in particular, regarding the
emotional needs, deprivations and conflicts of the child that we
must look for the most valuable contribution of psychoanalysis
to the cause of mental health. [Fairbairn, 1957, p. 61]

Fairbairn kept a disciplined focus on theory and indicated that the
application of his theoretical formulations is a different matter. He

was mainly acting as a metaphysician and leaving it to others to consider and develop the application of his theories.

He wrote clearly about psychoanalytic theory and his revisions of it, but, at least for me, his quiet tone and the close detail of his arguments requires repeated study and reflection in order to understand his meaning and its implications. However, given the extent of influential misconceptions about his ideas, it seems essential to go back to what he actually said. I often experience his writing as a call to reason, both through the outlining of previous misconceptions or partiality of theoretical focus and in the sense of encouraging me to think. He presented his reflections and conclusions for consideration. Some are startlingly different from what I had previously thought or been taught, and so clear once perceived, like experiencing for the first time the switch between figure and ground in a Gestalt image—for example, in "Observations on the Nature of Hysterical states", when he suggested: "If hysterical conversion can assume the form of sinusitis, what is there to prevent its assuming the form of anal retentiveness?" and went on to "submit for consideration the hypothesis that *the data upon which the theory of erotogenic zones is based themselves represent something in the nature of conversion-phenomena*" (Fairbairn, 1954c, p. 121).

Another "aha!" experience for me in this paper, inconspicuous in a footnote, was to read:

> It is a remarkable fact that psychoanalytical interest in the classical story of Oedipus should have been concentrated so preponderantly upon the final stages of the drama, and that the earliest stage should have been so largely ignored; for it seems to me a fundamental principle of psychological, no less than literary, interpretation that a drama should be considered as a unity deriving its significance as much from the first act as from the last. In the light of this principle, it becomes important to recognize that the same Oedipus who eventually killed his father and married his mother began life by being exposed upon a mountain, and thus being deprived of maternal care in all its aspects at a stage at which his mother constituted his exclusive object. [Fairbairn, 1954c, p. 116]

Reading and thinking, as a trainee, is influenced by individual trainers and by the *Zeitgeist* of the training institution. In Edinburgh in the early 1990s, the defining "open system" of the Scottish Institute of Human Relations continued, reflecting the liberal and empirical intellectual tradition in Scotland and evidenced by wide-ranging reading lists and seminars on attachment research. However, there was also a growing focus on Kleinian theory, and this felt like a "closed system" both in terms of its content and its proponents' seeming lack of interest in other theories. This combination of "open" and "closed" systems—or, to use a related terminology, pluralism and monism (which I will return to later)—constituted a complicated and conflictual setting for training. It led to polarizations in the training group that could be frustrating and inhibiting. Trainers influenced by Fairbairn seemed to study Klein seriously, but trainers with a Kleinian orientation seemed to dismiss Fairbairn from hearsay. This difference in attitude prevented serious debate. Furthermore, allegiance splits led to defensive foreclosure in case discussion. For example, as a trainee drawn to Fairbairn and developmental psychology (which seemed to me to provide considerable validation for Fairbairnian theory), I felt I was regarded as naive with regard to clinical material I presented if its focus was not on destructiveness. In retaliation, I thought of those drawn to Klein as aggressively defended against fear of weakness, in becoming indoctrinated by a fanatical, anti-therapeutic preoccupation with destructiveness.

Group splits were probably increased by the large size of our group and our heterogeneous aims in training, which ranged from private psychoanalytic psychotherapy practice, through psychotherapy within the NHS, to, in my case, applying psychoanalytic understanding in an NHS medical setting. I was at the end of the spectrum of training aims that made Fairbairn particularly appealing, given his integrated consideration of internal and external reality, the relevance of his clinical observations and theoretical formulations to somatic illness, and his emphasis on the usefulness of psychoanalytic understanding outside the analytic setting.

Not aiming to be a practising psychoanalytic psychotherapist protected me from professional defensiveness in response to Fairbairn's reformulation of psychoanalytic theory. I felt even freer after training, to the extent that I recently found myself suggesting that the logical conclusion of Fairbairn's reformulation is not psychoanalysis. On the other hand, my professional setting made me prey to defensiveness about not becoming a psychoanalytic psychotherapist, in situations touched upon in Fairbairn's 1958 paper on psychoanalytic treatment, "when the attitude is adopted that, if an analysed patient does not 'get better', it is necessarily because he is unsuitable for psycho-analytical treatment, and that, if a patient 'gets better' by some non-analytical form of psychotherapy, it is all very well, but it is not psycho-analysis". So I relish his characteristically succinct conclusion: "Such purism resolves itself simply into an apotheosis of the method at the expense of the aims which the method is intended to serve" (Fairbairn, 1958, p. 379).

Altogether, in the training group there were many types of differences: differences in training aim, in allegiance to individual trainers, in theoretical belief, and in attitude in the analytic setting. All these differences seemed to both reflect and exert a pull towards either Fairbairnian or Kleinian theory. This felt a self-promulgating process that could not be addressed in the training group, partly because it reflected differences in theoretical orientation among our trainers, in a period of particular change in the overall balance of theoretical orientation.

In *The Analyst's Preconscious*, published in 1996, Hamilton illustrates how such differences are widespread in psychoanalysis by describing, from 65 interviews conducted in Britain and America between 1988 and 1990, the beliefs and actions of different analysts in their practice in different psychoanalytic cultures or schools.

Hamilton found that "members of specific orientation groups, notably Kleinian and self-psychological, seemed to concentrate almost exclusively on the literature of their own orientation", and that American analysts read more widely and described a wider range of influences than did British analysts (Hamilton, 1996, p. 30). This fits with the striking fact that Fairbairn's work has become far better known in America than it is in Britain, and also suggests that British Kleinians are particularly unlikely to have read Fairbairn.

Analysing interview data concerning attitudes to the conduct of analysis, Hamilton delineated two principal dimensions of belief: "total transference versus relative view of transference" and "identification of psychic truth versus interpretations as hypotheses"

(1996, p. 309). The former dimension encapsulates one of the main differences between Klein and Fairbairn. With regard to the latter dimension, Hamilton's research indicates that Kleinian analysts tend to equate interpreting with identifying psychic truth, and they tend to disapprove of presenting interpretations to the patient as hypotheses. What about Fairbairn?

In "The Repression and Return of Bad Objects", published in 1943, Fairbairn spelt out in particular detail his thoughts about interpretative technique in the light of his theory:

> situations should be interpreted, not in terms of gratification, but in terms of object-relationships (including, of course, relationships with internalized objects) . . . libidinal strivings should be represented to the patient as ultimately dictated by object-love and as, therefore, basically if not superficially "good" . . . libidinal "badness" should be related to the cathexis of bad objects . . . "guilt" situations should be related by interpretation to "bad object" situations. . . . Caution should be exercised over interpretations in terms of aggression. . . .
>
> Interpretations in terms of aggression are liable to have the undesirable effect of making the patient feel that the analyst thinks him "bad". In any case, they become less necessary in proportion as the repressed objects are released; for in such circumstances the patient's aggression makes itself obvious enough. It will then become the analyst's task to point out to the patient the libidinal factor that lies behind his aggression.

He described the interpretative aims being:

> to enable the patient to release from his unconscious "buried" bad objects . . . to promote a dissolution of the libidinal bonds whereby the patient is attached to these hitherto indispensable bad objects [Fairbairn, 1943, p. 74]

Thus Fairbairn suggested interpreting in a way that involves internal and external reality together, linked by the relational focus. I think he would not have ruled out conveying such interpretations to the patient with certainty, but it seems to me that his emphasis on the importance of the "total relationship existing between the patient and the analyst as persons" (Fairbairn, 1958, p. 379), entails accepting variation in the degree of certainty conveyed to the patient, depending on the relational situation, including the patient's attitude to the analyst's interpretations and the analyst's actual degree of certainty.

Hamilton found that analysts' beliefs about transference and interpretation correlated with their theoretical orientation and with their "overall pattern of beliefs". She classified patterns of belief as "circumscribed", "wide", or "changed"—referring to analysts who had switched from one theoretical orientation to another, usually with no widening of their belief pattern (Hamilton, 1996, p. 310). She linked a "circumscribed" pattern of beliefs with a monistic attitude, and a "wide" pattern with a pluralist attitude, and she described a recent development of "an avowed commitment" to pluralism among analysts, "fired in part by weariness with the recurring ideological wars that have plagued the growth of psychoanalysis" (p. 24). But describing the British situation, she reflected that: "even in a pluralist society, monism tends to win out. Independents do not offer a grand explanatory scheme, and their force in the British Psychoanalytical Society has tended to be a mediating one, between the Freudian and Kleinian systems" (p. 25).

Perhaps part of the difficulty Fairbairn's ideas have met with is that he *did* offer a grand explanatory scheme, but one that is essentially pluralist in practice because it gives weight to internal *and* external reality and the relationship between them. It is this combination of clarity and inclusiveness in Fairbairn's explanatory scheme that I find so satisfying. However, in addition to its inherent challenge to the more monistic explanatory schemes of Freud and especially Klein, its sheer explanatory power and distinctly monistic emphasis on "the conditions of early childhood" as "the ultimate source of all disturbances of mental health" (Fairbairn, 1957, p. 61), this scheme may also be off-putting to analysts with a more pluralist disposition.

In a letter to Dr Brierley in 1942, Fairbairn wrote:

The point of view which I have developed is admittedly of Kleinian lineage, although privately I regard it as a definite advance beyond the Kleinian standpoint. I understand from Dr Glover, however, that the Klein group disclaim any paternity—or should I say "maternity"? I feel therefore somewhat of an orphan. Perhaps I have been disinherited as too independent-minded a child, whilst at the same time suffering the disadvantage of my lineage in the eyes of those who look askance at it.

He suggested that he had "fallen between two stools" in relation to the Klein group and the Vienna group, adding: "indeed between three, because I seem to have rather missed the boat so far as the Middle Group are concerned; and it is with the Middle Group that I should certainly align myself politically, if it is to become a question of politics. I remain quite unrepentant about my views, however, because I feel that they represent a genuine contribution" (Fairbairn, 1942, p. 444).

Hamilton emphasizes that beliefs cannot be severed from action, and that it makes no sense either to think of one unified psychoanalytic understanding nor to reduce theories to "mere metaphors".

> Beliefs seep into experience. Beliefs rarely exist in isolation; complex interrelationships connect beliefs with one another; in addition, I cannot choose my beliefs in the simple sense that I might choose to eat meat or fish for dinner. Moreover, beliefs depend on social connections. They are linked to people with whom we have formed strong ties, both loving and hating. [Hamilton, 1996, p. 24]

This seems especially the case in psychoanalytic training, which combines the learning of complex theories with experience in the intensely personal analytic setting. In contrast, philosophic training combines the learning of complex theories with experience in examining the basis of different theories. In both trainings, the experience acts as a gauge of theory, but to different extents. In philosophy training, experience, or skill in philosophical thinking is practised on the theories, including thinking about a theory's usefulness. In psychoanalytic training, experience in and outside the analytic setting is used to understand and in a sense test the theory, but this can easily be overshadowed by the simultaneous use of the analytic setting to practise the application of a particular theory—that is, understanding experience through the eyes of theory.

In the training context, it *can* feel that the main skills to be learnt constitute understanding what happens in the analytic setting in terms of particular psychoanalytic theory and interpreting accordingly. In my experience of training this happened with Freudian and Kleinian theory. It did not happen with Fairbairnian theory, which I think reflects how Fairbairnian theory does not lend itself readily to this use because of its emphasis on external as well as internal reality, past and present.

As a philosophy student, I went through different stages in relation to philosophical theories: taking each seriously, feeling drawn to some, and gradually understanding similarities and incompatibilities, which led to a sense of theories in relation to one another—like a kind of ideational jigsaw or map—none all-sufficient, though some particularly useful and personally appealing. I'd moved from a search for theoretical truth to an awareness of the presence and potential use of theory in the context of experience, and this felt an important learning.

Thinking about elements in psychotherapy training that helped theory not to dominate over experience, I remember Dr Sutherland's strong advocation in a seminar: "Forget the books and listen to your patients!", and Dr Wood's questions: "What is actually happening here?", "What is the patient communicating?", "What were you feeling then?"—to which he expected replies worded in the ordinary language of personal experience. His statement— "Technique follows understanding"—was not about theoretical understanding but about personal, relational understanding and encouraged a trust in this "personal knowledge" and a tolerance, in its absence, of not knowing. This teaching and practice highlighted how tempting it is, particularly when anxious and confused, to resort to a theoretical construct in order to gain the comfort and strength of a sense of knowing, and how different this is from an actual experience of understanding in the analytic situation, which may in a secondary way echo with psychoanalytic theory.

I think this attitude to understanding in the analytic setting is consistent with Fairbairn's theory, and I know the trainers who taught in this way were influenced by Fairbairn. But because this kind of teaching is characterized by encouraging a more natural, relational awareness in the analytic setting as distinct from theoretical knowledge, it makes sense that it was not explicitly identified with Fairbairn.

These training experiences influence my work as a liaison psychiatrist in an infectious diseases unit and in a department of neurology in Edinburgh. I work with doctors and nurses and other staff, seeing many patients for assessment and brief intervention and continuing with a significant proportion who seem to benefit from open-ended contact, usually once or twice a month for an hour, sometimes with their partner or a close relative. All the patients I see have some sort of physical problem. This may be organic illness, such as AIDS or epilepsy, or what is considered a non-organic illness, manifested in chronic pain and fatigue symptoms or multiple symptoms amounting to somatization disorder or a specific loss of function suggestive of conversion disorder. Organic and non-organic factors can also coexist. This work setting allows an unusual degree of access to both relational and psychosomatic processes, and I will briefly present some aspects of my work in this regard.

Being physically ill is like becoming a child again, thrown back into practical dependence on others and psychological dependence on authority figures—that is, doctors. Patients and their families, and doctors and other staff, vary greatly in their handling of this, and this is one area where Fairbairn's theory, together with attachment theory, influences my attitude in case discussion—not least in making dependency normal and important to take into account in clinical management. Apart from any other considerations, the widespread antilibidinal aggression towards dependency tends to worsen physical symptoms. For example, consider the effect on a teenager hearing that: "The GP wrote to ask if I was a difficult child—attention seeking". She described her emotional distress thus: "I lost trust in myself", and the concomitant increase in her physical symptoms can be at least partly explained by the physiological correlates of her suppressed distress.

I find it useful to think in terms of: "How much does this person need from us?" and "Who is in the best position to provide what?", and the more natural the provision the better, so I try to gauge the quality of the patient's family and social relationships together with what has been, and needs to be, provided professionally. Connected with this, I encourage the patient to think about what, relationally, has helped and what has not helped their physical symptoms. Thus, with a focus continuing on physical problems, we talk about relational problems, usually initially problems with doctors: experiences of disappointment, of having hopes of help and well-being raised and dashed, and many kinds of rejection, which may include feelings of humiliation about being referred to me as a psychiatrist.

Physical symptoms are there to return to from progression towards considering the endopsychic situation—how much the patient excites and disappoints him/herself by impossible *self*-expectations and the extent of self-rejection for any kind of non-physical weakness, including physical symptoms that are not both severe and organic.

One patient explained, in relationship to his severely disabling fatigue, judged non-organic: "If someone said there's such and such a process going on chemically", that would help, but in the absence of this: "I'm making it myself, I'm getting it wrong. It must be my fault." He emphasized the threat of "the invisibility of the illness—it doesn't exist, I'm mad, I'm lazy." Thus he was self-condemnatory in the absence of a monistic, physical explanation of his symptoms, which ran counter to his avowed acceptance of a multifactorial aetiology. His self-condemnation, together with painful internalized experiences—"Long periods of nothingness in childhood. I didn't have a role"—explained one terribly powerful vicious circle in his illness that he described thus: "The more tired I am, the more active I am. I bring up this energy to meet the tiredness. If I'm feeling really tired there's a fear of giving in completely. I've got a tremendous fear of disapproval—of being seen as not pulling my weight. Before, I don't think I'd have rushed things as I have since I've been ill, because I'd have had the confidence I had the energy."

Seeing the patient with their partner or a close relative can highlight the extent of their aggressive self-domination, including rejection of support: "She's always running round doing things for people", "He can't leave anything unfinished", "She never listens to me when I tell her to sit down and relax". Encouraging the partner or relative to speak out can help the patient more seriously consider their antilibidinal attitude as unhealthy, with elements of addiction, rather than unquestionable as moral virtue and that, in the face of this ruthless slave-driving, their body has had to do the protesting. One patient with severe back pain, and more recent headaches, fatigue, and widespread muscle pain, came to describe this: "I never said no to anyone, never refused anyone. I gave up holidays. People were always knocking at my door asking me to do more, and I always did." She summed up her accompanying inner feeling as "it's like you're running all the time inside", and she described dreams of "protecting people and getting in-between". Another patient emphasized: "It's terrible having to face yourself if you're not *doing* anything."

When the patient's self-domination and associated anxious focus on others makes sense to them as such, it is more possible to access relational tragedies in their personal history. Ferenczi's description of "the terrorism of suffering" often feels relevant. In "Confusion of Tongues between Adults and the Child" he wrote:

> In addition to passionate love and passionate punishment there is a third method of helplessly binding a child to an adult. This is the *terrorism of suffering*. Children have the compulsion to put to rights all disorder in the family, to burden, so to speak, their tender shoulders with the load of all the others; of course this is not only out of pure altruism, but is in order to be able to enjoy again the lost rest and the care and attention accompanying it. [Ferenczi, 1933, pp. 165–166]

The patient can realize that it is not, after all, a case of: "This is just *me*", "I've *always* been like this" or 'I was *born* like this". The ever-giving patient mentioned above came to reflect that: "Mum never showed any emotion. I was constrained so much I had to learn to hide my emotions", and she is now feeling freer, in a way that suggests that her libidinal ego is no longer so split off and repressed. She exclaimed recently: "I've no feelings of the *Great Rush* now. I'm far more contented than I've been for years." Similarly, the patient who couldn't face herself not doing anything exclaimed recently, about being with her first infant grandchild: "I'm amazed at the pleasure!" This patient was a "child of the manse", with a father who used to "soldier on" despite awful war wounds and a mother who "wouldn't stop at all ". A while ago, when I touched on the extreme expectations she would have felt as a child, she had exclaimed: "But I took it on!" Both these patients have made good

progress, and I think the support and encouragement that was
there in their key adult relationships to become personally—not
just physically—freer was an important contributing factor.

Winnicott, in "Psycho-somatic Illness in Its Positive and Negative Aspects", stated: "I have a desire to make it plain that *the
forces at work in the patient are tremendously strong*" (Winnicott, 1966,
p. 104). I feel this with my patients. In addition, I feel that some
patients are irretrievably caught up in a *tremendously strong* unsatisfying relationship, or relational setting, that perpetuates the
endopsychic situation and counteracts the psychotherapeutic process, apart from the measure of relief from antilibidinal self-attack
that can be felt with relational understanding when a respected
person comes to convey respect for the power of their external
situation, in conjunction with their endopsychic reality, including
their moral beliefs.

Finally, I will return to the young woman who described losing
trust in herself, and give you her conclusions about what helped.

She went through a great struggle physically and relationally
before leaving home for university. For example: "I was always
trying to *reach* somewhere, find some way to *resolve* things. Like
the time we stood up to Dad, thinking that would solve everything, and it didn't. It's like climbing a mountain and realizing
there's another mountain behind it." She felt she had to leave
home, and she had to work through considerable anxiety about
leaving. Talking, before she left, about her father and boyfriend,
she reflected: "It's like there's a big ghost that follows me
around and pops up—no matter what relationship I'm in."

A year later she contacted me during her summer holidays to
tell me she felt much better, and she explained why. She said: "I
needed this year to really *hate* my father." She told me about
important new friendships at college, which had helped,
through mutual support and confiding, whereas she'd felt her
old friends had been "dead reliant" on her, and she'd never
confided in them. She felt secure in her new relationships away
from home, knowing her family and boyfriend had survived
her leaving. She described recent invigorating dreams of "huge
tigers and huge snakes . . . and they'll *chase* me, and then I'll

stop—not a *giving-in* stopping. I'll turn round and *confront* them, and really *respect* them, and they don't *do* anything to me." She indicated that seeing me over a few years had been vital in her becoming freer in these ways, and she emphasized one element particularly: "I needed to know that there really *had* been problems, that things really *were* difficult." Knowing this gave her some freedom from self-domination.

Fairbairn's theoretical formulations lead naturally on to attachment theory and research, and the relational considerations I have presented with regard to psychoanalytic psychotherapy training and application, and philosophical and psychological theory and attitude, echo to a significant extent the distinction that Heard and Lake make in "The Challenge of Attachment for Care-giving" (1997), between "dominating/submissive" and "supportive companionable" patterns of relating. These terms are self-explanatory and also carry moral appeal, in that it is clear which relational pattern is better.

My primary aim here was to give tribute to the value of Fairbairn's theoretical contributions, but in the writing of it a related, subsidiary aim emerged, which is to call for a more collaborative form of relating, philosophically and pragmatically, in psychoanalytic psychotherapy training and application.

PART III

DREAMS AND AESTHETICS

CHAPTER SEVEN

Fairbairn, dreaming, and the aesthetic experience

Frederico Pereira

This chapter is made up of three parts. The first, which is extremely short, is dedicated to some aspects of classical psychoanalytic aesthetic experience; the second concentrates on Fairbairn's contributions on art and artistic creation; and the third sets out a scientific and mutual framework from which Fairbairn's thinking may have emerged.

In the first part, we are reminded that within the field of psychoanalytic thinking, the classic manner of living with art and literature is organized around a production aesthetic, which itself is based on the movement of *themes* and *contents*. It is, as used to be said, the "psychology of the artist" that is in question, and the issue of the dynamic of forms, while they remain such, is excluded.

The Freudian model of this production aesthetic is, it is understood, dreaming and reverie—where there is the ever-present movement of the central trio of repression–failure of repression–return of the repressed. It is therefore in the light of the internal conflicts of the creator that the aesthetic object becomes comprehensible, following a process of deciphering that enables one to surpass oneself while a mask. The logic of disguise and mask indeed constitutes the region in which art may arrive at meaning.

Within the permanent presence of these nuclear ideas, Freud looked at art, however, in different ways, which were successively in agreement with his own theoretical developments. We may therefore find three great moments in Freud's reflections on literature and art:

1. an initial moment where there is evidence of the idea of "family romance" introduced in a letter to Fliess on the subject of *"Die Richtering"* by Carl Ferdinand Meyer;

2. a second moment, from which emerges the principle of articulation of the fantasy and the daydream, as in *Gradiva*;

3. a third moment, which is characterized by its concentration on the analysis of the work's central, unconscious motif, and which ends up containing the nucleus of the classical psychoanalytic aesthetic.

Curiously, in this way of thinking, it is the work as such that is lost, and in particular its *formal qualities*—which are, after all, one of the central questions of aesthetics. On the other hand, an aesthetic of reception is completely disregarded, since this reception is reduced to the dimension of an *echo*, in the receptor, of the mental contents and creative processes of the creator himself. And finally, there exists in this classical psychoanalytic aesthetic a hysteria–art *analogy principle*, which one may believe to be lacking in the necessary preliminary basis.

If we now consider Kleinian developments, we witness a slight shift of attention from the problem of the motifs and logic of the masks, towards the study of the *conditions* so that internal reality may become transformed into an aesthetic object. If the inaugural work here, in 1929, is the work of Melanie Klein (1929/48); the paradigmatic reference remains that of Hanna Segal (1952). Although Melanie Klein's work is in fact presented as an *illustration*, within the field of art, of the theses developed within the clinical area, and therefore also based on the movement of the analogy, Hanna Segal's reflections seem to be attempting to achieve other objectives, insofar as they are interested, as stated, in analysing the *conditions* so that the conflict and the fantasy may become transformed into an aesthetic object.

The central idea, as arises almost immediately from Melanie Klein's theses, is that there is a narrow relationship between art and the depressive position. Art does not occur with splitting, fragmentation of the self, projective identification, nor with hate for the object, but, rather, in the relationship established towards the total object, which is lost but repaired and restored.

Retaining the dialectic of representation, we therefore add the issue of the internal conditions that are in place so that this dialectic may be possible. The problem of the *presentation of the object* (Pereira, 1997a; 1997b), the relevance of which I have been emphasizing—in other words, the problem of the *symbol as presence*—is disregarded once more, as well as the problem of the formal qualities of the aesthetic object.

I feel that it is something similar that is evoked by Paul Ricoeur when he enigmatically states, on the subject of da Vinci: "Leonardo does not recreate the recollection of his mother; he creates her as a work of art . . ." (Ricoeur, 1969, p. 205).

And furthermore, what qualities are inherent in Leonardo's aesthetic objects in order for them to be art and not a common scribble? This type of issue crops up regularly in the thinking of art philosophers—even when they are extremely sensitive to psychoanalytic thinking. Indeed, this is the case with H. Read, when he highlights the basic differences between aesthetics and psychoanalytic aesthetic. He states, paradigmatically:

> The obvious difference between our two Sciences [Psychoanalysis and Criticism] is that [Psychoanalysis] is only interested in the *processes* of mental activity, while Criticism is interested in the *product*. The [psychoanalyst] analyses the product only in order to reach the process: art is, from this point of view, as significant as any other expression of the mind. But not more significant: its significance does not correspond to its value as [art]. [Read, 1951, p. 73]

And more radically:

> Whether in the nature of things it is possible for such psychology to add anything positive to the principles of literary criticism is more in doubt. Analysis involves the reduction of the symbol to its origins, and once the symbol is in this way dissolved, it is of no aesthetic significance: art is art as symbol, not as sign. [Read, 1951, p.73]

The problem of aesthetic judgement and aesthetic value is thus forgotten. The issue of comparative aesthetic assessment is disregarded.

As Read asks as an example: What is the difference between *Hamlet* and *Death of a Salesman* by Arthur Miller, which both evoke the oedipal situation? "What is the difference? It is simple. *Hamlet* is poetry. *Death of a Salesman* is probably not even good prose" (Read, 1951, p. 79).

But it is Read himself who makes significant efforts, within the framework of psychoanalytic aesthetics, to push through the limits of classical psychoanalytic aesthetics. And, as we have already noted (Pereira, 1999b), it is Fairbairn himself whom he evokes.

Nevertheless, we will leave aside Read's thoughts on Fairbairn, but not without pointing out a very interesting passage where the *issue of representation* is strictly set out. In effect, Read states that psychoanalysis itself, *but above all as described by Fairbairn*, opened itself up to the idea that the symbol as such does not need to be *representative*: "it may be surreal, it may be completely geometric or abstract". I do not know if psychoanalysis did in fact open up to such ideas, but I would nevertheless add that the symbol may also be its *being-there in its surfaces* (Pereira, 1997b). It is, after all, this *being-there in its surfaces* that makes it possible to discuss, for example, the geometry of love in terms of Chirico's first work, or in terms of the "dream of a line", as the French poet Michaux used to say on the subject of Klee. . . .

* * *

But if, in the words of art philosophy, Fairbairn *innovates*—what does he innovate?

It is this that is now being addressed, with "Prolegomena to a Psychology of Art" (Fairbairn, 1938a) and the "grandiose", "The Ultimate Basis of Aesthetic Experience" (Fairbairn, 1938b), as starting points. In these works, whose titles immediately reveal Fairbairn's amplitude of ambition, multiple influences are indeed felt, from Aristotle to Hegel and surrealist thinking—and it is a pity that psychoanalysis has paid so little attention to them or understood them so badly. Remember that Hanna Segal does not even mention them and only mentions the name of Fairbairn, and that his most direct disciple considers them almost mediocre (Sutherland, 1989).

Recently, Ellinor Fairbairn Birtles and David Scharff recovered them (Birtles & Scharff, 1994), while an art historian, Levine (1998), explored them more completely.

* * *

The first aspect that should be highlighted—and which is more important than may at first appear—is the fact that in these works Fairbairn *seeks to characterize what he is talking about when he talks about art* and, rightly, *to pay special attention to the formal aspects of the aesthetic object.*

With regard to the first aspect—what is *art*?—Fairbairn's starting point is to attempt to characterize human activities as a whole, pointing out an axis that orients us in the specific direction of the aesthetic object. These activities may, according to him, be grouped into two broad categories: those that are performed *for their own sake*, and those which are performed for *"ulterior motives"*. The former are undertaken *"for fun"*, while the latter are *"serious activities"*. The central axis that enables us to differentiate one group of activities from the other is *instrumentality*, insofar as the "instrumental" is formed around the "re-sending to", and the non-instrumental therefore presents itself as "self-centred". In the same way, the aesthetic object may be defined as perceiving "for fun" something that was created "for fun".

Obviously, Fairbairn adds a *rhetoric of orthodoxy*, which creates an ambiguity of thinking that inevitably leads to confusion. But I think that the references to what he later qualifies as psychological hedonism are rhetorical expressions that camouflage what is implicitly already organized as being Fairbairnian.

An identical ambiguity is also encountered when Fairbairn seeks to characterize not only the nature, but also the *contextual framework* within which *art* operates. It is interesting to note that it is now the expression *social phenomenon* that stands out, only to seem to fade away as soon as Fairbairn affirms that a psychology of art can only be a psychology of the *artist*. This social phenomenon is characterized by four components, the presence of which require innovative developments". The term 'Art' is ordinarily employed to describe a social phenomenon embracing three component elements (1) the work of art, (2) the creative artist, (3) the percipient or audience." A fourth component is immediately added: "*technique,* which provides the means whereby the artist is enabled to embody his conceptions in actual works of art" (Fairbairn, 1938a, p. 381). This of course has essentially *formal* implications.

But leaving technique aside—which he nevertheless mentions in relation to Van Gogh, among others—Fairbairn concentrates on that which more easily seems to be a production aesthetic—in which the model is, as before, the dream as a fulfilment of desire. And it is with regard to the "tempo" of the return of the repressed in the dream object that Fairbairn describes his concept of art work with which, obviously, the concept of dream work reverberates. What should be pointed out, however, is the fact that art work is not only the process of *"rewriting"*, but also of *"writing"*, of radically *constructing*. Again we see the coexistence of two discourses: *camouflage and relief of tension*, and *revelation*, which is implicit.

In the same way, if a discourse emerges which leads the comprehension of art to that which is its production process, there also emerges the affirmation of *positive values* in the aesthetic object.

Later on, in *Reevaluating Some Basic Concepts* (Fairbairn, 1956), Fairbairn resurrects the notion of positive values now associated to a radical criticism of the *reductionist conceptions*:

> Reductive explanations of this type possess the great disadvantage of simply explaining away what they seek to explain. Whatever light they may throw upon the basic motivations of cultural activities, they make a minimum contribution to an understanding of the values involved in these activities themselves—as is perhaps most conveniently illustrated within the artistic field. Thus, quite apart from their failure to explain why the motivations of an artist should lead him to become an artist rather than, e.g., a philosopher, and what determines the degree of an artist's greatness, such explanations, as Herbert Read (1951) has pointed out, completely fail to explain what determines the specifically aesthetic value of a work of art, and characteristically provide no clue to any *scale* of aesthetic values. [Fairbairn, 1956, p. 130]

Ideas of this type are already evident in the works of 1938, even if *positive values* are seen merely as "tributes to the ideal-ego"—which indeed already introduces the relational principle into art.

But in fact Fairbairn goes further still in his innovative preoccupations, predicting that the *reductive explanation* is linked to the field of the contents of the representations, rightly disregarding the *dialectic of forms as such*.

And for this reason he can state—anticipating the criticisms themselves of art philosophy—that "this at once becomes obvious when we compare, say, the Madonna by Leonardo da Vinci with a picture entitled 'Maternity' by the Surrealist Joan Miró. In both pictures maternity is the theme; but, whereas the former shows considerable evidence of art-work, the latter, like most Surrealists works of art, shows comparatively little" (Fairbairn, 1938a, p. 387).

It does not seem to me—contrary to what Fairbairn *also* affirms—that the dimension of the "art-work" is co-extensive to the dimension of the processes of camouflage, especially since in another context he rightly evokes a *dual function* of this same "art-work": a function that *transforms* "trends and the system"—to use *Traumdeutung*'s expression—until they are compatible, but also another function, which is a *positive gesture*, of a truly uplifting production.

Despite the orthodox language he uses, Fairbairn is clearly conscious of the innovative character of this dual function of "art-work", since he states:

> So far as the psychoanalytic study of art is concerned, attention has been hitherto largely concentrated on the first function of art-work; and this fact has given rise to the criticism that, while psychoanalysis may shed some light on the nature of the unconscious urges prompting artistic creativity, the central problems of the psychology of art fall outside its purview. [Fairbairn, 1938a, p. 394].

However, these criticisms no longer apply once the other dimension of the aforementioned dual function is taken into account.

This permanent coexistence of the two discourses, one classic and the other innovative, perhaps allows us to think that Freudian but, above all, Kleinian theses are essentially a *convenience*, so to speak, based on which and with which Fairbairn begins to form his *specific* way of thinking. This *convenience*, as much as concepts, provides a language to express new thoughts that do not yet have their own words.

Alongside the dialectic of *representation* in the aesthetic object, Fairbairn already clearly feels *being-there* as a *presence* that requires its *contemplation*. It is not that to which the aesthetic object *re-sends* which is essentially in question—rather, the manner in which, in its specific aspect, it is *offered*.

And so much so that Fairbairn—almost contrary to what he himself states—finally develops an aesthetic of reception, which is secondarily made more complex, as we shall see. This aesthetic is incompatible with any expressionist or productivist vision of the aesthetic object, just as it is incompatible with its *reduction* to the dynamic of repair within the creative subject.

* * *

Prior to this, however, the basic problem of the work emerges. The problem is that when psychoanalysts talk about the aesthetic object, we may ask: *where* in fact is it? *Where* did it get left behind?

For Fairbairn, it is *ahead* of us, in its *being-there*. As far as he is concerned, understanding it is based, in part, on an almost physical dragging of Kleinian concepts to the visible surface of the work, which entails a functional re-formatting of these very concepts. Indeed, the aesthetic object will be—partially, of course—understood by means of an axis: the axis of *over-symbolization* and *under-symbolization* (note that it can only be felt by means of a systematic comparative analysis of different works) and, above all by means of another axis, the axis of fragmentation–integrity–unity, which are not seen essentially as psychological processes that lie at the profound heart of the work, but which are *immediately* present in the work exactly as it is *offered*. And the word that stands out here is precisely *immediacy*—an idea-word that is so often used in aesthetics and philosophy of art.

In fact, it is in this unity–integrity–fragmentation pulsation where the central dimensions of the meaning of the work emerge—not of its significance but of its *meaning*, which is exactly what will enable it to be opened up to the Other.

It is also in this movement of meaning in the formal pulsation of the aesthetic object, that the reception process itself, the presence of the audience, may become anchored (Pereira, 1997b): first of all, the internal audience—which again introduces the relational dimension into aesthetics—but also the *external audience*—which, based on the formal characteristics of the aesthetic object, will in its own way again render it semiotic.

Understanding this process, which I describe as again rendering the object semiotic is, in Fairbairn's text, a lengthy analysis—in which, once more, there are two discourses—of the surrealist "*objet trouvé*". "Symbol of fulfilment of desire" (but how? of which desire?): the essential aspect is that the analysis of the "*objet trouvé*" will be based on an almost *phenomenological* delimitation of this very object.

For Fairbairn—and I suspect that we all agree with him—the "*objet trouvé*" is "an intermediate point between the attitude of the artist and the attitude of the beholder" (Fairbairn, 1938b, p. 399). In fact, the "*objet trouvé*" is at large in the world stripped of all "art-work", and it is merely necessary to *discover it* and *frame it* (minimal forms of "art-work"). The basic problem immediately leaps out: for what reason will the artist *frame* the "*objet trouvé*", cut out of the world this small slice of the world? In addition to fulfilling emotional needs, it is cut out and framed first and foremost because it rapidly *acquires meaning*.

And why will it acquire meaning? Because it was discovered—a theory that, once again, seems simple, but which has multiple consequences. Fairbairn says: "['*objet trouvé*'] does not exist apart from the act of discovery; it is created by the discovery itself; and the discovery represents a creative act on the part of the artist" (Fairbairn, 1938b, p. 401). *Discovery is, therefore, where meaning lies.* And this is exactly what Fairbairn reveals, among other insights, in his analysis of Dali's "*Visage Paranoïque*", where only a *phenomenology* of the perception and *construction* of the object is present, and an aesthetic of production and significance is conspicuous by its complete absence.

To use other terms, I would say that the artist discovers the object because he *assigns a meaning to it*, and he *assigns meaning to it because he discovers it*—which is to say that anything that resides in the object, in the secret of its pre-existence, because of the vision with which one regards it, thus begins to speak (see Merleau-Ponty, 1964b).

Thus Fairbairn can almost affirm that for him the "*objet trouvé*" is the *basic model of the aesthetic object*. The subject–object symphony indicates from its union, where it is not fusion that is operating, it is a manifestation–constitution of a primordial relationship, which is indeed *perceived* by many creators. It is not the artist who sees the trees, but the trees that see the artist; it is not the artist who dreams but, rather, the lines, which he himself drew (Merleau-Ponty, 1964a). In the *"objet trouvé"* it is this *primordial relationship* that becomes abruptly *present*.

It is an intermediate object, stated Fairbairn, but not a bridge connecting two separate things: an intermediate object that is a thing where subject and object become *intertwined*. And this *intertwining* is perhaps the most singular and powerful form of relationship between the subject and its world.

And if it is so for the creator, so shall it be for the beholder, in which, over and above the reproduction of the artist's internal processes, there is also a demand for *construction by the discovery* of an *"objet trouvé"*—in other words, a demand for a new cutting from a new *being-there* in which the subject is the world and the world is the subject (see Sami Ali, 1985, 1989).

Perhaps it is because of this that the world of aesthetic objects is so *silent*. In fact, in the place where the aesthetic object and the subject that constructs or re-constructs it are located, there is not necessarily any talking at all. And if there is any talking, it is because the aesthetic object has been replaced by mundane conversation.

If the fragmentation present in Picasso's canvases awakens in the beholder perceptions and memories of internal processes of fragmentation, the object unity present in the works of Leonardo will awaken other perceptions and memories. But once these processes have been awakened in the beholder, within the context of their specific anchoring in the forms of the aesthetic object, the beholder's internal movements will follow their own paths, regardless of those formed by the creator.

Precisely because of this, a radical aesthetic of reception is itself inadequate because it transforms the multiplicity of the meanings into an undefined semiotic shift. It is the aforementioned anchoring that frames this shift and limits it for precisely this reason. The *"objet trouvé"* serves as a model insofar as at its side are the creator and the receptor: the creator who is the receptor and the receptor who is the creator, both enlivened by the *surprise* that is associated with cutting out the discovery, and which is followed by other-productions, other-meanings and other-narratives.

Upon thinking so forcedly about the *"objet trouvé"*, Fairbairn laid the roots of an aesthetic that, in addition to production or reception, *is an aesthetic of the Relationship*, open to the *polymorphism of meanings* (which are nevertheless not arbitrary), which are not enclosed in the ordering of the significations. And if Freud opened up paths for the possible understanding of that which is hidden behind forms as disguises, veils, or masks, Fairbairn opened up paths for understanding the being-right-there of forms on immediate surfaces that are its own.

* * *

We may now ask how the dynamic of dreaming contributes retroactively to broader clarifications of Fairbairn's aesthetic.

Setting aside the description of what could be called Fairbairn's "dream *princeps*", the actress's dream (Fairbairn, 1944), what is important for my purpose is the fact that, by means of different characters, it *renders present* some aspects of the functioning of the Ego. In fact, this dream, which appears like a true theatre of the mind, and which reveals internal and external relationships, also reveals an endopsychic structure characterized by the multiplicity of egos/objects that at the same time points out the polymorphous nature of the self. Upon *revealing*—rather than *camouflaging*—the endopsychic structure of this dream, it can be said that it is an "objectivation" of ourselves in the dream world, which at the same time is ourselves. A subjectivity encounters an object world, but this object world is an integral and *constitutive* part of that very subjectivity. The relationship between the subject and the dream thus evokes what could be called a *primordial relationship* (Pereira, 1999b). Just as the dreamer *is* his dream in its plural aspect, so the artist *is* also the aesthetic object, and the receptor *is* also this very object.

There is also such a relationship of construction–revelation—and once again not just of concealment—between the dreamer and the dream, which can to a certain extent be said to be a kind of theophany (a manifestation of deity to man) of the subject. Therefore, the dream is more than a mere manifestation–expression–

revelation: it is what I call a *subjectophany*[1] *appearing to be constitutive of the very thing that it appears to be.*

Therefore, nothing in the dream is in essence instrumental—just as nothing is instrumental in the aesthetic object. Everything in the aesthetic object is a progressive unfolding of itself. In the dream everything is a successive unfolding of the self, which is the dream.

For this reason, in the artist's movements—just as in the process of dreaming—the artist goes further than his own vision: he *is* vision, hand, paintbrush, paint, line, colour, or sound, or poetic melody, or proliferation in the narrative. He *is* all of this, and it cannot be said that he merely *uses* this to express conflicts, fantasies, desires.

As can be seen, these Fairbairnian derivations on the dream retroactively shed new light on initial intuitions, without cancelling them out but separating them from what was initially and fundamentally rhetoric.

* * *

The last problem on which I am going to dwell relates to knowing whether Fairbairn, in introducing inaugural relational principles, was as isolated as is believed. He was isolated in the psychoanalytic field, certainly; but to compensate, he was, without knowing it, plunged into a scientific and cultural environment that challenged classic categories and placed the relational dynamic centre stage in what became its own place.

The general theory of open systems itself points to a new environment, and the addition of concepts such as that of homeorhesis to homeostasis throws up new clues to understanding the relational processes and those relating to development. But perhaps the most important mark of this cultural environment is located in the so-called *dialogism*, which, at the same time as it opens up an aesthetic of verbal creation, outlines what perhaps may be called a relationship ontology. This *dialogism*, produced in isolation by

---

[1] By "subjectophany" I mean the *revelation* of the Subject to itself and to the world, which is constitutive of this same subject and of this same world. It is an ontological concept, and not an instrumental one.

Mikhail Bakhtin (1979; Todorov, 1981), indicates that there are solitary voices. Every voice, silent though it may be, can only prevail as a voice insofar as it is integrated into the complex of the already present voices. As has been stated, the almost ontological result is that "in the heart of the Being lies the Other" (Todorov, 1981). And for this reason, from Bahktine's point of view, it is not subjectivity that precedes intersubjectivity, but it is intersubjectivity that logically comes before subjectivity.

This being the case, the meaning itself of any statement, as well as containing the very act of statement, the code and the context, also implies a dimension that he called *community*—in which the other never takes on a passive role. On the contrary, this other, whether internal or external, makes up part of the formation of meaning in its polymorphy. Indeed, Bahktine states, "even the most primitive human statement made by an individual body is already organized *outside* [of this very body], and this is both from the point of view of its content, of its meaning, and of its signification". And Bahktine insists—which was extraordinary for the period—"even a baby's crying is already directed towards the mother".

It is for this reason that Tzetan Todorov can state, without hesitation, that "for Bahktine, *at the foundation of the human being is not the Id, but the Other*" (Todorov, 1981). It is clear that when one passes from the domain of language to that of meta-language, this *constitutive otherness of the sign* becomes more visible, and the dynamic of the formation of the meaning becomes broader. In effect, the meta-language literally *creates* a new object, which is not arbitrary, since it is not a question of pure description, nor of pure invention, but, rather, of *recreation-construction* assisted by anchoring.

The constitutive otherness of the self, this central *heterology*, is still to be found in another dynamic, which complements the former and is related to the different planes of organization of the *statement* (the "*saying so*"), in which it is not only the other as the other that is present, but still the other as the *statement–other*, which cannot be forgotten without the risk of entering a semiotic shift. This relationship with the statement–other is the basis of the *intertextuality* that is present throughout the whole text, the whole time, throughout the *talking*.

Every *statement* is related to the previous *statement*, with others that are possible and present and with others that are potential and of the future—and this recentres the *relationship as a relationship spiral*, the relationship of relationships, what could be called call *meta-relationship*.

If the human being is therefore Relationship and Meta-relationship, what can be said of the "locus" of meaning? The classic theory of interpretation considers that there exists *one* meaning as a signification, and some classic visions of the psychoanalytic process would further add that the *locus of this meaning is the production process of the meaning of the subject*. A dialogic sensibility would say that although the meaning is not arbitrary, it restores itself at all times in the *relationship* between plural *"voices"* of the self and the other, and in the spiral of this relationship.

This means—using this central concept of dialogism—that to the heterology of the self inevitably is added the *externality* of meaning. Meaning is never in a *here*: it is not unitary. It is present beyond the in-between. As a consequence, it is in relationship. And in the solitude of the subject, it is still a relationship, since it is another facet of the intrasubjective processes. And the relationship, more so than mere interaction, is the symphony of *multiple intersubjectivities*.

The aesthetic of verbal creation (Bakthin, 1979)—like any other aesthetic—cannot therefore be an aesthetic of production, nor an aesthetic of reception—*it is an aesthetic of relationship and an aesthetic of relationships between relationships*.

Bakthin's ideas are close to Fairbairn's developments, even if they worked in rather different scientific fields. Consequently, it would be interesting to see to what extent *dialogics* can provide the epistemological—or even ontological—model of Fairbairn's ideas, which seems even more powerful than the general theory of open systems.

In any case, the basic point is that "multiple voices", in multiple disciplinary areas, lead to the collapse of a subjectivism where the other appears as secondary, on the temporal or even logical plane, and also lead to the collapse of a theory of meaning that I would call *endotopic*.

The great challenge is therefore to seek to understand which aspects of the pulsation of knowing, which thus become organized as a rhizome, to use for the concept-idea of Gilles Deleuze and F. Guatarry (Deleuze & Guatarry, 1980), which is more than a mere reform of visions but, rather, emerges as a true paradigmatic revolution.

But even if an archaeology (Foucault, 1969) of the relational theories is yet to be performed, it cannot ignore the fundamental contributions made and reconstructed by Fairbairn during his solitude in Edinburgh.

CHAPTER EIGHT

Artistic process, dream process, and psychoanalytic process: Fairbairnian links

Emílio Salgueiro

I

One can view art as the result of a long, painful, and complex *intentional psychic work*, comparable to a process of "impregnation, gestation, and childbirth". It possesses conscious and unconscious dimensions, takes place in "psychic spaces" rooted in the whole body (Damasio, 1994), and reaches its zenith with the externalization or "delivery" of an "artistic object".

This artistic labour or artistic process uses specific expressive techniques (writing, painting, music, and so on), to transform internal representations pregnant with artistic potential, resulting from particular cycles of disturbance/turbulence/psychic re-equilibrium of the author ("state of inspiration", "state of trance") into external artistic objects. The creation of an internal creative state, endowed with a specific "surplus-value" propitiates the transmutation of the subject's innermost intimacy into a valuable object of art.

These *"cycles of alchemy"* will leave a luminous path inside the author; galleries will be dug in his deepest interior, from where can easily emerge *new creative states endowed with the specific "surplus-value"* that are capable of giving birth to new objects of art.

After their externalization or "delivery", the "artistic objects" become independent from the author, acquire a specific social, cultural, and sentimental value, and become capable of inducing *cycles of disturbance/ turbulence/ re-equilibrium* in those who appraise them. They promote *"psychic surplus-values"* that are related to those of the author: although they result from processes with inverted beginnings and endings, there is a certain parallelism between *the process of artistic production* and *the process of artistic reception and appraisal.*

II

Every artistic object necessarily has an *aesthetic* and a *dramatic* dimension—these are the dimensions that the public is looking for, these are the dimensions that the author has to *reveal* at a superlative level.

This is how Jean Genet describes these dimensions in Alberto Giacometti's work:

> At the origin of beauty there is solely the wound that everyone has sustained, singular, different from man to man, hidden or visible, preserved within each of us, and where one seeks shelter when a need emerges to exchange the world for a temporary but deep solitude. Outside any kind of miserableness. Giacometti's art seems to want to reveal that secret wound of beings and things, so that it becomes capable of illuminating them. [Genet, 1988, p. 18]

What "wound" is this that men keep in the depths of their beings *as if it were a treasure* and that Giacometti's art, and perhaps all art, illuminates?

I believe that this *"primal wound"* is what the "fatal beauty" of the child's primal love leaves behind. The "founding enchantment", the experiences of "the beginning-of-the-world-paradise", which were woven in the unique intimacy, in the great proximity of body and mind that happens between a baby and its mother, carry with them an intrinsic precariousness (Meltzer & Williams, 1988).

Inevitably, necessarily, these "exalted states of feeling" end up stained, slowly corroded by experiences of being out of tune, of misunderstanding, of disenchantment, by lack of interest, by deception, rage, and mutual dissatisfaction. It all ends up in feelings of estrangement, in a pressing need for detachment and solitude, even in the presence of one another—the great exaltation is over.

There is a *central detachment*, which is inevitable and necessary, bringing maturity to both partners; but there are also *disturbed and disturbing detachments*, resulting from specific historical circumstances of that baby and its mother. In these *long-lasting deceptions*, which are of a variable intensity and structure, there can emerge in the small child a deep and painful feeling of not having been sufficiently acknowledged and accepted, including in the recognition of his or her emerging masculinity or femininity. These disturbed evolutions are painful for both partners, but they are more difficult to bear for the baby or small child who does not yet possess enough resources of self-love from where to be soothed and find relief—the wound is open, and it will never again completely close.

The progressive detachment/extinction of the *"primal states of major encounter and sentimental exaltation"*, which seemed to be endless, are felt by the small child as the result of a very unfair justice and condemnation, as an unforgivable abandonment from lack of love, as an exile with no return. This fall from the "primal enchantment", which remains in the memory as a "wound that cannot heal", could correspond to the ontological fracture where the biblical myth of Adam and Eve's expulsion from Paradise acquired its roots.

Nevertheless, without this "wound", without this "fall", the child would never progress from the state of *being-turned-towards-its-mother* to that of *being-turnable-towards-himself-towards-the-world-and-towards-the-others*. The great pain might make the child a wandering being—like the hyperactive child, who endlessly strives to leave behind the sharpness of his suffering and find ahead, in a never reachable ahead, an acceptable alternative to the "Paradise Lost".

At this point, it is essential that the small child *discovers his father*, and that the father lets himself to be discovered by the child. The father is the lighthouse capable of illuminating the night of the *"primal deception"*: he is the solid column to which the small child can cling like a creeper and climb—the "wound" will not close, but the father can make it bearable.

It is essential that the small child find a paternal strength capable of focusing into his well-being; but it is also necessary that the child discovers and manages to accept and understand the strength of the liaison between his father and his mother. The acknowledgement of a strong link of love and desire between his parents opens up a "second wound", the "*oedipal wound*"—but this is a wound that can carry powerful healing elixirs to the "primal wound"....

The "primal wound" will not close: this wound cannot heal completely—it remains alive, although half-healed, softened, hidden, transformed, or disguised. This is the painful process the child has to go through in order, on the one hand, to maintain a good relationship with reality, and, on the other hand, to preserve a "linking cord" with his primordial source of aliveness. He still clings to the illusion of the possibility of a perfect match or understanding with the object of his primal love, a conviction that will *ad aeternum* reenergize his life-projects.

The child, but also the youth and the adult and the elderly person, need to keep on believing—in the most hidden part of their selves—that the *encounter of a perfect love* has once existed and that it *can happen again*—perhaps not in the immediate present, but perhaps in a not-so-distant future, on a glorious morning—that encounter, which will compensate for all the sufferings and will close all the wounds, may finally happen.

It is in this pain or suffering of "Paradise Lost" that the complex feelings of nostalgia and longing for become rooted and the "sebastianisms" and "millenarisms" gain strength.

The "wound", the "wounds", cannot be left without assistance for a long period of time: as a "background" for the needed help, there must appear the strength of the father's presence and the possible "reconciliation", both with the new mother, the *after-Paradise-mother*, and with the strength of the discovered affectionate connection between father and mother. In the "foreground", the discovery of *playing* has to appear, including the pleasure of *playing with others*, as well as the emergence of the *capacity for dreaming* and of an *aesthetic sensitivity and artistic capacity*.

These are fundamental soothing resources for the *pain-of-living*. But they also become propellers for a necessary *"psychic work concerning the wounds"*, establishing links, in a creative and fecund way, between the initial mythical past and the painful present and also with the future, which is feared as desolate.

It is here where a vital connection should be established between beauty and ugliness, where hope and despair should both become acceptable, where a *"capacity for regulating depression"* (Matos, 1985a) should emerge—a capacity for finding mental paths located at a safe distance both from exaltation and grand euphoria and from looming dark apathy and melancholia.

III

"Working-through" in this area of *"primal disappointment"*— perhaps close to the area of the "basic fault" (Balint, 1968)—can, therefore, be conducive to *creative ways of escape*, just as it may lead to *pseudo-ways-out* or *dead-ends*. In its *creative results* one can include play, humour, complex dreams, creative work, art, and love. Its *failures* could lead to nightmares or to the absence of a dreaming capacity, to the so-called "operational-way-of-thinking"(Marty & M'Uzan, 1963) that is present in some psychosomatic disturbances, to certain depressive states, to the addictions, including work-as-an-addiction, to the denial of art, and to the denial of love.

There is still a *neo-way of escape*, which is psychoanalysis.

I chose to look into three creative processes of resolution of the "primal wound", and to analyse what they have in common and what differentiates them: the *artistic process*, the *dream process*, and the *psychoanalytic process*.

Let us begin by searching for what links them.

Art, dream, and psychoanalysis all need the creation of a set of particular *previous conditions*, which will propitiate the emergence of its own specific processes. The individual has to put himself in an *internal state of special vulnerability*, where the processes might develop in a *background of safety*, in a protected situation.

In the *artistic process*, the individual must first put himself *in a state of isolation* (in a room to write, in a studio to paint) and will be protected by the use of *his technique*. He will also feel safe by the "presence" of *the group of his ancestors*, as Jean Genet tells us about Alberto Giacometti's (Genet, 1988, p. 27): they remain silent, waiting in no haste, obscurely surrounding the artist and gently prodding him forward by the attention they give to what he is striving to create. The artist will find himself in a state of "protected vulnerability" in the face of the empty sheet of paper or the white canvas, the plaster or the raw stone—the work of creation can proceed.

In the *dream process*, the individual searches for the isolation and silence of his room, the support given by the bed when he lies down, the comfort of the mattress, the enveloping by the sheets and the blankets, the bolster's support (paternal representative) and the pillow's complex caress (maternal representative of her lap and hands). The individual voluntarily places himself into a situation and a position of "protected vulnerability", and the act of closing his eyes and letting himself fall into the sleep allows for the emergence of a "virtual background canvas"—white, according to Bertrand Lewin (1946)—where a dream can take shape.

In the *psychoanalytic process*, the individual accepts submission to a number of characteristics of the "setting". They include the regularity, frequency, and payment of the sessions, and, within each session, the holding given by the couch to the supine position of the analysand, the firm support given to the head by the back of the couch and by the psychoanalytic pillow—generally harder than those used on beds—the ambivalent message given by the soft caress of the paper tissue that protects the pillow (this tissue is just for you, for nobody else but you, like the attention I give to you during this session, but it implicitly affirms that there are other analysands I have besides you). The whole "setting" shows a predominance of paternal representatives over maternal ones—in other words, it shows Freud's aegis over the process.

The weight of the psychoanalyst's silent presence outside the visual field of the analysand also contributes to the fact that he feels placed in a particular situation of *protected vulnerability*, in front of the "white canvas" of the beginning of each session. All of this allows for the safe emergence of progressively "freer associations" and the twosome creativity inherent in psychoanalytic work.

The common factor between art, dream, and psychoanalysis is, therefore, the possibility and the need for the creation of conditions favourable for the emergence, acceptance, and elaboration of a *creative vortex*. The main function of these vortexes is to allow for a *work of reconciliation with the "wounds"*, especially with "the primal wound", and to proceed with the healing process of the *"mal-de-vivre"*. *The reconciliation is done, under the aegis of the aesthetic, with the fatal beauty of the "primal encounter" between the baby and its mother* (Meltzer & Williams, 1988).

In psychoanalytic terms we can say that this *work on the vortex and through the vortex* makes possible the modification of the relationships existing between the "self" and its "objects", especially its "internal objects". To use a more Fairbairnian language, it permits the establishment of *new relationships between the "central self" and the "central object"* (Fairbairn, 1952a).

IV

How can this *relational rearrangement* be accomplished *under the aegis of the aesthetic*? Some diagrams of a Fairbairnian inspiration will help to clarify these concepts.

Figure 8.1 aims at representing the *primary mental organization*. There begins to emerge a separation between external reality and internal reality, due to the construction of the *"primal self"*, through the establishment of an *aesthetic link* with the *"primary external object"* and the progressive irradiation of that aesthetic quality to the newly discovered external and internal realities. The construction of the *"primal internal object"* proceeds slowly through a sedimentation process of how the concrete relational experiences with the "primary external object" are lived. The "primary external object" reveals itself as an object of enchantment and love, but also of deception, rage, and hatred—the *"primal aesthetic connection"* gives birth to the *"primal wound"*.

Figure 8.2 shows us the reinforcement of the separation between external and internal realities and the growing complexity of the internal organization, which is necessary for an efficient capacity of confrontation with the complex enigmas of the external and internal worlds.

The "primal self" gave way to an *"acceptant central self"* through the simultaneous construction of an *"acceptable central object"*. This

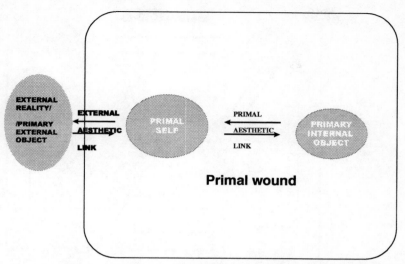

(Inspired by Scharff, 1982, and Scharff & Birtles, 1997.)

Figure 8.1

became possible due to the complex partial cleavage of the primal central structures into *"peripheral selves"* and *"peripheral objects"*. From the "central self" emerged an *"excited peripheral self"* and a *"rejected peripheral self"*, and from the "central object" an *"exciting peripheral object"* and a *"rejecting peripheral object"*. These *"auxiliary structures"*, full of dissociated or repressed strong affections, have a regulatory power over the whole psychic organization, as they keep a two-way special connection with the central structures.

These cleavages allow for the attenuation *and modulation of the pain inherent in the relation to the primary object* through the distancing of the intolerable aspects of the "primal internal object"— whether it be excessive excitement or excessive rejection. This process is also made easier by the creation of dynamic connections between the "peripheral selves" and between the "peripheral objects", enabling a *modulation of the "excessive" characteristics*.

All these partial cleavages and neo-connections make the system more flexible and capable of giving enriched answers, both in the encounter of the *"central self"* with external reality, where the *"maternal and paternal objects"* are progressively differentiated, and

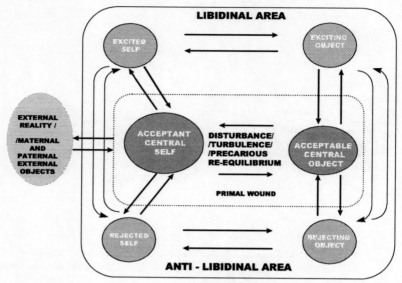

(Inspired by Scharff, 1982, and Scharff & Birtles, 1997.)

Figure 8.2

in its encounter with internal reality proper, which keeps on growing in complex networks.

Two functional areas emerge: a *libidinal area*, which has mainly to deal with excitement and desire, and an *anti-libidinal area*, faced with rejection and dejection. However, these are not closed areas: they have linked, overlapped borders, allowing for a *broad communication between the "excited" and the "rejected parts* in this *secondary mental organization*.

The *"acceptant central self"* maintains its privileged relation with the *"acceptable central internal object"* through the virtual space that exists between both, an area of *disturbance/ turbulence/ precarious re-equilibrium*—it is the *whirl area*, which is potentially creative and capable of transforming the *"primal wound"*.

V

In 1921, Luigi Pirandello wrote the play *Six Characters in Search of an Author*. In the Preface, he tells us that one day his imagination—which he calls "a maid at the service of his art"—placed a complete family in front of his eyes, without his having the faintest idea from where this family might have come.

The family was composed of a 50-year-old man with a dishevelled and humiliated appearance, a slightly younger woman wearing a widow's veil and dressed in black, with an expression of pain and misfortune all over her; she was holding by the hand, on one side, a 4-year-old girl, and, on the other, a boy little more than 10 years of age; there were also a very young woman, at the peak of her beauty and with a provocative look, although also dressed in black, and 20-year-old man, who kept himself at a distance from the group.

These six characters, as Pirandello reports (1977, p. 996): "frequently interrupting each other, kept insisting on telling me their problems, shouting their reasons, throwing their indecent passions at me. . . ." And he adds: "Which author can ever say how and for what reason a character was born in his imagination? The mystery of artistic creation is the same mystery of natural birth." He goes on: ". . . by the simple fact of being alive, an artist gives shelter inside himself to multiple germs of life, and he will never be able to say how or why one of these vital germs penetrates his imagination and becomes a live creature, in a level of existence superior to our ordinary way of living. I can only say that without having at all looked for them, I found these six live characters before me, alive to the extent of my being able to touch them, alive to the extent of my being able to hear them breathe. . . ." "And each one of them waited, with his secret torment, all united by the their birth and by the interlocking of their sufferings, they waited for me to make them enter the world of art. . . ." "Born alive, they wanted to keep on living."

And Pirandello goes on (p. 997): "Creatures of my spirit, these six characters had already a life of their own, which had ceased to be mine, a life that was no longer in my power to deny them."

The characters want to be heard: each one brings his own story and the way he sees it linked with the others' stories, and they all wish that someone would help them to find a sense and a way out of the deep pain that undermines them all. Pirandello refuses to assume the authorship of the drama's unfolding they want to impose on him, strongly believing that they are the ones who have to do it.

He does suggest that they present themselves on a theatre stage and act their drama right to the end, so that they can acquire a feeling of authorship of their discoveries and destiny.

The six characters end up accepting, and in an empty theatre—to the surprise of a stage director and several actors who were preparing to rehearse Pirandello's play *The Role Game*—they act their drama. The stage director and the actors end up accepting the role of a special public, although they comment on what they see, somewhat like a Greek chorus.

The characters start presenting themselves: the humiliated man was the first husband of the older woman, whom he pushed, almost 20 years ago, into the arms of the man who came to be her second husband, and who died recently, which is the reason why this woman is dressed in black. The 20-year-old man, who keeps himself distant from the rest of the group, was the only son of the first marriage; the seductive girl and the two children belong to their mother's second marriage. The son of the first marriage was rejected as a young child, both by his father and by his mother, having been given away to the care of other people—this *unhealable wound* is the cause for his distance from the others on stage.

The father did not remarry, resorting from time to time to the service of prostitutes.

The eldest daughter of her mother's second marriage fell into a golden prostitution, induced by an insinuating and blackmailing pander, Madam Pace, who eventually ends up enabling an encounter between the girl and her mother's first husband. Only the mother's *in extremis* arrival at the place of the encounter—Madam Pace's office—avoids the consummation of what, in the play, acquires a clear tone of father–daughter incest.

The accusations and counter-accusations that erupt in cross-fire, the abandonment and the lack of love, the jealousy and the moral battering, the erotic–incestuous underflow and the unbearable burning pain that everyone exhibits, as if it were caused by a red-hot iron, end up transforming the drama into a tragedy.

The younger children of the mother's second marriage die from lack of attention and love; and the characters who survive end up as wandering creatures who will have to carry a very heavy burden of repentance and guilt to the end of their lives. The prostitute daughter runs away, never to reappear, and the father, the mother, and the eldest son become locked in an eternal *huis clos*. The former family is only apparently re-established: its members became damned individuals, with no possible redemption.

The author's refusal in transmitting his own sense of the drama and helping the characters to come off the true "repetition compulsion" that moves them does not allow for "a good dream" to become organized: the whole scene becomes immersed in an inevitable nightmare. The possible analogy would be with a psychoanalyst who refused to intervene and interpret, leaving the patient alone with his internal characters' conflicts, with all the lack of personal resources to face them, which, by definition, brought him to analysis.

Let us try to organize and clarify this whole situation, using a new Fairbairnian diagram:

In Figure 8.3 we can see, on the left-hand side, the maternal and paternal "external objects" presented *as a couple*, which conditions the emergence of an *"oedipal wound"* immediately next to the "primal wound".

In the libidinal area the *need for closeness* becomes more apparent, just as in the anti-libidinal area the *need for detachment* gains definition and modulation.

The virtual space existing between the "acceptant central self" and the "acceptable central object"—a true *"potential space"* in Winnicott's sense, a melting-pot that transmutes lead into gold—allows for the emergence of a creative whirl, which can lead to an *artistic process*, a *literary one* in the case of the *Six Characters*. In this sense, the *Six Characters* can be viewed as partial aspects of Pirandello's *"self"* and *"artistic objects"*: under the strong light of the *"aesthetic organizer"* that he calls his imagination, he tries to put on stage his *"central artistic conflict"*.

Each character, placed in the situation of *protected vulnerability* that the stage allows, claims for himself the role of the *"acceptant central artistic self"*, pushing the other characters into the roles of the *peripheral dissociated aspects of both the "self" and the "object"*, accusing them of impediment to the construction of an *"acceptable central artistic object"*.

Pirandello's *"central artistic conflict"* surely has powerful, obscure, complex roots in the author's *"central psychic conflict"*, but there only an eventual personal psychoanalysis could shed some

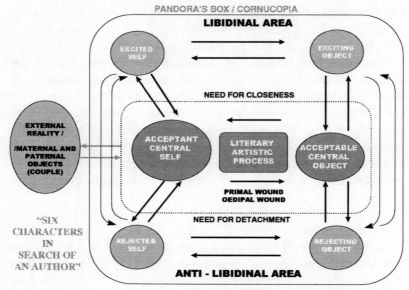

(Inspired by Scharff, 1982, and Scharff & Birtles, 1997.)

Figure 8.3

light. The *"complete artistic object"*, the theatre-play written by Pirandello, acquired an *exemplary autonomous value*, independent from the author's "central psychic conflict".

Its *incandescence* provokes in us a *receptive aesthetic whirl* that is complementary to Pirandello's *creative artistic whirl*: the frightful opening of *Pandora's Box* and our hope of its transformation into *a "Cornucopia"* add a *psychic surplus-value* to the necessary soothing work we keep on doing over our "wounds", especially over our *"primal wound"*.

Perhaps the six sectors that Fairbairn considered as constitutive of our minds—three of them belonging to the area of the "self" and the other three to the area of the "object"—*shape and give shelter to our main internal characters*, with their six fundamental aspects in a precarious dynamic equilibrium, in search for settlements and transformations. And we should not forget that everything that is in the unconscious, everything that is repressed and dissociated, *seeks expression*.

This is why we easily enter into *aesthetic consonance* with Pirandello's "six characters", emotionally watch the unfolding of the dramatic intrigue, and feel transformed at the end of the play.

Fairbairn's diagram would perhaps need to include a *clarification of the role of psychic bisexuality* in the organization of mental life and in the consolidation of the identification processes in order to give full justice to the dramatic richness of Pirandello's characters. However, we can imagine the rejected aspects of bisexuality to be placed in the dissociated, peripheral areas.

VI

With the production of the "artistic object", the writer has stated his aesthetic authority, stopped being at his characters' mercy, re-balanced his internal psychic structure, and softened the pain of his own "primal wound". This relief is only temporary, and very soon he will have to try to create a new "artistic object".

The "artistic object" can also be considered as a *propitiatory gift* primarily *to the "internal objects"*, secondarily to the *"inspiring external objects"*, to the "muses", and only at last to the public in general.

However, the "consumer"—the individual who appraises the "artistic object": in the present example, the reader or the theatre-going spectator—also acquires the possibility of changing the way his own "internal characters" relate to each other by means of a kind of *loan* or *aesthetic proxy* given by the author, through the establishment of an affectionate bond or painful attunement to the "artistic object". The pain of the "primal wound" is softened, and a feeling of authorship of his own destiny emerges: the "central self" stops feeling left at the mercy of the "central object" and acquires autonomy, also in what concerns the dissociated, "peripheral parts".

However, just like what happens with the artist, this *aesthetic surplus-value* acquired by the art-appraiser is temporary and needs successive encounters with new "artistic objects" to rekindle its effects: it is a never-never-ending process.

VII

The elaborate dream can be considered the "artistic object" of all of us. Nevertheless, the "artistic process" happens in daytime—needs a state of wakefulness—while the "dream process" is of nocturnal essence and demands the protection and support of sleep.

The "elaborate dream" gives an "iterative reinforcement of our identity", as Michel Jouvet (1992) has said. In other words, it allows for a creative, repetitive uptake and "work" on our conscious and unconscious psychic processes, linked to a "primal wound". On the *dream's stage* we try to obtain a better understanding and acceptance between the "central self" and the "central object", so that they can get closer to one another and recover, recreate, and modulate the conflictive beauty of the "primal aesthetic object".

Good dreams are those that transmit a *feeling of agency* to the dreamer—they help to close the "wound"—but it is not possible to know either how or when they will return. Repeated encounters with "dream objects" are necessary for a "good encounter" to come along, just as repeated encounters with "artistic objects" are necessary for the emergence of a true *transfiguring whirl*.

A feeling of *authorship in psychic reorganization*, more lasting than the one obtained through the "artistic process" and the "dream process", can only happen through the establishment of a "psychoanalytic process".

The "psychoanalytic process", just like the "artistic process", demands wakefulness. On the *session's stage*, the individual being analysed *attributes roles to his fundamental characters*, under the various shapes and disguises they can assume. He tries to give them life and authenticity, he relates them to each other and to himself, and, with the psychoanalyst's empathic and interpretative support, he becomes capable of understanding his old relationships and of establishing new ones. It is hard work, done session after session, and the changes become possible through the new ways of staging this drama of which the analysand is progressively *capable of assuming the authorship*.

In the "psychoanalytic process", in this neo-way-out of the "fundamental wounds" that was discovered by Freud, the aim is *the emergence and consolidation of a capacity for auto-analysis* that might permanently accompany the analysed.

In support of what has been said, let us look at a possible further development in the Fairbairnian diagram.

We can baptize Figure 8.4 as *"The rediscovered author"*.

The "internal stage" has significantly changed: a *creative space* was built between the "central self" and the "central object", where it became possible to propitiate the emergence of "artistic", "dream", and "psychoanalytic objects". These three types of "objects" have inherently a *transforming and re-equilibrating potential*, but they are all necessary, none of them being entirely capable of replacing or simply doing without the others.

The "central self", the one accepting of the "central object", also becomes *acceptable to the "object"*; on the other hand, the "central object" has become *accepting of its "self"*. The dissociated, peripheral parts of the "self" and of the "object" acquired the characteristics that other the pole opposed to them: the "excited self" becomes *"exciting" to its "object"* and the "rejected self" becomes *capable of rejecting*. The "exciting object" allows being *excited by its "self"* and

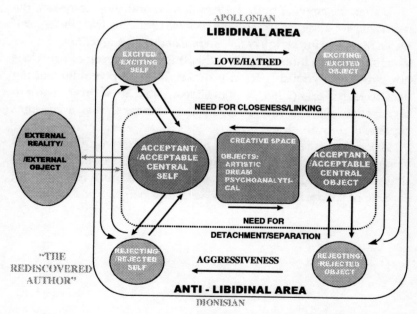

(Inspired by Scharff, 1982, and Scharff & Birtles, 1997.)

Figure 8.4

the "rejecting object" accepts *being rejected*—they all come closer to each other, the passive becoming active and the active allowing itself passivity.

These *Six Characters* have acquired a new mutual capacity for understanding and accepting the others' points of view. A rearrangement of bisexuality becomes possible, the bonds that unite and divide are clarified, love and hatred have an eased circulation, and aggressiveness becomes restricted. The value of each of the characters increases in the eyes of the others, being viewed with respect and admiration. On the other hand, the "external objects" acquire autonomy and gratitude from the *"renewed central self"*.

Jean Genet (1988, p. 18) said that "At the origin of beauty there is solely the singular wound. . . ." I believe that the opposite is closer to the truth: at the origin of the "wound" there is solely the singular beauty of the "primal character of love and hatred", the mother's beauty. And it is this "primal wound", which is impossible to heal, that leads to the never-ending quest for an *everlasting encounter with the mother's beauty*.

Under the aegis of both the Apollonian and the Dionysian, the *creative space* allowed for the *initial fatal beauty* to transform itself into a *transfiguring beauty of the internal and external realities*.

However, we must not forget that the transfiguring beauty does not cure the "wound"—it only makes it more bearable. Getting back to Jean Genet (1988, p. 18): "Giacometti's art seems to want to reveal that secret wound of beings and things, so that it becomes capable of illuminating them."

Art or dream or psychoanalysis reveal the wound; they uncover the wound, so that a new light might spread out. This revelation makes us richer and allows us to become more humane and capable of solidarity. It is already a starting point. . . .

PART IV

THE FUTURE
OF FAIRBAIRN'S CONTRIBUTION

Endopsychic structures, psychic retreats, and "fantasying": the pathological "third area" of the psyche

James S. Grotstein

In this contribution I seek to elaborate both upon the concept of normal and pathological psychic structures and upon their contents. In an earlier work I compared and contrasted Fairbairn's formal concept of endopsychic structures with Klein's less formal conception of internal objects (Grotstein, 1994b). In that same contribution I also hypothesized that a normal version of the internal world existed side-by-side with Fairbairn's endopsychic structures in the same personality, the latter of which inescapably indicate psychopathology. In other words, I proffered the notion that a normal libidinal self related to a good object existed side-by-side with a pathological libidinal ego related to a pathological exciting and rejecting object as well as to an ideal object, the latter three of which comprise a pathological (defensive) consortium. In other words, Fairbairn's central ego and ideal object were always intimately, though disingenuously, entangled with the rejecting and exciting objects and their respective subsidiary egos. What I failed to make clear in that contribution and what I wish now to clarify is the notion that, Fairbairn notwithstanding, Freud's (1900a, 1923b) two topographies (systems *Ucs, Pcs, Cs*, and id, ego, and superego) designate the cartography of the normal personality, whereas endopsychic structures, by contrast, constitute its pathological cartography. Thus, to use Bion's (1957) concept of the existence of a distinction between the "psychotic and non-psychotic personalities", one might say that Freud's two topographies apply to the normal personality and Fairbairn's endopsychic structures apply to the pathological sector of the personality.

Endopsychic structures as the "third area" of the psyche

I am postulating, following Winnicott (1971a), the existence of a normal unconscious internal world (dream world), which corresponds dialectically and complementarily to the external world. Side by side with this binary structure, however, there exists a third area of personality, that which has variously been called "endopsychic structures", "pathological organizations", "psychic retreats", an "internal gang" or "Mafia", or the area of pathological "fantasying".

The structure of the internal world and its relationship to character and psychopathology

Psychoanalytic theorists from Freud onward interpreted the onset of psychopathology from the economic vertex—that is, an excess of oral, anal, or phallic libido, an excess of projective identification, an excess of envy, and so forth. Others would impute an excess of parental impingement, an insufficient affective attunement, and so on. Permanent enclaves of psychopathology were assigned, furthermore, to pathological fixations and/or regressions to pathological fixations that unconsciously commemorated traumatic episodes in the patient's earlier history. The concept of "character", as distinguished from "personality", came to be used for the imputation of permanent on-going psychopathology and for psychoanalytic resistances. Behind this confusion between the psychopathological potency and effectiveness of the excessiveness of the drives versus character lay the issue of drive versus object, whether external or internal. Ultimately, the object-relations schools opted for the importance of character-as-internal-objects that were indistinguishable from the drives, thereby creating the conception of "dynamic structure" (Grotstein, 1995b). In other words, the drives, being unstructured, according to Freud (1923b), could not fit into a concept of a permanent psychic structure from which defences and resistances could predictably issue. Thus, the concept of character, as defined by the nature of objects with which the character was identified, was conceived to account for this series of defensive structures.[1]

Freud's (1937c) concept of the negative therapeutic reaction helped inaugurate our interest in character resistances against progress in psychoanalysis. The study of character resistances inescapably led to a need to re-examine our concepts of psychic structure—or, to put it another way, to re-examine the endoskeleton of character itself and its aberrations—as well as its more nearly permanent components and their relationships. Freud made two major attempts to deal with this internal anatomy. The first was the topographic model, in which he conceived of systems unconscious, preconscious, and conscious (Freud, 1900a). The second was his structural model, in which he elaborated the notions of the id, the ego, and the superego (Freud, 1923b). All the while, however, Freud had been emphasizing instinctual drives and their vicissitudes, yet he had hinted that the relationship of the id to the ego constituted an object relationship (Freud, 1923b), and in his final model he explicated the notion of an object relationship between the ego and the superego.

In the meanwhile, however, when Freud (1917e [1915]) published "Mourning and Melancholia", the foundations for an object-relations theory of psychic structure were firmly established. In this work, by distinguishing between the differing fates of mourning in the normal person as opposed to melancholia (the failure of mourning) in the narcissistically arrested character, he posited the first concept of pathological psychic structure: the narcissistic character,

---

[1] It is important to note in this regard that Klein and her followers link drive pathology as being embedded (because of projective identification) in archaic superegos.

unable to accept the loss of the object and thus to mourn it, creates an unconscious phantasy instead in which the object is not lost. It becomes internalized as two different entities within the subject: (1) as an internal object "in a gradient in the ego", which becomes identified with the ego ideal, and (2) as an internal object identified with the ego proper. Thereupon, the former behaves as a coalition and exerts a maximum of sadism against the latter couple, which must transitivistically and helplessly (masochistically) bear the inexorable torment—all in order for the subject to confabulate that the object is not truly lost.

The roots of psychic structure in Freud's "Mourning and Melancholia"

In "Mourning and Melancholia", Freud (1917e [1915]) emphasizes the failure of the narcissistically fixated subject to mourn the loss of its object. Because of its hatred of the object for the latter's putative desire, will, or intention to depart, the object becomes installed within the subject's ego and superego (originally ego ideal), and a maximum of sadism then becomes directed from the ego ideal-plus-internalized-object unit towards the ego-plus-internalized-object unit. Parenthetically, we must assume that the internalized object had already become subject to splitting—a concept that Freud had not addressed in his contribution.

But here we can see two sides to melancholia: one in which the subject is motivated out of narcissistic concern for its own welfare in regard to an intolerable or disappointing object and thus internalizes it in order to control it and transform[2] it internally (Freud's

---

[2] It is well known since Freud that in melancholia hostility that seems to be self-directed is really meant for the object with whom one has become identified. Fairbairn and Klein agree on this point. "What I believe they have all overlooked is that one of the probable motives for the internalization of the disappointing or departing object is magically or omnipotently to repair and restore it—after the subject has internally "taught it a lesson" by its morally cleansing sadism.

view), and another in which the subject, motivated out of love and an altruistic need to protect the object—either from the subject's own unconscious attacks (Klein) or from the subject's concern in regard to the object's realistic failures—will selectively absorb the object's failures by identifying with them as if they were the subject's failures, thereby "laundering" or "exorcizing" the object so that the subject can justify depending on it (Fairbairn's view). This "laundering" of the object amounts to a form of "depressive reparations", which is a counterpart to manic reparations.

In the first case narcissistic fears for the welfare of the self are involved, and the degree of sadism that is directed by the ego ideal-plus-object in a gradient in the ego towards the ego-plus-object in the ego constitutes an affective parity with the subject's anxiety about the prospect for the self losing the object. Moreover—and this point was never expressed by either Freud, Klein, or Fairbairn—the putative purpose behind the sadism is probably a desire to "reform" the object once it is internalized: that is, "teach it a lesson" by "blaming away" its endangering blemishes so that it can be restored to proper functioning. In other words, the purpose of primitive anger is to register a protest to an object, and the purpose of sadism is to control the object to one's will, where sometimes that will, albeit omnipotently fanciful, may often be to restore the object to duty as a container of "O".[3]

In the second case the subject is sensitive to the defective object's capacity as container (which is equated with object loss) and thus "exorcizes" or "launders" the putative or actual defects of the object by absorption and introjective identification in order to mythify the object and transform its image into one that is once again felt to be a good container for "O". In either case, a "true-self"/"false-self" schizoid dichotomy transpires. Consequently, "O" has at least two dimensions in the infant–mother relationship.

---

[3] I shall explicate Bion's (1965, 1970, 1992) conception of "O" as I proceed, but in the meanwhile I can hint at its ineffable nature with the following metaphor: imagine a toy machine at a children's arcade in which the subject steers the wheel of a make-believe, automobile while looking into its interior and experiencing a road relentlessly and unpredictably moving towards him.

One dimension is the mother's capacity to bear "O", as beta ele-ments[4] that the infant cannot tolerate and which it expels via pro-jective trans-identification into mother-as-container. The other is mother's ability to bear her own beta-element experiences in her own separate life. Here is where father-as-container assumes im-portance as well as container for the infant–mother couple.

The issue of the anatomy of psychic structure and its role in character resistances

Whereas virtually the whole opus of Klein's theorizing falls within the confines of this work of Freud's and whereas she elevated internal object-relations theory to new and more elaborate per-spectives, she did not supply an atlas of the psyche to account for the interrelationships between egos and internal objects in the in-ternal world. What was significantly new in her perspective of the internal world in terms of resistances, however, was her concep-tion that defence mechanisms can be understood as unconscious phantasies operating against other unconscious phantasies in which aspects of self and of objects constitute the repressed as well as the repressing—in contrast to Freud, who only spoke of "mecha-nisms" in an abstract and detached way. However, she did postu-late that the object of the toddler's initial curiosity and sadism was mother's internal anatomy (Klein, 1928). In another contribution I extended Klein's thesis to account for the ancient Greek myth of the labyrinth and the Minotaur, a constellation that is eminently suited to represent the anatomy of the internal world and es-pecially a "labyrinthine *cul de sac*" of pathological resistance (Grotstein, 1997d, 2000).

---

[4] Beta elements are Bion's (1962, 1963) terms for unmentalized or yet-to-be-mentalized confrontations with the reality of emotional experience, which he calls "O". Alpha function normally renders them into alpha elements suitable for mental processing. If they are not "alpha-bet-ized", they become the basic ingredients of psychopathology.

Background

Chronic resistance structures are implicit in Tausk's (1919) "anatomy of the 'influencing machine'", portrayed as the psychotic extreme of the transitivistic relationship between a sadistic, controlling superego and a masochistic, submissive ego; Reich's (1928, 1949) "character armour;" Klein's (1928) concept of the archaic Oedipus complex (adumbrated above), with particular emphasis on the internal "unborn infants" and paternal penis; Bion's (1962, 1963) concepts of –K (false knowledge or lies), "reversible perspectives", "alpha function in reverse", and the dissociation between the psychotic and non-psychotic personalities; Tustin's (1981) "confusional" and "encapsulated" defences used by autistic children to ward off the experience of separation;[5] Bick's (1968, 1986) "second skin", Rosenfeld's (1987) "malignant narcissism", Meltzer's (1973) "internal gang" or "Mafia", Winnicott's (1960, 1971a) concept of the "true and false selves" and of "fantasying", Steiner's (1993) "psychic retreats" or "pathological organizations", and Grotstein's (1997d, 2000) concepts of the "labyrinth", "orphans of the Real", and "Faustian bargain"—all placed together with Fairbairn's (1944) concept of endopsychic structure.

Fairbairn (1944), however, seems to have been the only one to have taken on the formal task of establishing the structure, function, and interrelationships of the personality so as to accommodate the interactions of internalized objects and selves in an organized anatomical structure or lexicon (Grotstein, 1993, 1994a, 1994b, 1998). Lamentably, his work seems not to have made a significant impact on Klein[6] and her followers. Steiner (1993) in particular, whose work on "pathological organizations" or "psy-

---

[5] Perhaps today we could say that the defensive phenomenon of encapsulation constitutes the phantasied presence of an object as the encapsulator of the self as a model for a psychic retreat.

[6] Klein (1946), though not fully comprehending the importance of Fairbairn's contributions, did acknowledge the importance of his ideas about schizoid phenomena and appended "schizoid" to her already established "paranoid position", though it must be pointed out that her concept of "schizoid" lacks the rich ontological meaningfulness that inheres in Fairbairn's use of the term.

chic retreats" veritably cries out for a "road map", as it were, of the internal object world, would do well, in my opinion, to utilize the one that Fairbairn had already established. Yet, when this possibility is contemplated, one begins to realize that Fairbairn's endopsychic structure *is* a psychic retreat or a pathological organization. One can readily observe, moreover, that, in Fairbairn's conception of the anatomy of the self's schizoid withdrawal from the object, we have the graphic portraiture of the structure of what Winnicott (1960) was later to call the "true- and false-self" dichotomy, which clearly Fairbairn adumbrated. Thus, whereas Freud (1917e [1915]) had established the anatomy of melancholy emphasizing guilt and repression, Fairbairn (1944), using Freud's format, transformed it into the anatomy of disillusion, which emphasized disappointment, schizoid withdrawal, splitting, and dissociation.

Winnicott essayed into psychic anatomy on three occasions: the first was in his distinction, as noted above, between the "true and false selves" (Winnicott, 1960); the second was his distinction between the normal antecedents of the former as the "being" and "doing" infants (1971b, p. 130); and the third was in his concept of the distinction between dreaming and reality on the one hand and "fantasying" on the other (1971a). Steiner (1979, 1987, 1990a, 1990b), in his study of borderline and psychotic patients, first conceived of a "borderline position" that occurs between the paranoid-schizoid and depressive positions to account for the genesis of borderline psychopathology. Later, following in the footsteps of Rosenfeld (1971, 1987) and Meltzer (1973), he conceived of "pathological organizations" or "psychic retreats" (Steiner, 1992, 1993). This latter idea all too closely resembles Fairbairn's concept of endopsychic structure and Winnicott's concept of "fantasying".

In this chapter, consequently, I seek to establish bridges between Fairbairn's and Steiner's (as well as Klein's) pictures of the internal world, also adding the relevant works of Bion (1962, 1963, 1965, 1970, 1992) on "lying", "–K", and transformations in "O", and of Winnicott (1971a) on "fantasying". This last idea, "fantasying",[7]

---

[7] "Fantasying" is used by Winnicott in an idiosyncratic way and therefore has a special meaning. It is not to be confused with "*ph*antasy", which, unlike fantasy, is entirely unconscious (Isaacs, 1948).

resembles but is not congruent with Freud's (1900a) concept of "day-dreaming". The difference between them is, at one extreme, important insofar as Freud's concept is one in which the day-dream is a conscious continuation or revision of the night-time dream, whereas Winnicott differentiates "fantasying" from "dreaming" and "reality" insofar as it is suggestive of the creation of an alliterative or pathological internal world—what I term a "third area of the psyche". I introduce "fantasying" because I believe that it constitutes the introductory chapter in the formation of psychic retreats and/or endopsychic structures. Furthermore, it constitutes a pathological alliterative to Winnicott's (1951)—and Fairbairn's alternative (1941) concept of transitional phenomena. "Fantasying" represents a disjunction from a relationship with an external object, whereas transitional phenomena seek to maintain the ties to the object.

In addition, I also suggest yet another addendum to our revised conceptualization of the internal world: that of Klein's (1928) idea about the infant's unconscious phantasies about the mother's internal anatomy, particularly that she is felt to contain "internal (unborn) babies", father's penis, and idealized as well as dangerous faeces. Elsewhere, I have elaborated this infantile phantasmal notion of mother's internal anatomy as suggestive of the ancient Greek myth about the Labyrinth and the Minotaur (Grotstein, 1997d, 2000). This unconscious phantasy about the insides of mother's body and its contents may conceivably be the source of the phantasies about a "gang" or the "Mafia"—tightly knit, secretly privileged "families" that wield omnipotent power. In other words, the "internal paternal penis" and the "unborn children" become transformed from an internal "noble" or "divine family" into a nefarious one by the subject's hostile and sadistic projective identifications.

Let me summarize: I believe that Fairbairn's endopsychic structure can include Steiner's psychic retreat within its embrace as well as offering a complementarity in conceptualizing the origins of pathological object relatedness, Fairbairn from traumatizing external objects and Steiner from the death instinct. Winnicott's "fantasying" offers yet another dimension: that of the idea of a conscious or preconscious "choice" on the part of the subject to enter into a false reality for protection. Bion (1965) refers to this phenomenon as "–K"—false knowledge and/or "alpha function in reverse (Bion, 1963). Klein's (1928) conceptualization about the infant's phantasies about mother's internal contents is yet another. However, we can now better understand that the libidinal ego's subservience to the split-off bad objects (exciting and rejecting) is due to its need to keep the ideal object ideal at all costs in order to maintain the illusion that the latter can be capable of containing "O" by repressively relegating it to the bad objects and bad egos respectively.

Fairbairn's contributions

Fairbairn, parenthetically, while formulating both a schizoid and a depressive position, may have unwittingly all but formulated a *transitional position*[8] that may well have prefigured Steiner's "borderline position between the two. Fairbairn's concept of endo-psychic structures is based upon the infant's capacity from the beginning to be realistic about its objects and about reality itself. Whereas the Kleinian infant seeks to achieve the "purified pleasure ego" by evacuating its unpleasant feelings into an object (thereby transforming that object to correspond to the evacuated feelings), the Fairbairnian infant realistically senses the discrepancy between his needs and the object who is supposed to address them. Because of its state of absolute biological and psychological dependency on the object, the infant, according to Fairbairn, has no option but to set things right by selectively absorbing and (introjectively) identi-fying with those traits in the parent that are felt to be inimical to its survival—thereby *becoming* that aspect of the parent. Put another way, those aspects of the parent that are unacceptable—and there-fore dangerous—must be *rejected*. The rejected object becomes in-ternalized within the infant as an *unacceptable object*, but although the object is rejected, it is also regarded as still needed; thus, it

---

[8] See Brown (1987) for his explication of a transitional position.

enters into a split or dissociation between a *rejecting object*[9] and an *exciting object*.

There are many consequences to this transformation. One is that the original innocent self has had to compromise itself by dividing itself between a "true self" and a "false self", the latter having to do with the disingenuous identification with the badness of the object—an act that amounts to a psychic surrender of one's innocence. Put another way, when the bad object is internalized as two seemingly different entities—but secretly are united as one—the very act of identification presupposes that autochthonous (native) aspects of the original self (ego) that would normally correspond to these objects—i.e. libidinal ego and assertive ego—are now pulled, as it were, away from their erstwhile healthy destinies to enter into "prostitutive" or corrupt collaboration with the enemy object(s) as antilibidinal ego or "internal saboteur"—with the rejecting object—and libidinal ego with the exciting object. This compromise on the part of the subsidiary egos—which have now lost their normal contact with the remaining central ego and its relationship with its ideal object—prefigured Winnicott's (1960) idea of the "true" and "false selves". It also amounts to a "Faustian bargain" or a pact with the devil, one in which one sacrifices one's innocence in order to survive, thereby really becoming an "orphan of the Real" (Grotstein, 1995a, 1995b, 2000).

Fairbairn's endopsychic model is driven by the primacy of an unbearable reality, whereas Steiner's, while acknowledging trauma and neglect, is based upon the primacy of the operation of the death instinct over the life instinct. Each system is persecutory, persuasive, hypnotic, compelling, compromising, and omnipotent. Each seems to threaten the self for attempts to escape from identification with them. Whereas Steiner's psychic retreats involves numerous subsidiary internal objects tightly grouped together in inexplicable configurations, Fairbairn's system of endopsychic structures is the first and perhaps only mapping of the internal

---

[9] The initially reject*ed* object becomes internalized as a reject*ing* object because of the subject's (infant's) projective identification of rejection into the object before internalization.

world that is characterized by anatomical precision and hierarchical lines of authority. For instance, the central ego, in alliance with its ideal object, represses both the antilibidinal ego and its rejecting object and the libidinal ego and its exciting object, the latter two of which are, in turn, indirectly repressed by the antilibidinal ego and rejecting object. Fairbairn states that the good object (ideal object) does not have to be internalized, a view with which I agree. *One normally internalizes the legacy of the experience one has had with a departed object* (my view). Fairbairn goes on to say, however, that the good object does become internalized as a defence against the absolute badness of the original internalized object, thereby transforming its image into a conditionally bad object. It is this last point that I have in mind when I suggest the existence of unconscious collusion between the central ego and its ideal object on one hand and all the other repressed objects and their subsidiary selves.

Winnicott's concept of "fantasying"

In his paper "Dreaming, Fantasying, and Living", Winnicott (1971a) states:

> Dream fits into object-relating in the real world, and living in the real world fits into the dream-world in ways that are quite familiar, especially to psycho-analysts. By contrast, however, fantasying remains an isolated phenomenon, absorbing energy but not contributing either to dreaming or to living. To some extent fantasying has remained static over the whole of this patient's life, that is to say, dating from very early years, the pattern being established by the time that she was two or three. It was in evidence at an even earlier date, and it probably started with a "cure" of thumb-sucking.
>
> Another distinguishing feature between these two sets of phenomena is this, that whereas a great deal of dream and of feelings belonging to life are liable to be under repression, this is a different kind of thing from the inaccessibility of the fantasying. Inaccessibility of fantasying is associated with dissociation rather than with repression. Gradually, as this patient begins to become a whole person and begins to lose her rigidly

organized dissociations, so she becomes aware of the vital importance that fantasying has always had for her. At the same time the fantasying is changing into imagination related to dream and reality. [pp. 26–27]

. . . It will be observed that creative playing is allied to dreaming and to living but essentially does *not* belong to fantasying. . . . For me the work of this session had produced an important result. It had taught me that fantasying interferes with action and with life in the real or external world, but much more so it interferes with dream, and with personal or inner psychic reality, the living core of the individual personality. [p. 31]

I included Winnicott's contribution because I believe that it belongs at the more conscious–preconscious range of the overall phenomenon of self-soothing self-deception. It strongly suggests an arrest at the transitional stage where self-soothing fantasies depart from normal illusion and imagination. How this happens, Winnicott leaves unclear. In this category we recognize a vast array of self-soothing phantasmagoria, one emblematic example of which is the compulsive day-dreaming by the protagonist in James Thurber's (1932) *The Secret Life of Walter Mitty*.

Psychic retreat

In introducing his work, *Psychic Retreats*, Steiner states:

A psychic retreat provides the patient with an area of relative peace and protection from strain when meaningful contact with the analyst is experienced as threatening. It is not difficult to understand the need for transient withdrawal of this kind, but serious technical problems arise in patients who turn to a psychic retreat, habitually, excessively, and indiscriminately. In some analyses, particularly with borderline and psychotic patients, a more or less permanent residence in the retreat may be taken up and it is then that obstacles to development and growth arise. [Steiner, 1993, p. 1]

Steiner cites the example of schizoid patients who are aloof, feel superior, and have an attitude of mocking dismissal. They enter into false contacts with their analyst. Their unconscious motivation is to avoid intolerable anxiety.

Parenthetically, the need for the infant *cum* patient to avoid intolerable anxiety—and what they do in phantasy to their objects: in reality as a consequence—seem to unite Steiner and Fairbairn, to say nothing of Winnicott. The term "false self" seems to unite the efforts of all three contributors, but, to my knowledge, Fairbairn (1941, 1943) prefigured that concept as well as the notion of transitionality, from which the false-self dissociation pathologically emerges. I discuss these connections further on.

Steiner then states:

> "[P]athological organizations of the personality" . . . denote a family of defensive systems which are characterized by extremely unyielding defences and which function to help the patient avoid anxiety by avoiding contact with other people and with reality. The analyst observes psychic retreats as states of mind in which the patient is stuck, cut off, and out of reach, and he may infer that these states arise from a powerful system of defences. The patient's view of the retreat is reflected in the description which he gives and also in unconscious phantasy as it is revealed in dreams, memories, and reports from everyday life. . . . Typically it appears as a house, a cave, a fortress, a desert island, or a similar location which is seen as an area of relative safety. Alternatively, it can take an interpersonal form, usually as an organization of objects or part-objects which offers to provide security. It may be represented as a business organization, as a boarding school, as a religious sect, as a totalitarian government or a Mafia-like gang. . . . [I]t is useful to think of it as a grouping of object relations, defences, and phantasies, which makes up a borderline position similar to but distinct from the paranoid-schizoid and depressive positions described by Melanie Klein (1952). [Steiner, 1993, p. 2]

The cost to the patient of using the psychic retreat is isolation, stagnation, and withdrawal. The relationship to the objects of the pathological retreat may be persecutory or idealized. "Whether idealized or persecutory, it is clung to as preferable to even worse states which the patient is convinced are the only alternatives" (Steiner, 1993, p. 2). Furthermore, the clinging to these retreats is an underlying factor in the negative therapeutic reaction, and, as a corollary, an analysis itself may be turned into a psychic retreat. In short, the patient who uses the psychic retreat becomes pathologically dependent on or addicted to the retreat. One of the consequences is that phantasy and omnipotence remain unchecked. These patients attempt to bewitch the analyst to assist them in organizing a retreat. Steiner asserts that, at bottom, the psychic retreat owes its power to the operation of the death instinct within the patient.

Steiner believes that environmental factors can play a significant role in the formation of retreats: "Traumatic experiences with violence or neglect in the environment lead to the internalization of violent disturbed objects which at the same time serve as suitable receptacles for the projection of the individuals' own destructiveness" (Steiner, 1993, p. 4). He then goes on to say: "In my view defensive organizations serve to bind, to neutralize, and to control primitive destructiveness whatever its source, and are a universal feature of the defensive make-up of all individuals . . . In normal individuals they are brought into play when anxiety exceeds tolerable limits and are relinquished once more when the crisis is over" (pp. 4–5). He goes on: "Trauma and deprivation in the patient's history have a profound effect on the creation of pathological organizations of the personality" (p. 8).

Steiner cites Bion's (1957) distinction between the neurotic and psychotic aspects of the personality as being applicable to psychic retreats.

With regard to the organizing or constellating importance of the death instinct in relation to the formation of psychic retreats, Steiner states:

> It was . . . Rosenfeld (1971) in his paper on destructive narcissism who gave the definitive description of this type of narcissistic object relationship based on idealization of destructive parts of the self. This important paper focuses on the problem of dealing with internal and external sources of destructiveness, which Rosenfeld relates to the activity of the death instinct. This theme goes back to Freud's early ideas on the death instinct which were elaborated by Melanie Klein. Although phrased in the now unfashionable language of instinct theory, the basic problem remains, central to our understanding of the deepest roots of severe psychopathology. It postulates the

universal emergence of internal sources of destructiveness manifested as primitive envy and threatening to destroy the individual from within. The part of the ego containing such impulses and phantasies is split off and evacuated by projective identification and in this way attributed to others. [Steiner, 1993, p. 45]

Finally, Steiner states:

In most retreats a special relationship with reality is established in which reality is neither fully accepted nor completely disavowed. I believe that this constitutes a third type of relation to reality ... and which contributes to the fixed character of the retreat. It is related to mechanisms similar to those which Freud (1927e) described in the case of fetishism and which play an important part in perversion. [p. 90]

Let me summarize Steiner's points: (1) psychic retreats represent schizoid factors in the personality resulting in false contacts with objects; (2) they are formed to avoid intolerable anxiety; (3) they constitute a family of defensive organizations and relationships between internal objects; (4) they are often portrayed as fortresses, deserts, and other images; (5) relief is achieved at the cost of isolation, stagnation, and withdrawal; (6) it becomes associated with the negative therapeutic reaction; (7) analysis itself can be turned into a retreat; (8) the causative forces behind it are environmental traumata and the activation of the death instinct; (9) one can analogize psychic retreats with Bion's concept of the distinction between the psychotic and non-psychotic parts of the personality; (10) the retreat is a developmental position (the borderline position) in its own right, one that lurks on the border between the paranoid-schizoid and depressive positions; (11) it constitutes a misrepresentation of reality akin to fetishes and perversions.

Ultimately, in Steiner's vision, the members of the organization are tightly bound together and constitute personifications of the patient's death instinct, the purpose of which is to fight the life instinct and the patient's seeking of "reality" and healthy adjustments to his real objects. In other words, the death instinct is morally perverse and anti-life from the beginning. From this point of view, Kleinian analysis resembles, as I have suggested, "pilgrim's progress" through "the forests of error".

Notes on the Kleinian basis for Steiner's thinking

From Klein's point of view unconscious phantasy is paramount, and external reality is secondary—despite the paradox that the goal of Kleinian analysis is to help the patient to become more "realistic"—that is, to recognize, accept, and adapt to external reality. Klein has frequently been accused of ignoring external reality. That is an untrue accusation, and Steiner's work amply confirms this. Her way of acknowledging it is in understanding how external reality preferentially selects the infant's corresponding, specific, unconscious phantasies as reactive counterparts. Bion (1962, 1963, 1965, 1970) was to establish a psychoanalytic theory of epistemology by amplifying these considerations. Put another way, while Klein thought she was following Freud in his concept of pure psychic determinism, she was really, according to Bion, following in the footsteps of Plato and Kant, especially in terms of inherent preconceptions and *a priori* considerations (which she overtly disavowed in conversations with Bion), which "format"—that is, anticipate—the stimuli of reality. In another contribution, I unite Klein's and Bion's endeavours with those of Winnicott with the idea of *"autochthony"*, the imaginatively self-creative act whereby the self, in the first instance creates itself and its world of objects (paranoid-schizoid position) before it becomes aware of its creation by parental intercourse (depressive position) (Grotstein, 1997b, 2000).

Hysteria versus melancholia

Fairbairn (1940, 1941, 1943, 1946, 1951) valorizes pre-moral splitting of the ego, as in hysteria, over moral issues of guilt, as in melancholia, as being of critical importance in the formation of the personality. Put another way, schizoid splitting is more important than guilt. Following from this hypothesis, schizoid splitting results from a default occasioned by failures of the *object*, whereas guilt issues from putative failures of the subject. Fairbairn leaned on Abraham (1924) for the concept of a "pre-moral stage", which he uses to support his notion of the prime organizing importance of splitting of the ego, yet he seems inconsistent when he suggests that the subject who has become schizoid does so because he had come to "believe that his love was bad". This clearly is a moral consideration, one that I have elsewhere described under the term "autochthony"—the phantasy that the subject has created himself and the object and is therefore responsible for all that happens to each (Grotstein, 1997b, 2000).

The psyche as whole and in parts: the fiction of splitting

To the above I should like to add yet another idea, that of *holography*. When we think of Freud's (1923b) psychic apparatus, we think of psychic determinism (choice, will, agency, intentionality) as originating in the id and progressing as a drive to the ego, which is being monitored all the while by the superego. What if we instead thought holographically—that is, that the psychic apparatus–self was paradoxically both indivisible as well as divisible at the same time (Bohm, 1980; Matte Blanco, 1975, 1988)? Thus, intentionality or agency can issue from any aspect of the psychic apparatus (id, ego, or superego) or from a supra-ordinate self acting holistically.[10] Winnicott's concept of "fantasying" seems to suggest this last alternative and consequently allows us to consider yet another alternative: namely, that the conscious–preconscious ego can initiate "fantasying" in order to escape reality, a phenomenon to which Bion (1962, 1963) refers as "–K" (negative knowledge) or at other times as "alpha function in reverse", which in either case constitutes an attack against the realization of truth on the part of the subject, presumably the conscious part. One of the most redoubtable characteristics of psychic retreats and/or endopsychic structures is the promulgation of –K or "anti-truth" in order to arrest progress, which is synonymous with change.

Put another way, the very existence of internalized objects and split-off egos or selves in the configuration of endopsychic structures or a psychic retreat (pathological organization) bears testi-

---

[10] By "supraordinate self" I mean to embrace the entirety of the first topography (Systems Ucs, Pcs, and Cs) and the psychic apparatus (id, ego, and superego) within the embrace of a single entity.

mony to the subject's fear of Absolute Truth or Ultimate Reality—
Bion's (1965, 1970) "O"—as suggested earlier, and can be thought
of as *default defective containers of "O"*. This implies, in line with
Fairbairn's and Winnicott's general theses, but not with Steiner's,
that all psychopathology can be thought of as unmediated "O",
either in the subject (infant, analysand) or in the mother (father
and/or analyst). Internal objects, therefore—particularly those en-
cased in endopsychic structures and/or pathological structures or
psychic retreats—constitute "renegade subjective objects" awaiting
repatriation by ultimate competent containment (Grotstein, 2000).

I also have in mind the coexistence of what Fairbairn (1940,
1941) termed the "original ego" and "original object" (before splitting) persisting (my idea, not Fairbairn's) alongside the six split-
off and split-up endopsychic structures: for example, a normal libidinal, *un*-split-off aspect of the original ego exists alongside the
already spit-off pathological libidinal ego, as I have already suggested earlier in this chapter. In other words, we must remember
that all six endopsychic structures are pathological, even the central ego and the ideal object. We must recall that they also were
internalized in order to mediate the unconditional badness of the
rejecting object. Furthermore, the very existence of the central ego
and ideal object is compromised by their de facto collusion with
their repressed "colleagues" whom they affect to disdain, disavow,
and repress (Grotstein, 1994a, 1994b).

Furthermore, we must not lose sight of the overarching fact that
splitting is a fiction of the mind. It does not really exist. It is really
only a phantasy or myth, which we arbitrarily superimpose on our
view of ourselves when we cannot reconcile with reality ("O").
We must consequently reserve room for the existence of the intact
subject who, unlike its twin, does not enter into the myth of splitting—and of projective identification, for that matter. That is why
I began this chapter with a modification of Fairbairn's single-
minded concept of endopsychic structure. Endopsychic structure is
the fictitious veil we superimpose upon our normal personality
structure in order to adapt to what we cannot otherwise adjust. The
normal personality structure perseveres as a viable hostage within
that fiction.

Overall, I am positing clinical entities in which the patient experiences a complex relationship, on the one hand between his own

ego and the legitimate objects positively associated with its welfare and, on the other hand, with other aspects of his ego, which are associated with chronic resistance structures that are seemingly intimidating, enthralling, compelling, exciting, tantalizing, and nefarious, damaging, sabotaging in turn. One of the main characteristics of these patients is the development of a dissociation in the ego so that they experience themselves to be a divided self characterized by a "true-self"–"false-self" schizoid dichotomy, a split in the ego that was adumbrated by Freud (1940e [1938]).

Internal objects as representations of failed containment: unmentalized "O" as the hidden order of psychopathology

My belief, following intimations from Bion (1965, 1970, 1992) is that, when an object becomes bad, it does so in a two-tiered way: (1) when the caretaking object fails to contain (neutralize) the infant's primal proto-affective experiences of "O" (Absolute Truth, Ultimate Reality, the thing-in-itself, "beta elements", "*Ananke*" [Necessity], "brute reality", life as it is, infinity, total symmetry and asymmetry, chaos, complexity, raw and unprocessed events awaiting the infant to experience them), the infant then introjects the failing object along with a heightenedly dreaded cargo of unneutralized "O", thereby creating internalized objects with "radioactive" "O"; (2) this dreaded and dreadful feedback loop is made worse by the infant's deeper realization that the caretaker not only cannot contain their (the infant's) "O"; the object also cannot bear their own personal experience of "O" and is therefore incapable as a parental caretaker, an ontological revelation of such magnitude that the infant must thereupon undergo an "infantile catastrophe" or undertake a factitious "repair" of its image of the caretaker by idealization but at its own expense—that is, giving up its own good qualities to the object and introjectively identifying with the selectively deficient aspects of the latter.

Fairbairn and Klein, from differing standpoints, have helped us understand this "exchange transfusion" or psychological "dialysis" very well. What I am adding is that the object that becomes internalized is not only always pathological, as Fairbairn avers, but also that its pathology consists in its failure to deneutralize (contain "O"). As a result, each internalized object represents (1) objects associated with uncontained "O"; (2) worthless objects that failed to contain the their own "O" as well as that of the infant; and (3) "O" itself as an unneutralized (unmentalized, unreflected-upon) thing-in-itself. A field theory naturally emerges from these hypotheses: *All psychopathology can be reduced to the subject's failure to have his proto-experience of "O" adequately contained by objects who themselves cannot contain either his or their own "O"*. I believe that this principle constitutes the hidden order of normal as well as pathological development and overarches both the infantile neurosis and infantile trauma.

The ego as "double agent"
between split-off selves and objects

A particular aspect of these chronic resistance structures is the phenomenon of the "double agent", in which the patient fearfully and sometimes collusively and disingenuously maintains an alliance both with the analyst and with the pathological internal objects. I am referring to: (1) what Fairbairn considered to be the divided loyalty of the self to the internalized objects of his repressed endopsychic structures on the one hand and his external objects on the other—that is, the covert as well as overt relationship between the central ego and its ideal object on the one hand with the other members of the endopsychic structure; and (2) what Winnicott (1960) originally referred to as the "true-self"–"false-self" dichotomy and later his work on "fantasying"; and Steiner's concept of psychic retreats or pathological organizations. In each case what seems to be operating is a state of conscious, preconscious, and/or unconscious collusion by the self with internalized objects whose seeming agenda is to keep the patient imprisoned, as it were, for the promise of protection and safety. Ultimately, this hierarchic relationship between the pathological organization and the subject begins to resemble the criminal "protection racket" made famous by the Mafia in which they "protect" their clients from the Mafia itself, all the while incriminating innocent scape-goats as the cause of their client's insecurities.

This is one of the reasons why agoraphobic anxiety seems to occur in patients suffering from imprisonment in psychic retreats or endopsychic structures. I have found a consistent tendency in these patients for them to experience the following unconscious phantasy: when the analysand begins to make progress in the analysis, fears will begin to emerge, frequently heralded by dreams in which the "Mafia objects" will project their very own bad charac-teristics onto the analyst and/or the good objects in the analysand's life, the end result of which is that the analysand seeks to remain in their persecutory but familiar retreat rather than risk danger from the external objects into which danger has been falsely attributed. Further on I demonstrate this phenomenon in a case example.

Fairbairn's (1940) concept of the schizoid personality and its metapsychological ramifications were a significant contribution in alerting us to the organizing and constellating importance of split-ting of the personality as a factor that he believed took precedence over the "moral factor"—that is, the issue of guilt being the organ-izer of the psyche, as held by Freud and Klein. Klein was later to adopt the schizoid emphasis for her own work, but the importance of the primacy of the division or dissociation of a unitary ego and its ramifications has never been fully appreciated. It must be re-membered that Fairbairn followed Abraham's (1924) conception that a "pre-moral stage" existed concurrently with the earlier oral phase, to be succeeded by "moral stage" coeval with the succeed-ing (biting) phase. It is as if for Abraham and Fairbairn the infant is helpless, transitivistic, and not responsible for itself and for its feelings prior to the second oral phase, in contrast to Klein, who believed that the infant experienced destructive and sadistic phan-tasies from birth. Consequently, Fairbairn envisions an innocent infant earlier on, one who is either the beneficiary or the victim of his/her caretakers.[11] In the second oral phase, however, Fairbairn

---

[11] Yet it would seem that this view of Fairbairn—one that seemingly ex-cuses the inchoate infant of phantasied damage toward mother—is incompat-ible with his statement that, in the schizoid position, the infant autochthonously believes that his/her *love* (rather than his/her *hate*) had been bad. I believe that Fairbairn never made up his mind about this dilemma.

allows for the infant's moral feelings of guilt for the phantasy of having bitten the breast.

Fairbairn was able to tap into what amounts to the feeling of shame in schizoids about being divided in the first place and in containing "bad" or defective internal objects. He was in effect elaborating the nature of a "true-self"/"false-self" dichotomy, which Winnicott (1960), without referencing him, went on later to formulate. Fairbairn (1941) also introduced the concept of "transitionalization", which Winnicott (1951) also "borrowed" from Fairbairn and was later to turn into the transitional object, transitional phenomena, and transitional (intermediate) space. Fairbairn's version of it was as a position that occurred between infantile dependency and mature dependency.[12] I mention these factors in order to help establish my theme: what Steiner (1993) calls the pathological dependency of "psychic retreats" or "pathological organizations" and what Winnicott (1960) calls the "true- and false-self dichotomy" and what he later refers to as "fantasying" all derive from object-related failures of transitionalization from immature dependency to mature dependency (Fairbairn, 1941). Furthermore, transitionalization failed not only because of external object failures as perceived by the infant (Fairbairn's and Winnicott's views) but also because of an addictive propensity by the infant to employ the death instinct to cut off his genuine contact with objects because they remind him only of pain and disappointment (Steiner's view).

While agreeing with Fairbairn and Winnicott, I also agree with Steiner. First, perhaps we can understand the death instinct as an adaptive force that becomes maladaptive only because of "precocious closure" or dissociation from the rest of the personality (Grotstein, 1977a, 1977b).[13] Put another way, to support Steiner's— and Klein's—point of view, the tenacity of the hold on the patient by the psychic retreats is due not only to the degree of frustrated

---

[12] John Padel related to me that, in a private conversation with Winnicott, the latter acknowledged Fairbairn's priority with regard to transitional phenomena and the "true-self/false-self" dichotomy.

[13] Many years ago I read a newspaper article about a Japanese soldier who was found existing in the jungle of Luzon in the Philippines. He had not heard that World War II was over. I believe that this event is metaphoric for the operation of resistance mechanisms, especially when precocious closure of the personality (dissociation) predominates.

need and dependency on these objects (as Fairbairn suggests), but also to how the external objects were experienced and internalized and to what was projected into them—the more that neediness is projected into them, the more tenacious, possessive and demanding they become (Grotstein, 1981). *It is my impression that Klein failed to understand that the death instinct could be employed defensively–adaptively to intercept and to destroy awarenesses of dangerous attachments with which uncontained "O" was indivisibly associated.*

We must also consider the secondary gain that devolves from experiencing a "grievance" with these objects, according to Steiner. This phenomenon can be understood as one in which the act of feeling sorry for oneself because of a needed object's mis-attunement becomes perversely (masochistically) and addictively satisfying in its own right.

The complementarity of all views

I wish in particular to show the existence of a line of continuity between the conceptions of Fairbairn on the one hand and Steiner and his Kleinian predecessors on the other: first, how the former's ideas prefigured the latter's, and also how they seem to form a complementarity with one another. Another motif in this contribution is the reconsideration of what the defence organizations really defend against—a subject to which I have already alluded. Despite their differences, orthodox–classical"[14] and Kleinian theories converge on the primacy of *psychic determinism* and its obligatory consequence, the primacy of *psychic reality*—a concept that underlies the organizing function of the *infantile neurosis*. While American ego psychology sought to modify the unilateral emphasis on psychic determinism with the provision of the concepts of adapta-

---

[14] "Orthodoxy" designates the earlier school of psychoanalysis, the one to which Freud essentially belonged, which was characterized by "id analysis". "Classical" is the standard analysis of today. It has variegated meanings and designates different assumptions, depending on its geographic locale. "Classical" American ego psychology appears to be radically different, for instance, from "classical" psychoanalysis in France.

tion, the average expectable environment, and change of function (Hartmann, 1939) while continuing to valorize libido theory and aggression, Kleinians remained entrenched with exclusive psychic determinism and psychic reality, valorizing the prime instigating intentionality of the operation of the death instinct while doing so.

Kleinians unwittingly often tend to become *de facto* moralists when they fail to consider the defensive or adaptive function of the death instinct, but Steiner does acknowledge what amounts to an adaptive motif for the formation of psychic retreats. Put another way, Kleinians recognize the reality of early traumata and environmental failures, but their theory and technique do not. Their awareness of the prime organizing importance of infantile and childhood trauma is, consequently, "unofficial". Relational theories, on the other hand, from Fairbairn through Winnicott and Bowlby, down to Sullivan, Kohut, and the followers of the current relational schools, such as Mitchell, Ogden, and others, conceive of an intersubjective matrix that is co-constructive from the relationship itself, a relationship that is considered indivisible. My own concept of "autochthony versus alterity" (self-creation and organization versus co-constructivism) is meant to rectify this gap in both Kleinian and relational theory (Grotstein, 1997d, 2000).

Returning to the Kleinian oeuvre, it was not until Bion (1962) conceived of the "container and contained" and the prime organizing importance of mother's reverie and alpha function that an adaptive dimension entered Kleinian theory and practice. In so doing, Bion not only normalized countertransference phenomena, he fundamentally enfranchised intersubjectivity itself. Nevertheless, when reading modern London Kleinians, despite their greater acknowledgement of environmental factors such as trauma and neglect, one still senses the emphasis they place on the prime organizing and structuring importance of the death instinct or of primal destructiveness. I shall argue that what appears to be primal destructiveness is really a primal defence against experiences that are even more profound: the terror of "O" (Bion, 1965, 1970, 1992)—thus, my argument that *internal objects constitute differing aspects of failed containers of "O"*.

Similarly, relationists, when interpreting to their patients about their experiences of trauma or neglect, often seem to fall back on explanations that position the patient as the actual victim of par-

ents who should have known better without considering the underlying unconscious phantasies of autochthony (sense of psychic
responsibility)—a phenomenon that dominates the landscape of
childhood abuse and trauma (Grotstein, 1997a, 2000).

Summary of the debate

Let me summarize what I believe is the debate between Fairbairn's
and Klein's conceptions about the formation of psychic reality.
Fairbairn begins with the primacy of external reality and the intactness of an original ego and original object. When intolerable experiences with objects occur, the infant splits the object (we would
have to say his *image* of the object) from the original whole object
into a rejec*ted* and accepted object, internalizing the former and
introjectively identifying with it, whereupon the latter is subsequently subdivided into a rejec*ting* and an exciting object, the two
together constituting what I have come to understand as a diaboli-
cally persuasive and "tantalizing" object. As these objects become
split, internalized, and further partitioned as part-objects, they become joined by corresponding counterparts derived from the original ego. Their draw to join their part-object counterparts in the
newly created endopsychic realm depends fundamentally on the
partially unrequited experience of a longing dependency on these
objects, despite the disappointments they (it) cause. Thus, a mythic
or phantasied endopsychic situation consisting of part- (parted and
de-parted) objects and subsidiary egos develops from a traumatizing reality.

The Kleinian legacy of Steiner's pathological organizations or
psychic retreats postulates the primacy of psychic reality (unconscious phantasy) and the secondary quality of external reality in the
following way: (1) the infant's psychic reality is constrained to the
succession of persecutory anxiety in the paranoid-schizoid position
to depressive anxiety in the depressive position; (2) the impingement of external objects will be registered in terms of the infant's
own personal, subjective capacity to experience the object: that is,
what particular aspects of the infant's inherent and acquired "hard-
ware" the object experience "selects". Thus, the Kleinian oeuvre

emphasizes the subjectivity and personalness of the manner in which the infant idiosyncratically experiences an event rather than emphasizing the primacy of the event itself. Perhaps we could summarize the debate this way: Klein and Steiner think of external reality as subserving, mediating, and modifying internal reality, whereas Fairbairn conceives of internal (endopsychic) reality as having been created in order to mediate and modify intolerable experiences in external reality.[15]

The difference between Klein's and Fairbairn's concepts of internal objects

Before I compare psychic retreats or pathological organizations with endopsychic structures, I should like to comment briefly on a comparison between Klein's and Fairbairn's conceptions of internal objects. Klein originally believed that the infant phantasied[16] that it incorporated the external object. Later, after she had become more aware of the importance of projective mechanisms and ultimately of projective identification, she began to realize that the infant's perception of the object is altered by projective identification, so that the object (image) that is incorporated and identified with has already been transformed by this projection (projective identification). The end result is a "third form" (Grotstein, 2000) or chimera whose altered nature reflects a metamorphosis from its original form in the subject's mind. This metamorphosis or transmogrification occurs because identification dissolves the defining boundaries of the projected subject and the object into which it is projected, which I have elsewhere termed a "rogue- or alien subjective object" (Grotstein, 1997c, 2000).

Fairbairn's objects, on the other hand, are always pictured as distinct from the subsidiary egos that relate to them, even though

---

[15] It would appear that the ideas of Kant underlie Kleinian (as well as orthodox Freudian) thinking, and Hegel Fairbairn's thinking.

[16] Although she never specified it as such, the *phantasy* of incorporating an object must be understood as *imagining* that one incorporated the object, i.e., as an *image*.

he considers that this relationship is one of identification. Notwithstanding this apparent difference, however, Fairbairn's picture of these endopsychic objects reveals hyperbole or exaggeration of their badness and excitingness—quantities that the subject must have projected into the object upon internalization. At first, Fairbairn states, the object is "unconditionally bad". Thereupon a good object is defensively internalized in order to modify (condition) the object's badness and, consequently, the badness of the endopsychic world.

There is one more point that deserves mention. Ogden (1983) proffered the subtle but profound realization that "objects don't think". What this means is that when we phantasize that we internalize an object—the intentionality and agency of that object, its "motor", as it were, is what the subject has projected into it. Thus, the subject (infant) is the unwitting puppeteer or ventriloquist of these internal objects, which subsequently exert such power over the subject. Put another way, the subject who is being beleaguered by internal objects is in a transitivistic paradox, akin to Tausk's (1919) "influencing-machine" phenomenon, in which he (the subject) is being hypnotically controlled by his own split-off subjectivity which he confuses with the object because of projective identification (Grotstein, 1981, 2000).

"Faustian bargains" and "pacts with the devil"

To the above I believe one should add the following factors: (1) the possibility of a latter-day "pact with the devil" or "Faustian bargain" on the part of the hapless subject who "bargained" for more than he asked; (2) the probability that the infant makes these shadowy deals because of a feeling even more imperilled than our older theories could understand. In this regard I have in mind that the infant's worst terror is not of bad objects or of his death instinct and its panoply of destructiveness. It is "O" (Bion, 1965, 1970, 1992), the ultimate ontological experience of "nameless dread", which I earlier described as the "black hole" experience (Grotstein, 1990a, 1990b, 1990c, 1991) and which I shall shortly explicate.

Intimations of the importance of "O"

In introducing these themes, I shall proffer the following hypotheses: (1) that the ultimate object of defence or resistance in all human beings is not the drives, affects, reality, or the "side effects" of human relationships per se, but, rather, a cryptic, unconscious terror of unmitigated (as yet uncontained) "O",[17] which lurks as a foreboding dark shadow cast over the preceding; (2) that so-called primitive, archaic, "cruel" internal objects are really pantomimic messenger-reminders of internal mental states ("O") that require recognition, attention, and repatriation, so that reparation and restoration of split-off states of the subject can occur so that they may return to their former holistic intactness; (3) the importance of drives as well as affects and/or feelings has been misunderstood because of the latter having become conflated with what they are addressing, recognizing, mediating, and regulating: "O". In other words, the importance of feelings is, ultimately, the ineffable experience that they intersect. The same is true for the drives. In other words, affects, feelings, and drives, according to this ontological view, constitute the "adjectives", not the "nouns", of experience. Yet, if I opt to use grammatical metaphors, I should quickly add that they really are the "adverbs" of experience, since I consider "O" to be a relentlessly ever-evolving "verb".[18]

Psychic retreats, like endopsychic structures, constitute "waste-dumps", as it were, of "radioactive 'O'"—that is, compromised and therefore compromising containers of "O", whose container capacity, in the subject's unconscious phantasy, has long since been overwhelmed by its content. Thus, the more the threshold[19] of the

---

[17] "O" is Bion's (1965, 1970, 1992) term for a variety of concepts; i.e., Absolute Truth, Ultimate Reality, the thing-in-itself, noumena, inherent preconceptions, Plato's Ideal Forms, and/or the godhead—to which I would add Heidegger's (1927) "aletheia" and "Being in itself", Ricoeur's (1970) "Ananke" (Necessity or Inevitability), Peirce's (1931) "brute reality", and Grotstein's (2000) "Indifferent Circumstance".

[18] Interestingly, Rabbi David Cooper's (1997) work, *God Is a Verb*, expresses a similar idea.

[19] The concept of threshold constitutes an inherent apparatus of primary autonomy in Hartmann's (1939) conception of adaptation. I link it with Hooke's Law for physical systems: "Stress equals strain times the modulus of elasticity."

container becomes exceeded by its contents (annihilation anxiety), the more the subsidiary egos in turn project into their objects so that the latter become pathologically internalized as defective-container-of-"O" objects that have to be reclaimed internally—that is, that which the central self cannot contain becomes repressively projected by its secret envoy, the anti-libidinal ego, into the rejecting object—with the help of the death instinct. In this transaction the rejecting object becomes progressively more cruel, rejecting, and intimidating the more the annihilation anxiety emerges.[20] Then a sexualization or masochistic accommodation takes place in which the libidinal ego becomes all the more infatuated with the exciting-object aspects of the rejecting ego. This configuration bears some resemblance to Bion's (1958) portrait of the "bizarre object" of psychosis. The purpose of internalizing these defective objects is not merely to control them from within, as Fairbairn claims, but, in my estimation, magically to repair, restore, and reclaim them by one's sadistic hatred—to "blame away" their blemishes", so to speak. From this perspective one can view the endopsychic world as a virtual "purgatory", in the sense of Dante.

If these hypotheses have merit, then it is possible to hypothesize further that all pathological defensive organizations and/or endopsychic structures are testimonies to failed—and failing—containment of "O" by infant, mother, father, family, culture, or any combination of them. Furthermore, the subject "suffers" them internally as he suffers *from* them, all the while believing that he is (magically) restoring them. This dynamic constitutes the raison d'être of *martyrdom*.

Yet another hypothesis can be put forward: (4) that, when endopsychic structures, pathological organizations, or, for that matter, internal objects generally, form, they are imbued with separate life—almost as if they become separate, live, humanized (personified) individuals within the self, yet paradoxically seem to display a dehumanization and automatization, so that they are experienced as relentless, persuasive, compelling, omnipotent, wilful,

---

[20] In Christian theology this dialectical oppositionality can be equated with (1) the concept of the Christ, who transforms and thereby transcends the projections thrust into him as the paschal lamb, and (2) the devil, who becomes transformed by the projections (Grotstein, 1996a, 1996b, 2000).

intentional (with their own agendas), and possessive automatons or robots and occupy the so-called moral high ground. They seem hypnotically to hold their host, the subject, in an unconscious trance-state of submission or thralldom. They also seem to have a transitional-object quality of reassuring familiarity, about which one or more of their unconscious spokesmen is quick to remind their host when the latter attempts to undergo change—particularly analytic change. Finally (5), these internal structures are formed through the subject's projective identification into internal images of real objects with subsequent introjective identification of that transformation on a gradient—that is, in the ego and the superego.

* * *

In summary, psychic retreats or endopsychic structures—and "fantasying"—have as their purpose the obliteration of the experience of the relentless evolutions of "O". They allow us to believe that time stands still and that we live in a world of our own making, no matter how persecutory it may be experienced. The persecutors, at least, know us personally. Yet we must also keep in mind that psychic retreats and/or endopsychic structures also constitute sentinels of desperation inaugurated in the whirling vortex of infantile catastrophe.[21]

The ontological dimension of endopsychic structures and psychic retreats

There is yet another dimension of the problem that needs clarification. No matter how psychic retreats or endopsychic structures develop, one thing they have in common is the existence of an ethical and ontological issue for the defensive subject. This issue can be explicated as follows: whereas existential analysis emphasizes it, traditional psychoanalytic techniques imply that it is of

---

[21] Recall footnote 13, in which I cite the incident of the Japanese soldier who had not realized that World War II had been over for years.

utmost importance for the analysand to accept his feeling states with regard to *"reality"*, whether internal or external. This principle has achieved the state of a moral categorical imperative among analysts. Whereas defences seem to be acceptable, there is a tendency for analysts to consider resistances on the part of the patient as almost sinful in an existential way. "Facing reality" constitutes a psychoanalytic version of the "Stations of the Cross" in Christianity. Winnicott's (1951) concept of transitional objects—which Fairbairn [1943] prefigured—helped modify this "religious" aspect of psychoanalysis by advocating, in effect, that the infant needed to be bonded before it could be weaned.

Thus, resistances can be thought of as residues of incomplete or unsuccessful bonding and attachment (Bowlby, 1969, 1973, 1980). From this point of view, psychic retreats and/or endopsychic structures are automatized residues of failed bonding and attachment and adaptive/maladaptive attempts to achieve a compromised transitionality between bonding and attachment and weaning into reality. In other words, psychic retreats and endopsychic structures form because of trauma, whether the origin is internal or external, but they persevere as chronic resistances because they have become split-off, dissociated, enlivened, authorized, and automatized, following which they become used as "psychic addictions" by the subject, who existentially "stalemates" in order to avoid life's "checkmates".[22]

What I am getting at here is that I believe that endopsychic structures, fantasying, psychic retreats, and labyrinths form innocently enough—on the part of the hapless subject—but, once formed, they seem to develop an automatized and dissociated life of their own and wield unusual influence over the subject, who, after a while, "gambles" on them and then remains with and within them because of a fear of cutting his losses by becoming real, during which time the retreats seem to acquire progressively more power and authority over him. The hapless subject, whether infant, child, adult, or patient, then feels trapped in a labyrinth of self-deception, knowing the truth but feeling unable to forswear the

---

[22] In an earlier contribution I referred to pathological automatizations in infant development as "precocious closures of the personality" (Grotstein, 1977a, 1997b).

loyalty to his "only true friend and companion"—the misery that has been his/her silent partner and secret double all his life, the only witness and consolation to his parade of sorrows.

Discussion

What endopsychic structures have in common with psychic retreats or pathological organizations is that they are split-off or alien ("rogue") subjectivities mislocated in the images of internal objects that constitute veritable unconscious fortresses or redoubts that exert omnipotent, hypnotic influence over the subjectivity of the patient (Grotstein, 1997c). These "rogue subjective objects constrain thoughts, feelings, and behaviour toward others and exert a powerful centripetal force of pulling the patient back within their sphere—almost as if the patient is stuck in an orbital trajectory and thus cannot leave the gravitational pull of the dreaded and dreadful nucleus of their nemesis. They also have in common the putative promise of solace or sanctuary to the patient if the latter remains loyal to the "organization", despite the latter's often punitive, perverse, and threatening nature. That quality is what Rosenfeld, Meltzer, and Steiner had in mind when they used the term "Mafia" to designate that the organization offered a "protection racket": "Remain loyal to us and we'll protect you—from them, who is really us!"

Clinical examples

I once had a difficult-to-analyse patient whose negative therapeutic reaction began to dissolve when I began to understand the "protection racket" of her psychic retreat.

In one dream *she found herself passionately kissing a boyfriend while both were seated in an automobile. Suddenly a robber with a gun confronted her (she was on the driver's side), took her money, and then knocked her out by hitting her head with the butt of the gun.*

When she awoke, the robber was still there. He pointed to her boy-friend so as to implicate him as the one who had struck her. The patient believed him. The boyfriend, of course, was I. She became a double agent during the rest of the session, going back and forth between believing me and the robber.

Here we can see that she was overtly identified with her libidinal ego caught in a forbidden relationship with her analyst, who was identified as her exciting object. The antilibidinal ego, in its rela-tionship with the rejecting object, forbade her relationship with me, superficially condemning her for an alleged incestuous rela-tionship with the analyst–father but really forbidding her, at a deeper level, from cooperating with me in the analytic process, in which case I was also an ideal object relating to her central ego.

In another dream this same patient had a nightmare in which *she was being chased by a dangerous-looking man, who had got out of a car, which looked as if it belonged to the Mafia. There were others in the car. They looked ominous and dangerous. She ran into a nearby radio station to get help. She found herself at a live microphone, but when she began to broadcast for help, she found herself frantically exclaiming, "Help, he's grabbed the microphone!" As she uttered this, her voice changed to that of the man.*

Background information of relevance is as follows: she had two older male siblings, one of whom had aggressively abused and taunted her during her whole childhood. She subsequently be-came frightened of men and never married. In the analysis we became aware that the aggressive and threatening objects of her endopsychic world consisted not only of images of her menac-ing brother but also of her own cryptically counter-belligerent self, indistinguishably combined with that of her brother. While this image *threatened*, it also *warned* her about unions with men because they would be dangerous for her. In so "warning" her, this object (or objects) was projecting its own dangerous charac-ter into the new external objects. Furthermore, it emerged in many dreams that she was unconsciously punishing her brother for his intimidation of her, on one level, while he retaliated against her on other. The "Mafia" reference devolved into asso-ciations about her belief that her parents privileged her brother over her, causing her to feel unprotected as well as envious of their privileged position.

Later in the analysis this patient had another dream in which *she was a prisoner in a mental hospital*. In this particular dream *she attempted to escape at night, but once she was free, she became overwhelmingly anxious and sought to return unnoticed*. This latter aspect seemed to be the acme of her anxiety—that she would be discovered (by the agents of the psychic retreat) as having attempted to escape in the first place.

Another similar patient was able to fathom the duplicity of the psychic retreat in a dream. *She and I were in a room together. We were both silent. As time wore on* in the dream, *the patient's view of me changed back and forth and then ultimately remained bad. At one point she was able ever so slightly to catch a glimpse of a light reflection on a thin sheet of glass that she suddenly became aware existed between us. She then realized for the first time that she had been encapsulated within an invisible glass bell jar and then began to realize that the bell jar was organic*, was, in other words, an internal object or organization that was "brainwashing" her by projecting images of itself onto me so as to imply that I was the dangerous one.

Towards a reconciling synthesis

Notwithstanding the avowed differences in the respective explanations of how the origin of endopsychic structures differs from that of psychic retreats, what unites them is the primacy of terror or anxiety. From the Kleinian point of view it would be what Bion (1962) called the "fear of dying"—an infantile catastrophe ("nameless dread") in which the infant experiences the presence of its death instinct before it is able to project it into mother-as-container, but, if the latter fails to contain it, the infant now internalizes a very bad, destructive, and obstructive object consisting of the uncontained death instinct at one remove. This is the beginning of a psychic retreat. This object is then felt to make evil alliances with other objects (if parental intercourse is enviously attacked, then a bad, retaliating parental couple emerges that begins to populate the Hell of the unconscious. The Fairbairnian infant, all too realistically aware of its neediness on the one hand and felt endangering discrepancies of attunement by the parent(s) on the other becomes aware of a problem not unlike "Sophie's choice" (Styron, 1979)—an impossible choice put to a mother concerning which of her two children to sacrifice.

Acceptance of the reality of the situation of an unsupportable environment in the face of its absolute neediness without compromise condemns the infant to an infantile catastrophe (Bion, 1959), a "failure to-going-on-being" (Winnicott, 1962), an "orphandom of the Real", with consequent detachment or "divorce" from one's objects (Grotstein, 1995a, 1995b). The alternative—the "Faustian bargain" or "pact with the devil"—allows the self to "die a little" as a self in order to survive, but with the felt consequence of having forfeited one's authenticity, one's right to joy, happiness, liberty, freedom, or success. One has forfeited one's passport as a soul and is vulnerable to predation, shame, and guilt—and is forever constrained to being the unconscious martyr–scapegoat for one's objects, the unfairness of which one does not perceive as such since they have become the object as well as its harsh superego.

What the two differing views have in common, consequently, is the conception of the infant's sense of not being able to tolerate its feelings—actually its proto-feelings, feelings that have not yet been sufficiently attuned by being recognized, accepted, mediated, and usefully transformed by the mother. Here is where a dilemma arises. After I had attended a "Conference on Affects" sponsored by the International Psychoanalytic Association, I came away with the sad realization that the essential feature of affects was, in my opinion, essentially ignored. This essential feature seems also to be neglected, I believe, in much of the recent infant development literature, which highlights "affect attunement". What does "affect attunement" mean? What is the essential feature to which I refer? What I am getting at is that affects and feelings must be considered as "adjectives" of experience rather than as the ultimate nouns— that is, feelings about what?

Feelings are not important merely because they are feelings. Their importance for us is as mediating sentinels of what Bion (1965, 1970, 1992) calls "O", Absolute Truth, Ultimate (unknowable, ineffable) Reality, or, as I would put it, the Utter Inevitability and Indifference of Circumstance or Necessity. Feelings personify our encounter with "O" so that we can have a personal, subjective relationship with the ineffable world of indifferent cosmic reality so as to get our bearings (feelings in terms of relationships to ourselves and objects) and can allow ourselves to continue to be sovereign selves in the face of the ineffable. Feelings do that for us—with the help of the mediating drives, which offer us the illusion of personal will and a sense of agency (Grotstein, 2000).

I believe, consequently, that the Fairbairnian infant is endangered by having become too prematurely aware of "O" because its objects failed sufficiently to protect it. Therefore it has to undertake a fictional transformation of itself and its relationship to its objects (within rather than outside) and compromise its authenticity and innocence—all in order to create ideal parents who are capable of shielding the infant from the "Sodom and Gomorrah" of "O". If this hypothesis is correct, then the club that the endopsychic structures hold over the infant's ego is that they really contain—or really *are*—"O" and threaten to doff their disguise, should the infant not heed their entreaties. Thus, the fear of the unveiling of "O" constitutes, in my opinion, the hidden order that organizes and preserves the endopsychic situation.

What about psychic retreats? I have already dealt with the Kleinian belief that the death instinct is the prime mover of the psyche and the prime source of anxiety. Bion himself seems to accept this verdict but modifies it in terms of container–contained considerations. Thus, a psychic retreat would be formed in the default of a sufficiently containing (attuning) object. What the object is supposed to attune or contain is the infant's fear of "O", as Bion states elsewhere. Thus, "O", or the fear of unmediated "O", causes the formation of a psychic retreat. The conclusion is obvious: in both cases, in the formation of the endopsychic situation and of the psychic retreat, the infant undergoes a fictional transformation *in order to protect his objects from his awareness of their failure to be able to countenance "O" in him and in their own lives*. In other words, endopsychic structure, as "psychic retreats", is a defence, not against the risk of encounters with objects so much as premonitions that the latter will eventuate in exposure to "O". In either case, the handling of "O" (life as it is) is the ultimate problem.

At this point I should like to state a general hypothesis that naturally emerges from the above considerations. *"O" in the first instance just is—and evolves. How we countenance it—with the help of our objects—is what ultimately matters in mental health or in psychopathology—and all other considerations occupy only secondary roles of importance.*

Summary

"Psychic retreats" or "pathological organizations" is but another way of referring to endopsychic structures of split-off and internalized "objects", which really constitute split-off alien or "rogue subjective objects"—that is, alienated subjective aspects—of the original subject. The main difference between the conception of endopsychic structures and psychic retreats or pathological organizations lies in the tradition and "politics" of their formulators, the former (Fairbairn) relational and the latter (Steiner) death instinct. Winnicott's concept of "fantasying" augments our understanding of these organizations by revealing that they seek to avoid reality, whether external reality or psychic reality. At the same time these organizations originated on a path that deviated from a failed attempt to maintain a transitional attachment to the object. They paradoxically are would-be protectors and zealous as well as jealous guardians of the subject—and intimidating enemies when the subject seeks freedom by progressing in analysis.

The concept of "O" and its relentless evolutions being the ultimate content of the repressed—and not the death instinct—allows for a reconciliation between the relational and the Kleinian–classical views of psychic retreats/endopsychic structures. Ultimately, therefore, the infant is either terrified of its own experience of "O" and/or of mother's inability to contain its "O" or her own experience of "O". All trauma proceeds from this failure in one way or another.

CHAPTER TEN

Towards a theory of the self: Fairbairn and beyond

J. Alan Harrow

> I have said that the soul is not more than the body, and I have said that the body is not more than the soul. And nothing, not God, is greater to one than one's Self is.
>
> Walt Whitman, *Song of Myself*

As expected from the nature of the subject, the literature on the self, both psychoanalytic and philosophical, is vast, an overview of which cannot be attempted here. Instead, for the purposes of this chapter, a particular line of psychoanalytic thought is followed, focusing in particular on the work of Ronald Fairbairn and Jock Sutherland, with other theorists being drawn upon as the chapter develops.

Some initial theoretical considerations

Before considering Fairbairn's contribution, let me draw attention to some thoughts from Masud Khan and Donald Winnicott on the subject of the self. Khan states that "no matter how zealously, or critically, one studies the varied and perplexing literature on the subject, no clear definition of the self, as a concept, crystallizes, though each of us feels very sure about what we mean when he uses the concept of self, it is hard to communicate our particular meaning to another" (1981, p. 294). In his attempt to describe the self, Khan prefers to use the term "notion of the self" when someone claims to know him or herself. He does not share the Utopian notion of selfhood described by Ronald Laing during the counterculture years of the 1960s, but he does believe that each human individual has a distinct sense of the wholeness of his or her self. He has some reservations about the use of the concept of self in the clinical context and is uneasy about those who tend to treat the self as an idyllic, non-conflictual pure state. He states that even Winnicott is not free of this bias. Khan thought that Winnicott's concept of the true—in contrast to a false—self carried the implication of a pure, unadulterated state that is attainable in ideal circumstances. He expresses grave doubts about the existence of a hypothetical true self, saying that his clinical experience inclines him to believe that sometimes a "notion of self", which is quite illusional and delusional as well as quite untrue, can establish itself in a person (1981, p. 303). In clinical practice we know how successful and convincing the false self can be. In fact, the falsity can, in extreme cases, be so well established that it can pass for the true self. The development of a genuine working relationship between patient and analyst in these conditions can be a difficult—at times impossible—task to achieve.

Khan also refers to Winnicott's thinking on the subject of the self in his concept of "the capacity to be alone". The basis of the capacity to be alone is a paradox: it is the experience of being alone while someone else is present. Winnicott (1965) uses this concept to describe the analytic situation, in which the patient realizes and experiences the analyst as there, present and real. The analyst (although present) can be disregarded, this being in Winnicott's view the necessary condition needed in the analytic situation for what he describes as a "true-self experience". Winnicott is advocating creating conditions in which experiences of the self should be allowed to emerge and develop in a personalized (analytic) relationship without unnecessary intrusions or impingement from the analyst. (Late in his life he significantly reduced interpretation and concentrated on creating the conditions whereby the patient's growing sense of self could be realized over time in a trusted relationship.) He states: "It is good to remember that playing itself is therapy ..." (Winnicott, 1971b). For Winnicott, impingement (or a not-good-enough holding environment) would result in a false, or compliant, self formation, exploiting a biological endowment towards survival, which dissociates the person from his or her true self. Following Khan's unease regarding Winnicott's tendency to view the self-experience in somewhat idyllic terms, there appears to be a corresponding idealization of the analytic relationship reflected in his essentially non-interpretative clinical approach. While Winnicott's concept of true and false self continues to be relevant and useful in clinical practice, it may not be as reliable as once thought.

This is an appropriate point of departure to begin a consideration of Fairbairn's theory of the nature of the self.

Fairbairn's contribution

Fairbairn's starting point is a philosophical one, in that he believed that "the study of the person, at a personal level with his or her subjectivity had to be the essential focus of psychoanalysis. Concepts that reduced personal phenomena to impersonal processes were not acceptable to him" (Sutherland, 1994b, p. 335). This essential focus underpins all his psychoanalytic theorizing. According to Sutherland (1994a), Bruno Bettelheim, in *Reflections: Freud and the Soul* (1982), takes the view that Freud's early theorizing did include the significance of a personal self, but this was lost when he introduced the impersonal ego as part of his structural theory. The "I", as Freud termed it, was clearly the self in all its richness of meaning (p. 304).

It was on the self and its primary need for an object that Fairbairn built his theory of the person. His observation that the infant has, from the very beginning, to be unconditionally loved for him / herself is his theoretical starting point. Along with the innate endowment that the infant brings to the relationship with the mother, there has to be a personalized loving response to the infant as a whole person in its own right. In other words, the essential emotional ingredient is a personalized and genuine relationship such as a good-enough mother knows spontaneously how to provide. Fairbairn stated clearly that the real libidinal aim of the self is the establishment of satisfactory relationships with objects. According to Sutherland, Fairbairn accepted the self as a more appropriate term since it refers to the whole from which sub-selves are split off Sutherland (1994b, p. 342). Richard Rubens comments that the self, and its relationship to the other, constitutes the only meaningful unit of consideration for Fairbairn. This unit of self, other, and the relationship in between becomes the pattern for Fairbairn's understanding of the form of all systems within the self (1994, p. 154).

A deprivation of the mother's subjective personalized responsiveness and the infant's frustration of its need for such a relationship result in a splitting of the self. These splits in the self occur at a very early stage of dependence and reflect a failure in a relationship with an external person, which results in the formation of internal object relations. Fairbairn describes the first split being of the object, and a second stage involves a splitting-off of parts of the self related to the splits in the object.

The dynamic internal structures that Fairbairn describes are, in his view, required to organize the infant's early experience of relationships in the real or external world. These are real objects in interaction with the infant, which are internalized and form unconscious dynamic structures, constantly interacting internally and with the environment. Fairbairn seems to be pointing towards the idea that an innate or instinctual potential drives the infant to seek objects, and the subsequent transactions between infant and environment give rise to these internal dynamic structures. In other words, as stated by John Padel (1995): "those who set up a dichotomy between object relations theory, or instinctual drive theory, are misrepresenting Fairbairn's thought: the theory of object relations does not deny the instincts, it simply insists that they are not external to the structures of self or sub-selves but are inherent in them (p. 177)". The id-ego paradigm has no place in Fairbairn's theory. Sutherland commented that the function of the self is the adaptation of primal instinctual activity to outer, essentially social, reality (1994b, p. 338).

Mitchell thought that "it could be argued that Fairbairn's object seeking is a kind of drive in much the same way Bowlby has argued that attachment is driven instinctually" (1998, p. 116). Fairbairn went on to describe how early deprivation of the needs of the whole self results in a withdrawal of investment in external objects. The apparent lack of genuine interest in external relationships displayed by schizoid, or borderline, patients is well documented. This is a defensive reaction to emotionally frustrating experiences between infant and mother and involves the turning to the inner world for emotional satisfaction. Fairbairn points out that it is accompanied by an increase of omnipotence, although this may be fairly well hidden. It is often well into an analysis before such effective concealment is uncovered. It follows that the lack of personal relations and detachment from real people results in feelings of emptiness and futility. Fairbairn thought that these feelings of futility were based on a loss of trust in others. He is emphasizing the patient's feeling of failure and sense of defeat regarding ever being able to achieve a sustainable internal/external attachment to a good object.

This loss of trust in being able to form satisfactory relationships, resulting in the formation of a schizoid dynamic, is more specifically the outcome of the infant's experience of being unloved by mother or, perhaps even worse, of having his love for the mother not valued by her. When this failure occurs in the early oral phase, the infant feels that it is his love that is at fault—that is, the infant's emotional neediness and intense early dependence must have been too overwhelming for the mother. Love becomes an unacceptable (to the object) bad oral greed.

Fairbairn distinguishes this phase from a second, late oral phase, which involves biting and is a potential for aggression. When failure to form a satisfactory relationship in this phase of development occurs, the infant's hatred is felt to be to blame because it is experienced as destructive. In contrast to the schizoid fear of the effect of love upon the object, the effect of hatred results in a depressive dynamic. These failures to form a satisfactory relationship undergo a process of internalization, repression, and splitting, which involves the child in taking control of bad object experiences, which then results in the badness becoming permanently established in the child, and in the adult which he or she eventually becomes. This essentially desperate manoeuvre Fairbairn described as a "moral defence". The critical factor here is that the illusion of goodness is maintained at the expense of the child. In other words, the self is devalued and, as a result, diminished. Or, as Grotstein puts it: "there is a laundering of the image of the object at one's own expense" (1994a, p. 115). The external relationship with parents is too powerful to resist, so the critical factor is that they are internalized simply because the child cannot do without them (Sutherland, 1989, p. 121). The alternative is an unthinkable exist-ence, which includes the threat of an annihilation of the self. Better, in other words, to cling assiduously to the bad internal object and the associated painful experience than to have no object available at all. This "obstinate attachment" as Fairbairn (1944, p. 117) called it, is, in effect, a compensation, in that the child struggles to protect the gratifying or satisfactory experiences with parents while de-priving, unsatisfactory experiences are controlled by the establish-ment of internal objects, with their attachment to split-off parts of the self. This solution is in keeping with Fairbairn's observation of particular delinquent children with whom he worked, who were extremely reluctant to admit that their parents were bad, even when there was a substantial weight of evidence of abuse, violence, and cruelty.

Fairbairn thought that guilt about the inner feeling of badness acted as a resistance to the release of bad objects. He thought that the therapist must have become established as a good object whose non-persecutory attitude allows the (transference) projections to be transmitted. Until this is possible, the patient remains locked into a painful closed system of early internalized attachments, which per-sist because of the loyalty and devotion the patient has towards these bad objects. Any hint of blame or criticism being apportioned to parents by the therapist often produces an aggressive protective defence of them from the patient. Fairbairn came to regard the greatest of all sources of resistance to be the maintenance of the patient's internal world as a closed system. This closed system involves the perpetuation of relationships between aspects of the self and respective internal objects, as well as between one another. He states: "it becomes still another aim of psychoanalytic treat-ment to effect breaches of the closed system which constitutes the patient's inner world and thus to make this world accessible to the influence of outer reality" (Fairbairn, 1958, p. 380).

Fairbairn emphasized the internalization of bad objects as the first line of defence against negative experiences, but he also implied that an early "primary identification" between mother and infant involves internalization of a good object, which can be seen to be used as a layering or foundation for the early structuring of the self.

Sutherland's theory of the self

Let me now move beyond Fairbairn and devote some time to Jock Sutherland's wide-ranging contribution to a theory of the self. Sutherland had seen the whole tenor of Fairbairn's work as moving towards a conceptualization of the self, which, he adds, was, after all, where he—that is, Fairbairn—started. He thought that psychoanalysis lacked a theoretical account of the person as inseparably interwoven with the fabric of society (Sutherland, 1994a, p. 304).

Sutherland's thinking, was, of course, influenced by both British and American theorists (Balint, Fairbairn, Guntrip, Winnicott, Erikson, Kernberg, and Kohut). He comments that "these theorists had contributed to the understanding of the self by advancing the theory from where Freud left it" (Sutherland, 1994c, p. 258). His early attempts to formulate a less-than-tidy theory of the self are reflected in his paper, "The Self and Object Relations" (Sutherland, 1983). His starting point is based on clinical work with a number of patients whom he saw as being greatly preoccupied with insecurity about how other people accepted and valued them. All these patients had a powerful need for a positive responsiveness from others, although this need was often concealed behind extensive negative denials and aggressive defensiveness. He went so far as to say that this was a central issue for most, if not all, patients who seek psychotherapy.

Sutherland appears to leave open just how coherent the self is in its early stages (although he assumes that there is a unity from the start), and he emphasizes how the self soon acquires divisions, or sub-selves. The splits originate in environmental mismatches.

These sub-selves contain needs that press to be accepted as vital parts of the self, but some of these needs are unacceptable to the infant's parents and can lead to painful consequences, if expressed. So these needs are kept away from parents and are coped with through fantasy activity or, later on, through secret expression. Sutherland thought that the goal of therapy involved helping the person to integrate the visible dominant self with the hidden and shameful sub-selves.

Sutherland also thought that a basic feature of the self from the beginning was its active initiating role with the environment. He supports the view that there was increasing evidence suggesting that there was no lack of differentiation between self and others at a very early stage of development. He quoted Daniel Stern (1985), who describes how the infant's boundaries are differentiated from birth. This is based on it being difficult to see how two separate psyches could be undifferentiated, but also findings of infant–mother studies confirm this (Sutherland 1994a, p. 327). It may be, of course, that from the beginning this differentiation is concealed by the infant's early attachment and physical dependence on the mother. What he called the self-system strives to interact and establish compatible and reciprocal relationships with its surroundings. He comments that if in early life everything that is given is rejected, then the adult person seldom offers itself to others.

The self can thus be seen as a complex system that has internalized the important figures of the external world. Sutherland's view was that there is an inherent social relatedness of the self from the start. It is worth noting here that Fairbairn, followed by Sutherland, parted company with Melanie Klein, who, while emphasizing the importance of object relations, did not agree that the need to be in relationship was primary. Balint, Winnicott, Fairbairn, and Guntrip all supported the view that what is important to us at birth is to be recognized and loved for oneself. A search for the object is a more basic motivating force than the gratification associated with the discharge of instinctual tensions. While at one with this view, Sutherland thought that the views of these theorists lacked an account of growth over time—that is, through the numerous growth opportunities presented by a variety of relationships throughout the life cycle.

In his paper "The Autonomous Self" (1994a), Sutherland provided a framework for considering the self as a process. His theory of the self involved two key concepts—namely, the autonomous self and open self-organizing systems. He saw man as a social animal, whose sense of self is his central organizing principle. In other words, Sutherland viewed the whole personality as being in a state of constant flux and interaction with the environment. Starting with the infant and mother and then extending into adult life, there is an incessant mutual exchange between self and environment.

Influenced by Lichtenstein (1977), Sutherland conceptualized the self as our innate bio–psycho–social process, which allowed the infant to search out, firstly, a primal identity, and subsequently, social identities, which eventually included professional work identities. While the self developed and remained more or less constant through social connectedness, Sutherland thought that we adopted, as we matured, different identities throughout the life cycle, such as those of father, mother, sister, brother, doctor, nurse, teacher, and so on. His view was that these various identities were components of a core self, but the "core self" or sense of "oneness" transcended them.

An initial primary identity fashioned in the phases of infantile dependence and a later social identity patterned by environmental experience are, as it were, built on the back of an innate self process. Sutherland thought that just as there appeared to be an organizing ground plan operating for anatomical growth, so there must be a similar or parallel process operating, which integrates the self's interaction with reality. Thinking in such terms, the development of a self-organizing system could be likened to the development of the respiratory system, in that they are both simply there from birth, and, like breathing, the self is by and large outside our awareness (Scott, 1999, personal communication). Sutherland describes the autonomous self as having a "perpetual inherited presence" (1994a, p. 323). It could perhaps be said that the infant's first breath triggers the rudimentary innate self's interaction with its human environment.

So, to begin with, you have self-development, which is necessary for us to relate to the environment, and then, in turn, social identity is essential for maintaining the integrity of the self. The two concepts of self and identity are inextricably linked, but the existence of a core self in interaction with an adequate environment remains the necessary and sufficient condition for adaptive identity development for the individual in a social group.

Sutherland quotes Lichtenstein's suggestion that "the infant self innately expects to find the constellation of a mother responding to it and it responds at once to the mother. Correspondingly, the mother begins to personalise the infant" (1994a, p. 310). Infant research confirms just how competent the early infant self is in evoking attachment responses from the mother. Particularly human is our capacity to conceive of ourselves as having a self, a continuity of self-feeling that we take for granted. It perhaps goes without saying that this vital human capacity is precisely what cannot be taken for granted by many patients who seek psychotherapy. They suffer from serious disruptions in the sense of continuity of self, and here, as far as Sutherland is concerned, we are talking about the disruption of the development of an autonomous self. He took the view—and this is a central part of his thinking—that interference with the steady development of an autonomous self-process elicits intense aggression. Threats to the self-process evoke, he thought, the defensive ferocity of an animal faced with a lethal predator. Aggression, for Sutherland, results from the self's struggle for its autonomy. Jill Scharff comments that this self-determined dynamic is inevitably frustrated by the facts of infantile dependence, even when parenting is more or less satisfactory (1998, p. 173). Also, the infant's innate characteristics may be a factor in disrupting a steady development of the self. While Fairbairn emphasized that aggression is a response to frustration in general, Sutherland goes beyond this to suggest that the origin of hate and aggression is a response to the specific frustration of the self's innate striving for autonomy.

Within an evolutionary perspective, Sutherland demonstrates that, among other elements, the unique property of the human mind is consciousness of "the self" and the capacity to transcend that self, to look at it in its relationship with aspects of itself, with others, and with the physical environment. The self's relationship with the environment, he thought, was evolution in action. Sutherland comments that we have reached a point in evolutionary development whereby humans largely determine the environment (1994a, p. 322).

Sutherland set the core of the self within a relational perspective and emphasized not only that the self could not exist in isolation, but that it needed other selves in order to thrive and develop. The self is an innate process that constantly seeks autonomy. It is, as Sutherland states, "at once revealed if (the 'autonomous self' process) it is threatened or ignored".

Sutherland defined the self as "the heart of the matter", regarding the organization and functioning of subjective experience— that is, of the self as being at the core of the individual. With this proposition in mind, I would now like briefly to reflect on Steven Mitchell's description of two very distinct ways in which the self has been thought about in psychoanalytic literature in recent times. He has described how the self has been considered, on the one hand, to be layered, singular, and continuous and, on the other, to be multiple and discontinuous (1991, p. 126).

Most relevant to this chapter is his description of self as multiple and discontinuous, which is grounded in a temporal metaphor. Selves are what people do and experience over time, rather than entities that exist in definite or fixed places. Oneself is nothing more or less than the subjective organization of the meanings one creates as one moves through time doing things, such as having ideas and feelings, including self-reflective ideas and feelings about oneself. In other words, the self is experienced and develops throughout life. There can, on the one hand, Mitchell (1991) states, be substantial feelings of a sense of self that feels framed and complete, while, on the other hand, selves change and are transformed continually over time.

This would be in keeping with Fairbairn's and Sutherland's concept of the self, which emphasizes both multiplicity and discontinuity, by their portraying the self as embedded in, and fashioned within, different relationships. Sutherland in particular has emphasized that we become persons through our interaction with others. Different experiences of self with different others is, in effect, describing the self as discontinuous, and yet there also seems to be a sense of a constant thread that gives us the feeling of being the same person. It can be argued that a multiplicity and discontinuity of relationships in effect supports, enriches, and sustains the self.

Sutherland concluded that, for the eventual integration of the self, the relationship between the parents and their joint attitudes towards the child are almost as critically important as that of each parent separately (1994a, p. 326).

In clinical terms, when severe discontinuities of self-organization have occurred, patients frequently express fears of fragmenting, of feeling unanchored or dislocated.

While the experience of the self can be disrupted, Mitchell comments that most of us do seem to have, and perhaps need to have, a singular sense of self as constant and unaffected by time, as continuous and unvarying, even though from a temporal perspective there is discontinuity and constant change (1991, p. 138).

He refers to the paradox alluded to earlier, that Winnicott described regarding the infant's capacity to be alone in the presence of the mother, and he comments that when we feel most private, most deeply "into" ourselves, it is then that we are most deeply connected with others through whom we learn to become a self. This is in keeping with Sutherland's emphasis on the self as only being able to thrive in a genuine relationship with other selves. At the beginning, this involves the inter-subjective relationship between the infant's rudimentary self and the self of the maternal object.

Both Fairbairn and Sutherland emphasize the importance of a genuine relationship between infant/mother–patient/analyst— nothing less will do if the self is to thrive and fulfil its innate potential.

In the final part of this chapter I would like briefly to consider Sutherland's interest in the wider application of psychoanalytic insights and his (life-long) concern for the future of psychoanalysis.

Freud (1926e, p. 248) said that "the use of analysis for the treatment of neuroses was only one of its applications". Fairbairn, influenced by Freud, was interested in applying psychoanalytic thinking as widely as possible, and, like Freud, he lectured to mental health professionals and the educated public. Both hoped that mankind as a whole would benefit from these unique and potentially far-reaching ideas. Sutherland's approach to this task goes beyond them and is more sophisticated and wider in its scope. Writing over 30 years ago, Sutherland (1969) was concerned about the growing reaction, now even more a reality, against the slow and painstaking process of psychoanalytically oriented therapeutic work. In response, he thought that it was crucial that psychoanalytic knowledge be made more available to the public, and that this could be an effective way of engaging support for the continuing development of psychoanalysis. In his view, "the image of psychoanalysis was pejoratively linked in the public mind with neuroses and should instead be more identified with growth and development" (Sutherland, 1969, p. 680).

Using key aspects of his theory of the self, he advocated that psychoanalytic institutions should seek reciprocal relationships of mutual dependence with the communities to which they belong. In other words, psychoanalysis, in his view, must have a social relevance if it is to continue to develop. The underlying objective was that the application of psychoanalytic insights to, for example, community mental health services, could be an effective counterbalance to a growing trend towards psychoanalysis being perceived as less relevant and on its way out.

Kenneth Eisold has described a widespread tendency for psychoanalysts and, by implication, psychoanalytic institutions to see themselves as apart from social reality. As a result, psychoanalysts devalue and fear institutions that connect them with the real world (1994, p. 785). Sutherland's open-systems approach is an attempt to correct this—in some respects understandable—social disconnectedness. As implied above, psychoanalytic institutions should do more than simply produce psychoanalysts: this, in his view, constituted a closed system. He thought that an interactive process, between an institution and its environment, has the potential to produce change and growth in both. An open-systems perspective was, he believed, essential if psychoanalysis, like the self, is to realize its potential.

In summary

Sutherland's contribution to a theory of the self involves two basic features: its autonomy and its concurrent membership in a community (1994a, p. 310).

His conception includes the need to be valued as a person and to feel oneself to be of significance in the lives of others and to be attached in varying degrees of intensity to others while also having a capacity for autonomous functioning. These relationships determine how coherent or otherwise a sense of self will be. Threats to the autonomy of the self, which is synonymous with survival, are seen as the origin of hatred and aggression. Sutherland has built on and gone beyond Fairbairn's object relations theory in his attempt to develop a theory of the self. He has offered a valuable contribution to what he thought was the essential next step in psychoanalytic theorizing.

Finally, it occurs to me that Walt Whitman and Jock Sutherland have something fundamental in common: both attach particular importance to the self. They emphasize the self as the essential reality—"the heart of the matter" and the ultimate essence of all being.

CHAPTER ELEVEN

Fairbairn and the self as an organized system: chaos theory as a new paradigm

David E. Scharff

A s he lay down on the couch, "Donald" said: "I don't know if you know this, Dr Scharff: the mind is a very interesting thing. It occurred to me while I was driving over here that I have a really great life. I have a lot of good things going for me. I thought that was an interesting way to feel, because I complained about everything last week. "My cat licked me first thing this morning. Last week it annoyed me. This week it felt like a sign of closeness and familiarity. Last week I complained about the stress in my job. Today it seems to me it has lots of possibility for creativity. With Ellen, last week I told you about the big problems in our relationship. This week I feel like she's a wonderful person and I'm lucky she loves me. . . . Last week I went from feeling very positive Monday to very negative Wednesday. Now I'm positive again. When I'm down, each little roadblock seems insurmountable, so I lose confidence. I'm afraid of the opinion of some authority figure at work, afraid that I'll lose a vote of confidence. Then I have success in solving a problem, and my confidence comes back.

"So what has happened to take me from this state to another state and back again? I've tried to figure it out: who is the authority figure that makes me lose confidence? My sister who persecuted me, or my father or mother? Actually my mother was a pretty big booster, but when she did say something critical, like 'You should get a Master's Degree', I'd get upset and defensive."

In our psychoanalytic work together, I've experienced the oscillation Donald is reporting. On most days he complains about his job and his girlfriend, but this state of mind alternates with an almost unbearable self-confidence. In his grandiose state of mind, he dismisses the difficulties in love and work with a mental wave of his hand that makes me feel also dismissed for having doubts that his life could really be that easy. I feel then that if I expressed my doubts, I'd be a spoilsport like his mother when she occasionally questions the wisdom of his choices. On the other hand, when he's down, there isn't so much to say either, because he is so harsh about his objects that it feels as though it would be easy to become one of the ones he is attacking.

This session with Donald happened when I was looking for a way to present the relevance of chaos theory to Fairbairn's object relations theory of the personality. I believe that chaos theory presents a paradigm shift of major consequence to psychoanalysis, and that it offers a particularly rich set of organizing ideas to those of us who follow Fairbairn in placing relationships at the centre of human development and psychology.

Ellinor Birtles (1998) has written of the scientific and philosophical paradigm shift that occurred from Freud to Fairbairn. Philosophically, the shift involved moving from Freud's nineteenth-century Platonism that described man in conflict with society and within himself, to the Aristotelian view of man as a social animal embedded naturally in society. Hegel's description of each person motivated by an inborn desire to be the object of the other's desire lies at the heart of this vision. Scientifically, Freud's nineteenth-century model that derived from Newton, Helmholtz, and the laws of thermodynamics no longer serves as an adequate paradigm. Fairbairn took from Einstein's theory of relativity, $e = mc^2$, the fundamental relationship between the structure of matter and energy, and in a parallel way he replaced Freud's scientific model with a psychic model centred on the inextricable relationship between the structure of mental content and mental energy.

In his MD thesis (1929a) and again in his one long clinical study written in 1931(a), Fairbairn referred to the self as an "organized system". This was a starting place for his work. He did not specifically restate this principle in his papers on object relations, in which he went on to develop a remarkable schema of the endopsychic situation as a system of internalized part-objects attached by tell-tale affects to parts of the ego. Mental structure and its contents are inextricably related in this model, and energy resides in the relative forces of the dynamic organization, closely related to the role of affects. Fairbairn's idea of "the self as an organized system" is given form in this model by the way this internal system of parts of the personality was in dynamic flux, subject to the central ego as the agent of splitting and repression. Later, Fairbairn (1958) added that the goal of maturation and treatment is to heal the splits and promote integration of the system—an ideal that can never be fully realized but remains a guiding principle. And, he said clearly, it is the therapeutic relationship that is the principal agent of change and integration, because all the specific techniques of therapy owe their power to the relationship between patient and analyst.

Fairbairn concentrated on the relationship between structure and content. Where Freud (1923b) had described structure as the principal issue, with content almost as an incidental afterthought, Fairbairn posited the complete interrelationship of structure and content (Scharff & Birtles, 1994). While Fairbairn only described a few aspects of the dynamics and mechanics of the mutual influence of the sub-units of personality, it is the fact that he described a dynamic system of internal object relations that comprises his most radical shift in theory. It is this contention that makes mind itself a cybernetic system rather than a fixed structure derived by linear principles of construction. In his theory of endopsychic structure, he named the central ego as the agent of repression of the anti-libidinal and libidinal objects and egos. Then he added to this original dynamic the attack of the anti-libidinal ego on the libidinal constellation in hysteria, and the way the ideal object combines dynamically with the anti-libidinal self and object to form the func-

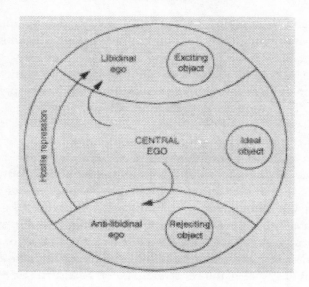

Figure 11.1.   Fairbairn's original Endopsychic Model
of the Personality.

Note short arrows depicting the dynamic that the Central Ego represses both the
Libidinal and Anti-Libidinal relationships between object and ego. In hysteria,
Fairbairn described secondary repression, the further attack (long arrow) of the Anti-
Libidinal Ego on the Libidinal Ego and Exciting Object. (From Scharff, 1982.)

tions of the superego in a changing and flexible pattern (1944,
1954c, 1963a) (Figure 11.1).

While Fairbairn opened the possibility of seeing mind as a self-
organizing dynamic system, he did not generate a general theory
of the dynamic relationship between all sub-units of self and object
organization. Nor did he expand the picture to include the way the
individual is in dynamic flux with the social context in which each
person lives, although here too, he opened the door. Pathology, he
said, often consisted of the "static internal situation . . . self-contained situations in inner reality, which persist unchanged indefi-
nitely, and which are precluded from change by their very nature
so long as they remain self-contained" (1958, p. 87). A patient of his
called these "frozen dramas". In the same paper, his only one on
clinical practice, Fairbairn wrote:

[P]sychoanalytical treatment resolves itself into a struggle on the part of the patient to press-gang his relationship with the analyst into the closed system of the inner world through the agency of transference, and a determination on the part of the analyst to effect a breach in this closed system and to provide conditions under which, in the setting of a therapeutic relationship, the patient may be induced to accept the open system of outer reality. [p. 92]

Fairbairn formulated the principle of dynamic systems in this way, comparing the healthy open and self-organizing system with the frozen, static system that characterizes the repetitive patterns of mental ill health. It seems to me that any attempt to formulate a more thorough set of dynamic principles at the time would have led Fairbairn back to the linear reductionism of Freud's original principles that separated psychic energy, structure, and mental content. They would have been inadequate because the models did not yet exist. The self-organizing principles of complex dynamic systems had not yet been described in the realms of physical science and mathematics.

Chaos theory

This brings us to a consideration of the contributions of chaos theory that now make possible a more sophisticated understanding of the internal dynamics of self-organization and of interpersonal interaction that both creates personality and is at the same time organized by it. Chaos theory derives from developments in mathematics and physics during the last quarter-century. It offers a shift in scientific and philosophic models comparable to the shift from Helmholtz to Einstein. Just as the theory of relativity and new philosophic writing (Birtles, 1998) offered new vistas in the middle of the twentieth century, so chaos theory offers new ways of seeing psychologically and psychoanalytically. It aids our efforts to apply new research findings, and it supports recent developments in applying information-processing theory to relational and object relational theory.

Let me now review some elements of chaos theory, before I return to the clinical vignette with which I began, to see whether applying some tenets of chaos theory extends our reach in understanding the clinical situation. Specifically, I want to view Donald's oscillations between positive and negative views of his internal and external worlds, and his transference oscillations that convey these shifts in psychic organization, in a new way.

Chaos theory brings together findings from the fields of mathematics, physics, and such diverse areas of research as weather forecasting, astronomy, and population studies. It comes from the study of non-linear mathematical equations that cannot be solved, and from non-Euclidean geometry. Let me introduce some terms from chaos theory that can richly inflect the language of psychoanalysis (Briggs, 1992; Gleick, 1987).

1. The first principle is: *Dynamical systems are characterized by continuous feedback*. Mathematically, an *iterated equation* is such a system.

In an iterated algebraic equation, where X is the unknown, the equation is solved, and then the answer is taken as the next value of X in the next run of the equation. For instance, $X^2 + 2 = Y$ is solved. Then Y becomes the new X. This becomes more complex when many of the numbers involved are small complex numbers, located not on the familiar two planes of an x and y axis but in more than two dimensions. *An iterated equation is the basis for a continual process of feedback in a system.* Such a system always begins the next cycle at a place determined by the solution of the previous cycle. To bring home the relevance of this process, we can say that all biological life is an iterated system. Individually, as a community, as an entire human species, we begin the next moment of life by starting at the point we have arrived at so far, and then we usually employ the same old processes or equations to take the next step. We begin with a new X that is the sum of everything that has happened to us so far. So do our patients, and so does an analytic dyad. The most common example of the process of iteration in the psychoanalytic process occurs when the analyst "mirrors" a thought of the patient. Just repeating a statement or question the patient made suggests that the patient start the equation at the point just reached, although the analyst has also inevitably introduced a difference through the small inflections in tone or phrasing that always attend even supposedly "neutral" interventions, such as the proverbial "Hmm".

2. Such small vocal inflections or verbal changes make an enormous difference because of the next principle: *Sensitive dependence on initial conditions*—the "butterfly principle".

The weather researcher Edward Lorenz ran a computer simulation model of long-range weather forecasting on his computer and got an answer of a certain pattern of weather. He wanted to validate it by running the same program again. He set it running, went off for a cup of coffee, and came back a while later to a completely different outcome. Why? In rerunning the program, he finally realized that he had very slightly rounded off some of the numbers after several decimal points. He formulated what has come to be a hallmark principle in chaos theory: in complex systems, very small differences in initial conditions produce completely different and unpredictable results. In complex systems, it is not possible to predict what difference these small—even unnoticeable—differences will make, but the differences are enormous. This gave rise to Lorenz's "butterfly principle": the flap of a butterfly's wings in Brazil can produce a small current that will be unpredictably amplified, until it becomes a hurricane in Texas (Gleick, 1987).

To return to our human examples, we can easily say that humans have a life-long sensitivity to initial conditions. Small differences in neurobiological events and constitution, small differences in the way a parent treats a child, small differences in school or in adolescent relationships change a person's life in unpredictable ways. Clinically, small differences in analyst–patient interaction make distinct differences in the condition of the following iteration, and over time the small incremental differences have a large impact that profoundly affects the unfolding analytic experience.

3. The third principle concerns *predictability*.

Periodically, psychoanalysis has been criticized for being unable to predict the outcome of development of a treatment. Can chaos theory explain how we can know so much and be so helpless to predict? Human factors, like complex physical phenomena, are far too complex to allow us to predict. But it is often possible to understand what has happened in retrospect because of the kind of pattern recognition that can be explicated using chaos theory.

4. The fourth principle holds that *chaotic systems tend to self-organize.*

Nineteenth-century physicists predicted the drift of the universe towards a heat death of entropy, but Darwin and others showed how, on earth at least, more and more complex structure evolves. These contradictions have been addressed by chaos theory, which has elaborated the way that energized chaotic activity spontaneously produces structure and complexity (Briggs, 1992). Self-organizing systems seem to organize out of chaotic patterns. The emergent self-organizing property of the self was identified by Sutherland (J. Scharff, 1994) as a quality that also characterizes human beings. The self does not tend towards self-destruction influenced by a death instinct, as Freud and Klein proposed. Chaos theory applied to human development and psychoanalysis suggests that the self and the collective self of humanity exhibit properties of progressive and emergent organization. How does this work?

When complex equations are solved and iterated millions of times, the solutions can be plotted—something that has only become practical in the computer age. At first the solutions may follow a definable curve on the xy axis or on the xyz three-dimensional axis. The curve then splits at a place called the *saddle point*, as two groups of solutions show up in a double or saddle curve. Then each curve doubles at another saddle point, resulting, as the process of progressive doubling continues, in a *cascade of doubling*, until suddenly the orderliness of the process breaks down into chaos. The pattern becomes random. If the points continue to be plotted, the successive solutions are completely unpredictable. If we keep iterating, solving, and plotting, suddenly out of the edge of chaos a pattern emerges that sooner or later comes to resemble the original one. This is called *self-similarity*. A computer plot of such equations demonstrates the alternation between chaos and form.

5. The fifth principle describes *fractal scaling*.

If such equations are plotted with the use of a computer by iterating such equations millions of times, the most interesting feature of all emerges: the patterns that emerge show *self-similarity at different scales of magnification*—a feature chaotologist Bernard Mandelbrot has called *"fractal scaling"* (Gleick, 1987). Mandelbrot invented fractal geometry, the geometry of dynamical systems. This is the non-Euclidean geometry of the universe. The *self-similarity across different orders of magnitude* in these systems forms patterns that characterize this process called "fractals". This aspect of the mathematics of chaos is easier to show in pictures than in mathematical formulas. For instance, a leaf has a pattern of veins and their branches at varying levels of magnification that is similar to its overall shape and that resembles again the pattern of leaves on twigs, the twigs on larger branches, and the trees in the forest. We can see this effect everywhere in nature and art, in the pattern of mountains, the rocks that make them up, and the microscopic structure of rocks, of small and large waves. In art, too, self-similar fractal patterns at differing orders of scale—as for instance in the detail of exterior decorations of the Paris Opera matching its overall architectural structure—often produce the most aesthetically satisfying images (Briggs, 1992).

6. The sixth next set of principles refers to the concept of *attractors*. Attractors determine the form of organization of a system. There are three main kinds of attractors:

A *"fixed attractor"* is a point, the kind of pattern to which a pendulum powered by gravity tends. As the pendulum runs down, its arc acts as though drawn by the point at which it will eventually stop.

A *"limit cycle attractor"* is a fixed pattern that holds all the points through which movement occurs. The arc of a pendulum powered by electricity is a limit cycle attractor. There are more complex limit cycle attractors that can be plotted, such as the shape of an inner tube—a pattern known as a torus.

The attractor most relevant to our interest in object relations theory is the *strange attractor*—a pattern generated by complex nonlinear equations. It is characterized by irregularity. The solutions to its equations—for instance the place one would find planets or stars, the pattern of drips from a faucet, or the pattern of simulated weather situations—cross random, non-repeating, unpredictable points. Eventually, however, pattern begins to develop—even though the exact answer to the iterated equations is not repeated. The results can be plotted, and the resulting strange attractor often forms beautiful patterns. The first paradox I want to call to your attention is this: *Strange attractors have a predictable overall form, but that form is made up of unpredictable details* (Briggs, 1992).

The most famous strange attractor is the *Mandelbrot set*, which shows *fractal scaling*—that is, self-similarity across different orders of magnitude, and repeating patterns of great intricacy and beauty that emerge at the edge of chaos. The strange attractor has a second paradoxical characteristic of great importance to analytic theory: *A strange attractor is produced by the system of which it is a part, but it appears to be the thing that organizes the system* (Gleick, 1987).

Most rhythms in biology and physics are not regular: a marcher's pace, a singer's vocal frequency, so-called regular heart rate, EEG rhythms—all healthy biological rhythms show chaotic irregularity. The frequencies are ever-changing and can be plotted only by the patterns of strange attractors. Only in disease do these biological rhythms become essentially regular. Chaotic irregularity seems to confer a much higher degree of potential for adaptability than regularity. Current neurobiological research is beginning to demonstrate that the brain is also organized by the principles of chaos theory (Schore, 2000).

John Sutherland, Fairbairn's disciple, described the autonomous self as an emergent self-organizing system that tended to evolve to levels of progressive organization towards that which he called "the autonomous self" (J. Scharff, 1994). This adds richness to Fairbairn's concept of the ego that is present from the beginning. Now we can see that the "pristine, unsplit ego" of the beginning of life is a complex system with the central property that is designed to be self-organizing at increasing levels of complexity. This self-organization shows fractal scaling: there are inherent patterns that are self-similar at different orders of magnitude. In many patients, for instance, one can demonstrate that the speech pattern demonstrated in a clinical moment is self-similar to the pattern of an overall session, and again shows a similarity to the pattern of a person's life and to the transference pattern (Galatzer-Levy, 1995).

Applying chaos theory to the clinical situation in a Fairbairnian mode

Let us return to the clinical situation with my patient Donald, who was asking how it is he can so rapidly and unpredictably shift from one sense of himself to another. Fairbairn's theory of the self as a dynamic system of object relationships and chaos theory go well together to help us conceptualize this. Donald has a fundamental split in his personality, in which he alternates between libidinal and antilibidinal organizations, hardly pausing for a central ego experience. His experience resembles the plot of complex non-linear equation that has a saddle point, the beginning of two alternate solutions to the same problem.

Donald's relationship with his mother had two organizations: sometimes she was his "booster", at other times she was critical. Fairbairn (1944) noted that the hysteric's early object relations presented a rapid and repeated alternation between excitement and rejection. The relationship characterized by excitement and arousal on the one side, or by frustration and rejection on the other, provide the perturbation that tends to push patterns into and out of emotional turbulence, or from patterns of one emotional attractor to another. This perturbation is like the friction that can slow, accelerate, or change the direction of a moving object. So when Donald experiences an increase in arousal or hope or a sense of disappointment, for instance, this sets up the pattern for period doubling—that is, for two patterns that alternate. The patterns of excited, grandiose relating and dejected, persecuted relating alternate, cascade, and then move into regions of chaotic non-organization. Then, suddenly, a new pattern may emerge, one that will have elements of self-similarity with other sets of Donald's personality patterns on various levels of scale. We can also say that the strange attractor pattern Donald described—of being either overly pessimistic or overly optimistic—alternates between two spheres or components of the overall attractor, with relatively little time spent in the central region. This is another way of saying that Donald cannot achieve an integration of his mental experience or of his interpersonal relations. He operates by oscillating between two attractor patterns, but he cannot experience the ambivalence that would represent Fairbairn's conception of an integrated object relationship. This pattern is in evidence when he describes the denigrated and sexually tantalizing women he seeks and the idealized but critical or disappointing women he ends up with and then avoids. It is in evidence about his mother and his father, and it is intrinsically interwoven with the transference when he seeks an ideal relationship with me, only to face disappointment—a time when he treats me with the denigration otherwise saved for the women he then comes to desire. The pattern repeats, but never in exactly the same way, and it is demonstrated in microscopic and macroscopic ways.

The strange attractor that organizes Donald's mind and that is equally the product of his organized self in interaction with a split object has an alternating shape rather than one that might dwell predominantly in the central areas, with less frequent excursions into the complex areas of libidinal and antilibidinal forces.

The forces that throw Donald from one pattern to another—the perturbation that moves him from emotional turbulence to an organized pattern—may be the detection of a slight criticism or praise in the voice of his girlfriend, boss, or analyst. Small perturbations produce changes from non-organized to patterned areas and are exquisitely dependent on initial conditions—that is, these small factors in each rendition of a relationship's interactions.

The influence of a new relationship—the therapeutic relationship—is a destabilizing influence that can be expected to change fundamentally the existing patterns of organization. The only thing we can confidently predict about these new patterns is that change will come in essentially unpredictable ways.

The dyadic interpersonal field in which we work is exceeding complex. If we work in group or family therapy, the interpersonal system is even more complex, although the same factors of complexity theory apply. We cannot hope to maintain control of the factors or to exert influence on the organization of personality in any simple or direct way. Rather, we work by introducing a fundamental destabilizing influence, often by beginning a cascade of small changes that eventually throws our patients into emotional turbulence. This has been called "regression in the service of the ego", but I believe it is better thought of as a return to chaos that allows for the development of new attractor patterns. When I say "a return to chaos", I mean that primordial pre-integrative state with the quality of healthy randomness, like a heartbeat that has a chaotic quality that holds the greatest potential for adaptation to need. When the personality can let go of the relatively limited attractors into which it has been frozen as a result of traumatic or overwhelming experience, the potential for new organization—for the growth of new psychic strange attractors—is restored.

Conclusion

Chaos theory offers a paradigm for psychoanalysis that improves our powers of understanding. Because it offers an explanation for the essential unpredictability of complex dynamic events, it relieves analysis of the burden of prediction and at the same time enables it to offer enhanced understanding of complex and repetitive patterns of psychic organization and interpersonal interaction. Fairbairn's endopsychic model of personality introduced the idea of dynamic flux of endlessly complex factors into psychoanalytic theory. The clinical concepts of transference–countertransference exchange and of the analytic process are best theoretically explained by his model. Chaos theory offers to ground these ideas on the firmer support of a model of the organization of complex self-organizing systems as they tend towards higher levels of organization—a fitting model for the psychoanalytic process.

Psychoanalysis works because it introduces a new organizing pull into the patient's internal system that throws him away from the rigidly repetitive, narrow patterns into the chaos he has often feared, but from which, with our help, he can recover with a new self-organized pattern, more adaptive, more integrated.

Clinical epilogue

In the session after the one I reported in which Donald told me that the mind was a strange and wondrous thing, he came in with unusual enthusiasm.

"Dr Scharff, I discovered something in that last session," he said. "I realized that I use one state of mind to cover up another."

I was pleased to hear him corroborate things I had written (in this chapter) in the interval between these two sessions. In my enthusiasm, I started to interrupt him to elaborate on my previous interpretation: I was about to repeat an old pattern between us—I would tell him how things were in a way that repeated a pattern with his mother. But he stopped me, and in doing so, he altered our pattern of interaction:

"Wait, I want to tell you what I figured out. When I start to care about someone, I get worried that that person is going to criticize or reject me. So I get angry at them, or I put them down. That way, I avoid hoping they will care about me, that they'll return my longing for them. So I use this way of feeling and thinking on myself to cover up my worry and to keep from feeling hurt and lonely. And it works for a while. And then I try to move on quickly to a new relationship before the hurt settles in. So I have these two ways of thinking, and the one protects me against the other, and that's also why I lapse so easily into being angry or critical myself—to keep someone else from doing it to me. That happens in here too. I do it to myself so you won't do it to me."

When Donald stopped me from talking, he demonstrated a capacity we hope to facilitate in every therapeutic process—the capacity to self-organize. Paradoxically, the capacity for a person to grow, to self-organize, has to be grown in the soil of a mutual relationship—one like the mutually organizing process of psychoanalysis that has the capacity to alter the attractors that organize our patients' repetitive patterns. The work we offer to facilitate is to help patients move from their fixed organizations to another more functional and more complex level. It is not that they are not organized, but that the pattern they come with lacks the higher levels of integration they need. To get help get them there, we do as Fairbairn suggested: we try to breach their closed, repetitive inner worlds and introduce a functional chaos, out of which they can form new attractors and new adaptations.

CHAPTER TWELVE

Fairbairn and the problem of agency

Stephen A. Mitchell

F airbairn's enormous contribution to contemporary psychoanalytic thought was, for many decades, hidden in the
shadowy background of analytic discourse; in recent years
the originality and generativity of his work has begun to be noted
and given its due. Of central significance has been Fairbairn's radical shift from an understanding of mind built out of impulses and
regulatory defences to an understanding of mind built out of relational configurations composed of versions of the self in relation
to objects and versions of objects in relation to selves. Fairbairn's
breakthroughs in these areas was truly revolutionary, and, for
many analysts in the United States, the convergence between
Fairbairn's theory of internal object relations and Harry Stack
Sullivan's theory of interpersonal relations has sparked the emergence of what has come to be known as Relational Psychoanalysis.

What I would like to do in this chapter is a little different: to
explore Fairbairn's contribution to a central issue within psychoanalytic thought, the problem of agency, even though Fairbairn did
not himself address it directly, as far as I know. I am undertaking
this task because despite the fact that agency was peripheral to

Fairbairn's major concerns, I have found key aspects of Fairbairn's system extremely helpful in my own struggles with the problem of agency. This chapter has three parts: first, I indicate why I have come to regard this issue as one of *the* major psychoanalytic problems—in fact, a central dilemma for anyone living in our time; second, I suggest what I believe Fairbairn's object relations model teaches us about it; and, third, I present some clinical material that illustrates these problems and the usefulness of Fairbairn's contribution to the clinical struggle of both patient and analyst with them.

The problem of the will

Agency became problematic for us largely through Freud's de-centring of the individual within his own mind.

Freud himself provided what is probably the best-known—even if self-aggrandizing—account of the larger impact of his work upon human self-perception. The Copernican revolution decentred man from his special place in the very middle of creation; the Darwinian revolution dislocated man from his special status among all creatures. With his discovery of unconscious motivation, Freud argued, psychoanalysis exposed the illusory nature of man's claim to be master in his own house, in control of his own mind.

"I am the master of my fate/I am the captain of my soul", intoned Freud's contemporary, the poet William Ernest Henley (1903), crippled by tuberculosis of the bone but undaunted. But belief in the Victorian, Enlightenment-based ideal of an omnipotent, autonomous will-power, overseeing and in control of a mind transparent to itself, has faded, in no small part because of the pervasive impact of the psychoanalytic notion of the unconscious on contemporary culture.

Sartre's attack on psychoanalysis in *Being and Nothingness* (1956) represented a brief, spirited defence of the belief in an omnipotent will. Existence precedes essence, argued Sartre, and we are self-created beings, generating ourselves in time. All claims to an essence, a nature, any limits to that self-creating process, certainly any notion of unconscious forces acting upon us and delimiting our self-control, constitute "bad faith". Sartre did not challenge the *content* of Freud's analysis of motives—Sartre's biographies of Baudelaire, Genet, and Flaubert and his own autobiography are filled with depictions of psychodynamic processes and motives and an emphasis on early infantile experiences. What Sartre does challenge is the elimination of personal agency, the failure to recognize the architect of the life in question, the person who chooses to be motivated by this or that event, circumstance, longing. By contrast, existential psychoanalysis, as Sartre characterizes it, is "a methodology designed to bring to light, in a strictly objective form, the subjective choice by which each living person makes himself a person" (1953, p. 58). Thus, Sartre's vision drew on Freud's insights into psychodynamics while preserving, even extending, the belief in an omnipotent, autonomous, agentic self. On the whole, as measured by the recent evolution of human self-understanding within Western culture, we would have to say that Sartre has lost and Freud has won.

If the individual does not control his own psyche the way a driver, say, controls his car, who does? Freud dethroned the naive belief in an omnipotent will steering a transparent and pliable mind—what looks like a driver became a cardboard dummy—but it left him with an enormous problem that psychoanalysis has been struggling with ever since. Is the psyche really *out* of control, lurching this way and that? Or is there a remote control, a hidden controller inside the mind, unbeknownst to the now merely titular owner?

In the many concepts and metaphors he generated for thinking about mind, Freud went back and forth on this question. Early on, Freud (1892–93) imagined a secretly defiant "counter-will" (p. 122)—a kind of saboteur generating unconscious conflicts and troublesome symptoms. But in his formal, "metapsychological" theorizing of the 1910s, Freud rejected the term "subconscious" precisely because it implied an alternative consciousness operating in hidden recesses of the mind. Unconscious thoughts are not organized into a single hidden or secret subjectivity, Freud argued. They are fragmentary and dispersed. But the tension in Freud's struggle to visualize a decentred mind remained. In 1923 he introduced the concept of the "id" as the repository of instinctual drives and the core of the unconscious (Freud, 1923b). At times the id has qualities of an "it" (the literal translation of "id")—a kind of perverse, hidden imp that drives the psyche according to its own secret agenda. [This was the original meaning intended by George Groddeck, from whose *Book of the It* (1923), Freud borrowed the term.] And Freud at times pictured the relationship between the ego and the id as like the relationship between a rider and his horse. The horse, as anyone who has ridden horses well knows, operates as a powerful "counter-will". But at other times, Freud portrays the id as diffuse and fragmentary, a "seething cauldron", or like the ocean itself—the Zeider Zee—which civilization slowly exposes, organizes, and brings under control.

Thus, in dethroning the Enlightenment/Victorian ideal of an autonomous, omnipotent will-power, Freud created a conceptual vacuum in our ways of imagining our own minds, a vacuum that his subsequent images and metaphors of "the unconscious" never quite succeeded in filling. And neither have his descendants. Is there a hidden controller somewhere in the mind, a secret operator other than the titular owner? Or is the sense we have of ourselves as singular individuals, as "selves", with an individually grounded coherence and agenda, completely illusory? Post-Freudian theories, like Freud himself, have tended to gravitate to one or the other position. And the different approaches to this issue have come to define some of the fundamental schisms within contemporary thought, within and beyond psychoanalysis.

On the one hand, within some currents of American psychoanalysis, there has been a restoration of a psychic centre. In Freudian ego psychology, the reigning psychoanalytic ideology in the United States from the 1940s through the 1970s, the "ego" was granted many more powers and resources than Freud ever had in mind. Whereas Freud's ego was essentially a mediator that emerged at the interface between the id and external reality to negotiate their very different aims, the ego of Freudian ego psychology has a powerful agenda of its own, synthesizing, adapting, and creating what Erik Erikson famously termed "identity" (1959). And in Kohut's self psychology, an off-shoot of Freudian ego psychology, the self has a core, a nuclear destiny, not the pre-Freudian omnipotent, autonomous will, but a psychic control centre of a new sort.

On the other hand, within many currents of fashionable post-modern thought influenced by French post-structuralism, the philosophizing of Foucault, and the psychoanalytic theorizing of Jacques Lacan, there has been a complete obliteration of any meaningful sense of agency, psychic centre, or coherent self. The persons we take ourselves to be are merely "discursive" positions generated by the linguistic, regulatory practices of culture. Or, alternatively, what is most authentic about us is the churning fragmentation of unconscious processes that perpetually disperse the false coherences, the illusory subjectivities, the dichotomously gendered, compulsively heterosexual identities that society subjects us into. There is no "doer behind the deed", as Judith Butler (1990) puts it. Lacan repeatedly mocked ego psychology precisely for attributing to the "self" a narcissistic illusion, qualities of substance and control.

And the unconscious has also been depicted in many different ways. Freud's vision of the Unconscious was shaped by his instinct theory of "drives" and most frequently portrayed as a "seething cauldron" of intensely imperious infantile sexual and aggressive impulses. Jung's version of the unconscious has served, since the early decades of the twentieth century, as a counterpoint to Freud's. For Jung, the deepest unconscious is constituted by universal archetypal symbols that shape human consciousness cross-culturally, generating the same stories told in many different ways, the "mono-myth", as Joseph Campbell (1990) put it, the "hero with a thousand faces".

In recent decades psychoanalysis has generated new, distinctly different visions of the unconscious, among them: Melanie Klein's startling portrayal of a complex phantasy world of inner spaces, substances, cataclysmic interior wars and couplings; Jacques Lacan's linguistic unconscious, with transpersonal clusters of "signifiers" shaping personal desire; and the unconscious of contemporary relational psychoanalysis, informed by Fairbairn's object relations theory, a latticework of self–other configurations, internalized from interactions with significant others and perpetually transformed through the impact of temperament, affect, and imagination.

We have been considering different positions on conscious agency and different images of unconscious processes. But what of the *relationship* between conscious and unconscious mental processes?

During the middle decades of the twentieth century, as Freudian psychoanalysis slowly became absorbed into modern consciousness and popular culture, consciousness was often portrayed as a thin veneer beneath which lurked true, unconscious motives. Psychoanalytic interpretations of Freudian slips, dreams, neurotic symptoms, or literary texts could be employed as a parlour game in which the *real* hidden meanings were exposed. In the pre-Freudian world, consciousness was all; in the heyday of pop-Freudianism, unconscious was all.

In many currents of contemporary psychoanalytic thought, consciousness has made something of a comeback. Rather than a discardable veneer, conscious experience has been portrayed increasingly in a richly dialectical relationship with unconscious processes. Our "sense" of self is complexly related to disavowed selves; the story we tell ourselves about ourselves is complexly related to the stories we foreclose (Donnel Stern, 1997). The manifest does not merely cover over the latent; the surface is generated by underlying processes, out of awareness, and the depths are continually impacted upon and transformed by current experience. Thomas Ogden has used the practice of *Pentimento*—the painting over and changing of an earlier painting by a subsequent painting on the same canvas—to compare the Lacanian understanding of relationship between consciousness and unconsciousness with his own:

> the Lacanian project can be likened to an effort to see through the intervals or chips in the surface presentation of a painting over a painting. In contrast, ... [Ogden's] project can be conceived of in terms of the hermeneutic circle in which the original is contextualized by background and vice versa ... every part is related to, informs, and is informed by every other part. [1994, p. 29]

One impediment to a satisfying framework for thinking about agency has been the tendency to assume that agency is, in fact, just one sort of thing. We have many different theories of object relations, but they generally presume a singular agent in interaction with different objects, or attribute the same kind of agency to objects themselves. Most authors seem to be arguing about whether or not it is meaningful to think of human beings as agents. Some think it is; some think it is not. But I think we get a bit further if we consider the *kind* of agents we are talking about.

For example, some adherents of Freudian drive theory argue that Freud's concept of "drive" preserves a place for agency; drives are active: they *do* things. If we didn't have drives pushing us as agentic forces from within, we would be merely passive, responding to external social forces, shaped completely by others.

Yet, consider Fairbairn's revolutionary statement: "Libido is not pleasure-seeking but object-seeking." In what ways might an object-seeking agent be different from a pleasure-seeking agent? The pleasure principle, as presented by Freud, has an automaticity about it. Pleasure and pain were defined originally as simply quantitative decreases and increases in tensions within somatic tissue. Later, in trying to account for the problem of foreplay, Freud redefined pleasure as a rhythmicity of rises and decreases in tension. But throughout, Freud always defined pleasure in purely somatic, quantitative, objective terms. The pleasure-seeking agent does not make any decisions or choices about what to find pleasurable or what to commit himself to. Of course, the meaning of somatic experiences is determined by conscious and unconscious associations to somatic events. But whether something is pleasurable or not is a purely quantitative, somatic affair.

What is an object-seeking agent like? What do we seek objects *for*? Fairbairn has been criticized for being vague about this (e.g. Greenberg). There are places where Fairbairn seems to suggest that object-seeking is driven by oral dependency, but I think this is not the deepest or most interesting way to read Fairbairn. Fairbairn insists that we seek objects because it is our nature to do precisely that: our lungs breathe air, our eyes see light, our ears hear sounds, and our minds seek out other minds with which to interact. We are built that way, and, in one sense, we cannot choose to do otherwise. We seek the objects that are available in the ways they make themselves available. Fairbairn tells of a patient who dreams he is starving and confronted by poison pudding; he eats the pudding.

So, in one sense, Fairbairn's object-seeking agent, like Freud's pleasure-seeking agent, does not make decisions or commitments but does what she is compelled by her nature to do.[1]

But Fairbairn has more to say on this issue. The object-seeking agent takes what she can get, but her preferences are not indiscriminate. She is looking for something more specific, and what she is seeking is to love and to be loved. Implicit in Fairbairn's theory is the sort of intersubjective recognition Jessica Benjamin, drawing upon Hegel, has written about. Fairbairn's object-seeking agent is searching for an object that is a subject in her own right—a subject that can love and treasure love. Thus, implied in Fairbairn's theory of object relations is a theory of agents, different agents for different sorts of object relations.

When Fairbairn's object-seeker's first choice, a loving and loveable subject, is thwarted, he accepts what is available. In these psychopathological situations, Fairbairn has suggested two different ways through which agency becomes compromised: (1) in situations of extreme relational deprivation, the object-seeking agent becomes a cynical, sheer pleasure-seeker, as relatedness disintegrates into impulses; (2) as the object-seeking agent encounters a world of thoroughly bad objects, the sense of helplessness in the face of chaos or injustice is unbearable. Through what Fairbairn terms the moral defence, the object-seeking agent internalizes the badness inside himself, taking responsibility for it in order to control it. The moral defence preserves the illusion that a good object who could love him would be available if only he, himself, could be good and not bad. Through the moral defence, the object-seeking agent becomes a grandiose, guilty, illusion-bound agent.

Additionally, Fairbairn points out that object-seeking agents develop allegiances to their objects, even "bad" or unsatisfying objects. In fact, the allegiance to bad objects is, Fairbairn suggests, the deepest source of resistance to change in analysis. Of all Fairbairn's rich insights, I have always found this the most clinically useful and intriguing. Despite the fact that the object-seeking agent

---

[1] Similarly, in contemporary versions of Bowlby's attachment theory, there are no insecurely attached children, but only attachments to insecure objects.

had no choice but to internalize her bad objects, she becomes loy-
ally devoted to them. Despite their unsatisfying qualities, she has
come to be a person only through her relatedness to them. She has
become her objects, and, because of the quality Freud evocatively
termed the "adhesiveness of the libido", she can develop richer
forms of relatedness and enter into loving relations with other
objects only at the cost of the considerable psychic pain and grief
involved in giving them up.

Thus, unpacking some of the implications of Fairbairn's theory
of object relations with respect to agency leads to the conclusion
that it is a mistake to frame the question of agency in terms like: are
human beings agents of their own experience, yes or no? Rather, it
is more useful to differentiate various forms human agency takes
in the complex dialectics between consciousness and unconsciousness, nurturing and depriving care-givers, choices and necessities.

James Grotstein (1997b) has recently introduced a concept he
terms "autochthony", which sheds some interesting light on Fairbairn's clinical observations concerning both the allegiance to bad
objects and the moral defence. Grotstein suggests that there is a
fundamental sense in which the human mind assumes authorship
over all its experiences, good and bad, pleasurable and traumatic.
Grotstein does not regard autochthony as a defence against anxiety
or helplessness, like the moral defence, but rather as a basic operating principle of mind—like Freud's notion of the pleasure principle.

I find it interesting to think about Grotstein's notion of autochthony in connection with Hans Loewald's (1980) understanding of
what he terms "primary process" (and Bessel Van der Kolk's (1987)
recent work on the neurophysiology of attachment). Loewald suggests that both early in infancy and also throughout life at the most
basic level of organization, intense emotional experiences are not
sorted out in terms of boundaries between internal and external,
self and other. When intensely exciting things happen, both in
ecstasy and in horror, our brains are bathed in endorphins, and,
Loewald suggests, at the deepest levels of organization, those intense experiences becomes ours, become us, regardless of who did
what to whom on a higher, secondary process level of organization. Thus, victims of abuse tend to seek out situations that are

likely to recreate the abusive experiences as a form of self-regeneration and addiction. What was done to us becomes us, and in some sense what Fairbairn described as allegiances to bad objects are really allegiances to what has become oneself.

Thus, I am suggesting that there are many different forms of human agency:

— agency in Loewald's primary process organization: "I am what I have experienced";

— agency in Grotstein's principle of autochthony: "Because I am what I have experienced, I assume responsibility for and create what I experience";

— agency in Fairbairn's allegiance to bad objects: "I am devoted to painful experiences that keep my bad objects alive because they are the only objects I know and objectlessness is intolerable";

— the omnipotent, guilty agent of Fairbairn's moral defence warding off unbearable helplessness: "I am bad so I don't have to believe you are bad or crazy";

— the cynical, self-regulating agent: "I don't anticipate others being available to me for the sharing of pleasure and intimacy, so I carefully monitor my own sensations, hoarding my satisfactions and avoiding frustrations";

— and the cynical, other-regulating agent: "I don't anticipate others being available to me for the sharing of pleasure and intimacy, so I involve myself in controlling them and subjecting them to my own will."[2]

I find it useful to assume that none of us are singular agents of one specific type, but that all of us have different versions through which all of us *are* agents of all these types.

---

[2] In his important work on agency, Leslie Farber (1976) distinguishes between "will", a contextualized intentionality, and "willfulness" entailing illusory, omnipotent efforts at control of oneself and others. Roy Schafer's (1976) work on "action language" explores these same problems with the distinction between "action" and "excessively claimed action".

Clinical vignettes

The following two clinical vignettes illustrate some of the ways in which agency operates as a key dimension of object relations and analytic change.

Fred

"Fred" begins a session by expressing puzzlement at his own behaviour. Among the reasons for which he had entered psychoanalytic treatment a year earlier was the almost complete lack of sexual contact between him and his wife. He understood this as deriving largely from her fears of sex; she had been raped as a teenager and was quite fearful. She had little interest in sex for long stretches of time and always left it up to him to take the initiative. He experienced her response as a tepid compliance, and he had lost interest. Yet Fred was aware of deep constrictions in his own emotional life and felt that he might also play a part in their problems.

Over the course of the year's work, important issues had been explored, and there had been an opening up and deepening of the intimacy between Fred and his wife in several major respects. Yet sex remained virtually non-existent. The evening before his session, Fred's wife had made a tentative overture, which he had declined. He experienced her tentativeness as anti-erotic and off-putting—the very quality that had extinguished his desire. Yet when he thought about it afterward, he realized that her overture was probably a very difficult initiative on her part; he had declined what might have been a movement in the direction of precisely the sort of intimacy he had longed for.

Psychoanalytic inquiry is based upon the fundamental principle that our minds are extraordinarily complex. There is always much more going on, many more resonances and reverberating meanings, real and imaginary, past and present, than we can possibly be aware of. Yet, we are constantly making choices. These choices are made, necessarily, with only a very partial, often exceedingly dim, awareness, of their significance to us.

For a psychoanalyst, Fred's puzzlement about himself, his sense that he seemed to be operating at cross-purposes, was a precious development, a very satisfying outcome of a year's work. We might say that it was an opening into a sense of himself as decentred; he is not simply the rational, controlling agent of his own experience; there is more going on. And many of the sessions in the months that followed explored features of his experience that had bearing on his choice that night.

Fred declined his wife's overture because he was waiting for something else to happen—the emergence of a sexual display from her that would be dramatic, expressive, unmistakable, and bold. Her tentativeness betrayed her conflict, and he was fearful of responding to something that might soon vanish. What if he reconnected with the intense desire he had felt for her in the early days of their relationship? Could he bear the pain of losing their intimacy if she retreated once again? Could he control the rage that her possible future withdrawal might arouse in him? Her tentativeness signalled the absence of any guarantee against the riskiness, the endangerment he felt about his own desire and possible disappointment.

In another vein, her tentativeness resonated for Fred with his experience of his mother, who, during his childhood, oscillated between periods of vitality and exuberance and bouts of depression and withdrawal. He had become adaptively accustomed as a child to a wary, emotional distance from his mother. He had renounced the moments of exhilaration to protect himself from the searing loneliness he felt at her withdrawals. Fred had similarly accustomed himself to a renunciation of sex with his wife that had become familiar, almost comfortable. Despite his longings, he began to realize how fearful he was of shaking up that renunciatory equanimity.

What if Fred's wife actually had produced the kind of approach he longed for? What would that be like? Along that line of exploration, we discovered that Fred's experience of sex, even

at its best, was complex and conflicted. Sex at its most passionate felt "animalistic" and a bit sadistic. His most exciting lovers
were women for whom he had little respect and regard; he
tended to become devoted, as an asexual saviour, to women he
held in high regard. He experienced love as a worshipful con-
scientiousness; he experienced passion as a kind of reckless
exploitation. Fred began to realize that although he longed for a
fully expressive, unrestrained sexual intimacy with his wife, the
unresolved tension in his experience of love and desire made it
difficult for him to imagine how he could have such passionate
intimacy with her without also losing her.

Yet another key feature of what was at stake for Fred in his
rejection of his wife's gambit came to light several months later.
Fred's father had been orphaned as a teenager and had a stereo-
typical, almost caricatured masculine style, macho and with-
drawn. But the father's distant demeanour would crack on rare
occasions, often at extended family events when he had been
drinking. He would then speak tearfully about his fantasies of
an impossible reunion with his parents, and Fred had a deep
feeling of connection with him in a sense of isolation and longing he felt they both shared.

As invariably happens in psychoanalysis, key features of his
relationships with others began to appear in his relationship
with me. There was often quite a warm quality between the two
of us that I experienced as deepening over time, as we worked
through various issues related to trust and anxiety. However,
Fred found my professional approach to our work, which he
appreciated, also off-putting—as if I, like his father, were remote and hiding from him the emotional places in which I
really lived. And Fred began to search for fragments of information about what might be my secret pain, the longings I must
be hiding from him and everyone else. These imaginings of his,
some of which were more accurate than others, surfaced in our
work over the course of two years, when I began to notice
changing feelings in myself about them. Earlier, our exploration
of his fantasies about and perceptions of my hidden emotional
recesses felt vibrant and important to me. As my fondness for

Fred deepened, I began to find annoying his sense that what actually took place between us was less real than his imagined connection with my pain, which he was sure would never take place. So I began to point to the ways in which an imagined intimacy through private suffering served to undo real intimacy that might actually develop.

This exploration of a search for intimacy resulting in distancing between us proved very useful and, it soon became apparent, served as an analogue to the way Fred positioned himself *vis-à-vis* his wife. He loved his wife deeply and longed for a more open closeness, sexual and otherwise, with her. And he was certain, almost, that she also loved him deeply and experienced a similar, poignant longing. Such a longing was the most intense imaginable feeling for him, like the longing he glimpsed at rare moments in his father. We came to understand that Fred's experience of himself and his wife, both longing for each other in a perpetually frustrated state, was his ideal of the most intimate relatedness imaginable. Actual sex between them could only result in a falling off, a diminution of that exquisite, complementary longing that locked them together. Thus, he felt he would have much more to lose than to gain in reciprocating his wife's sexual gambit.

Any productive analysis generates endless ripples of motives and meanings that bear on nodal choice points. Psychodynamic interpretations are infinite. The question is: how do they bear on Fred's struggle for self-understanding and a more satisfying life? Where is *he* in the middle of all of this?

Fairbairn has contributed to helping us see that Fred, through his multiple object relations and the multiple versions of agency implicit in them, is actually in several different, conflictual places at the same time. Fred was a fearful, cynical, self-regulating agent, tamping down what he experienced as his own ravenous desire and lethal destructiveness; Fred was a devoted and loving agent, preserving his tie to both his mother in her depression and his father in his strangulated, secret longings; and Fred was an autochthonous agent, preserving the intensity of his own longings as the deepest, most precious thing about himself.

Charles

A second clinical example captures some of the complex factors involved for someone in the process of expanding the sort of agent he can experience himself as being.

"Charles" has been in analysis for several years. His relationships with women had become depressingly redundant. He found not being in a relationship intolerable, and he would become obsessed with the hunt for a girlfriend. He was adept at evoking women's interest in him and would easily become infatuated, particularly with someone somewhat remote or inaccessible. As the latest object of his desire became more interested in him, he would enter a thicket of dense ruminations about whether she was, in fact, the right woman for him, about whether he really excited by her and did love her. The more he ruminated, the less he felt and the more suffocated he became by the woman's feelings towards him. Towards the end of the cycle he longed for the escape that ending the relationship would provide, so that he could be free to hunt a variety of women once again. But almost as soon as he found himself unattached, he would begin to court a new commitment. He exemplified the sort of "in-and-out program" Fairbairn (1952a) and later Guntrip (1969) described in schizoid personalities.

Over the course of several years of analysis, the futility of this pattern became increasingly clear to Charles; he was able to remain for periods of time in situations where he could suspend his meta-level obsessions about whether he felt enough for the woman he was with to actually have more authentic feelings for her without breaking off. Currently, he had been with "Sarah" for almost a year, and with her he had experienced stretches of pleasurable experiences of some intimacy. She then confronted him with a dilemma. They were at the point in their relationship where, she felt, they should be saying to each other, "I love you." She had said it several times, and he seemed to have retracted. So she stopped saying it. Sarah, who struck me as a woman of considerable emotional maturity, was not interested in coercing protestations of love from Charles. But she felt that the fact that such verbal expressions of love were not forthcoming was not unimportant and probably put a ceiling on what was possible in their relationship.

Sarah's confrontation created something of a crisis for Charles, and he, and then he and I, spent quite a bit of time trying to sort out exactly what he *did* feel about her in different situations. There were times, he noticed, when "love is in the air". I became very intrigued about what this meant.

These moments, when love was in the air, often followed intense shared experiences, like engrossing conversations or exciting sex. It was an affective outcome of complex interactive sequences between them in which they were both active participants, both pre-symbolically, in the subtle choreography of successful emotional and sexual intimacies, and symbolically, in the conscious and unconscious ways in which they had come to understand each other and themselves in relation to each other. The love that was "in the air" was a feeling that was clearly an interactive product of the relatedness between them; but who, exactly, was feeling what?

The most familiar, easiest way for Charles to approach this question was to assume that Sarah, not he, felt the love; he felt *her* feeling love for him and therefore felt pressured to declare a love he did not really feel. But—we came to understand—that description did not really do justice to the situation. It was not easy for him to know what he felt because he felt so obliged to gratify and control what he imagined was her need for him. (He fantasized about taking a polygraph test to discern what, in fact, he did feel.) When he could free himself from his largely self-imposed pressure to say things he did not feel, he came to realize that he certainly did feel something for Sarah in these moments. But was it love? It had elements in it, as he struggled to sort them out, of warmth, dependency, gratitude, security, exhilaration. But is it love? *Does* the feeling of love come in a pre-packaged form, waiting to be correctly identified and named? Or does the naming itself make it into love (Spezzano, 1993)?

One could approach this situation via the concept of projective identification. Of course Charles loves Sarah, we might assume, but he is too anxious to allow himself that feeling. So he projects his love into her, experiences it coming from her, and controls it *in* her by distancing himself from her. Love is "in the air" because that it where Charles projects it. I believe there is some value in this formulation, but that it is also misleading. I came to feel that the love that Charles felt *in* Sarah was not just his projection; it was not just a fantasy of his affect residing in her. She also seemed, in fact, to be feeling love for him at those moments. The more we explored the situation, the less useful was the effort to choose between the view that the love "in the air" was *hers*, which he was afraid of, or *his*, which he evacuated outsides the boundaries of his experience of himself. We were speaking about affective experience that could exist only if it operated in both of them—an experience that, in fact, *requires* two participants to ignite and fuel. So, in an important sense, this feeling they have in relation to each other *is* "in the air"; it is not simply in either or both of them; it has a transpersonal quality and operates in the field that they comprise together, in the kind of shared affect that crosses the semi-permeable boundaries between self and others, agents and their objects.

Yet, there is an important difference in the ways in which Charles and Sarah are processing or organizing their affect. Sarah wanted to say, "I love you" and also wanted Charles to say this to her. The more Charles and I mulled over the implications of Sarah's wish, the clearer it became that saying "I love you" is not just a report on a pre-packaged feeling, but also a linguistic "performative". Saying "I love you" has, built into it, various other messages and actions. It says: "I like loving you" ... "I want to love you" ... "I accept and embrace my loving you" ... "I want to evoke an expression of what you might be feeling for me." Saying "I love you" entails the emergence of Charles as a different sort of agent, committed to engaging Sarah in a more fully developed intersubjective event. It is self-reflectively self-defining and calls for a recognizing response of one sort or another from the other. Becoming that sort of agent entailed for Charles a giving up of much more familiar versions of himself as a cynical, self- and other-controlling agent and, at a deeper level, a devoted agent, preserving his tie to his mother, who, he secretly suspected, wanted to preserve him for herself, in union with her own depressive longings.

The relationships among affect, behaviour and language are enormously complex and contextual. The conventional pressure to say "I love you" often *does* have a coercive, deadening impact on relationships. What was crucial for Charles was to decide whether or not he wanted to enhance the vitality of his relationship with Sarah and to become the sort of agent who could do so, with all the attendant risks; if he did, he needed to find a way, with or without language, to do so. In this sense, Sarah was right. Saying "I love you" or something equivalent to each other is not just a report on what has happened; it contributes to determining what sort of objects they can become for each other, what sort of agents they can become *vis-à-vis* themselves, and whether their relationship will deepen or whether certain paths of development will be foreclosed.

* * *

In the traditional psychoanalytic literature on what is technically called the "therapeutic action" of psychoanalysis, or "how it is supposed to work", the analyst's interpretation of unconscious conflicts generates "insight", which undoes repression of unconscious motives that are causing the trouble in the first place. If the patient is not changing, then, the traditional analyst can safely assume, the correct interpretations have not been arrived at. But there is more to it than that.

Analyst and analysand struggle to collaborate on a narrative of the patient's experience and their experiences together. This must be a narrative that explores, in an often painstaking fashion, the complex reasons for the analysand's choices—their motives—yet at the same time holds the sense of the analysand making choices in the context of conscious and unconscious meanings. We exercise our will, at best, embedded in situations, the meanings of which we often only dimly grasp or, sometimes, are quite oblivious of. Much of the craft of the psychoanalyst lies in the collaborative discovery with the analysand of a voice that traces the operations of the will, through its varieties of agency, which, at the same time, entails both the assumption of responsibility and the avoidance of moralistic blaming.

So, the problem for both Fred and Charles is not simply to arrive at the perpetually illusive ultimate interpretation of their motives, but to find a way to enable them to connect up with a sense of themselves, to experience themselves, as the agent of their motives, alternatively willing them or else wilfully insisting upon them (and then disclaiming) them. The ultimate yield of good analytic work is less a particular understanding, the correct interpretation, than the emergence of a self-reflective form of experience that breaks through what Fairbairn described as the closed circle of bad object relations and sustains the tension between agency and unconscious motivation, in which willing perpetually shapes often opaque and fragmentary psychic processes into the complex, often surprising, lives we lead.

Fairbairn's object relations theory helps us understand that we are neither singular autonomous agents consciously running our lives, nor passive foils for unconscious impulses seeking discharge. Rather, we are multiplicitous, object-seeking agents of various types, with deep allegiances to significant others and the forms of relatedness through which we were able to find and connect to them and to become ourselves. The more we understand of our allegiances to those others and to the versions of ourselves we became to maintain them, the more freedom we find to overcome those constraints and to enrich our experiences of self and self with others.

REFERENCES

Abraham, K. (1911). Notes on the psycho-analytical investigation and treatment of manic-depressive insanity and allied conditions. In: *Selected Papers on Psycho-Analysis*. London: Hogarth Press, 1948.

Abraham, K. (1924). A short study of the development of the libido. In: *Selected Papers on Psycho-Analysis* (pp. 418–501). London: Hogarth Press, 1948.

Anzieu, D. (1984). *The Group and the Unconscious*. London & Boston, MA: Routledge & Kegan Paul.

Anzieu, D. (1990). Lettre aux rapporteurs. *Revue Française de Psychanalyse, 54*: 1592.

Bakhtin, M. (1979). *Esthétique de la Création Verbale* (French translation, 1984). Paris: Ed. Gallimard.

Balint, M. (1968). *The Basic Fault*. Tavistock Publications.

Bauman, Z. (1987). *Legislators and Interpreters: On Modernity and the Intellectuals*. Cambridge: Polity Press & Blackwell.

Bauman, Z. (1991). *Modernity and Ambivalence*. Cambridge: Polity Press & Blackwell.

Bégoin, J. (1987). Névrose et traumatisme. *Revue Française de Psychanalyse, 51*, 999–1019.

Benjamin, W. (1934). "The Author as Producer". Lecture given at the Institute for the Study of Fascism, Paris. In: F. Franscina & C.

232   REFERENCES

Harrison (Eds.), *Modern Art and Modernism* (pp. 213–216). London: Harper Row & Open University, 1982.

Benjamin, W. (1936). The work of art in the age of mechanical reproduction. *Zeitschrift für Sozialforschung, 1*. In: F. Franscina & C. Harrison (Eds.), *Modern Art and Modernism* (pp. 217–220). London: Harper Row & Open University, 1982.

Berger, P., & Luckmann, T. (1967). *The Social Construction of Reality: A Treatise in the Sociology of Knowledge*. Harmondsworth, U.K., & New York: Penguin Books, 1985.

Bergeret, J. (1994). *La violence et la vie: La face cachée de l'oedipe*. Paris: Payot.

Bergson, H. (1889). *Time and Free Will: An Essay on the Immediateness of Consciousness*, trans. F. L. Pogson. London: Sonneschein (Swan), 1910.

Berlin, I. (1969). Two concepts of liberty. In *Four Essays on Liberty*. Oxford: Oxford University Press.

Bettelheim, B. (1982). Reflections: Freud and the soul. *The New Yorker*, 1 March, pp. 59–93.

Beveridge, C., & Turnbull, R. (1989). *The Eclipse of Scottish Culture*. Edinburgh: Polygon.

Bick, E. (1968). The experience of the skin in early object relations. *International Journal of Psycho-Analysis, 49*: 484–486.

Bick, E. (1986). Further considerations on the function of the skin in early object relations. *British Journal of Psychotherapy, 2*: 292–299.

Bion, W. R. (1957). Differentiation of the psychotic from the non-psychotic personalities. *International Journal of Psycho-Analysis, 38*: 266–275.

Bion, W. R. (1958). On arrogance. *International Journal of Psycho-Analysis, 39* (2): 144–146. Also in *Second Thoughts* (pp. 86–92). London: Heinemann, 1967.

Bion, W. R. (1959). Attacks on linking. In: *Second Thoughts* (pp. 93–109). London: Heinemann, 1967.

Bion, W. R. (1961). *Experiences in Groups*. New York: Basic Books.

Bion, W. R. (1962). *Learning From Experience*. London: Heinemann.

Bion, W. R. (1963). *Elements of Psycho-Analysis*. London: Heinemann.

Bion, W. R. (1965). *Transformations*. London: Heinemann.

Bion, W. R. (1970). *Attention and Interpretation*. London: Tavistock Publications.

Bion, W. R. (1992). *Cogitations*. London: Karnac Books.

Birtles, E. F. (1998). Developing connections: Fairbairn's philosophic contributions. In N. J. Skolnick & D. Scharff (Eds.), *Fairbairn Then and Now*. Hillsdale, NJ: Analytic Press.

Birtles, E. F., Fairbairn, E., & Scharff, D. (Eds.) (1994). Introduction to Part V. In: W. R. D. Fairbairn, *From Instinct to Self: Selected Papers of W. R. D. Fairbairn, Vol. 2*, ed. by E. F. Birtles & D. E. Scharff. London: Jason Aronson.

Birtles, E. F., & Scharff, D. E. (Eds.) (1994). *From Instinct to Self: Selected Papers of W. R. D. Fairbairn, Vol. 2*. Northvale, NJ, & London: Jason Aronson.

Bohm, D. (1980). *Wholeness and the Implicate Order*. London & Boston, MA: Routledge & Kegan Paul.

Bowlby, J. (1969). *Attachment and Loss, Vol. 1: Attachment*. New York: Basic Books.

Bowlby, J. (1973). *Attachment and Loss, Vol. 2: Separation Anxiety and Anger*. New York: Basic Books.

Bowlby, J. (1980). *Attachment and Loss, Vol. 3: Loss: Sadness and Depression*. New York: Basic Books.

Braunschweig, D., & Fain, M. (1971). *Eros et Anteros*. Paris: Petite Bibliothèque Payot.

Braunschweig, D., & Fain, M. (1975). *La Nuit, le Jour*. Paris: Presses Universitaires de France.

Brenman, E. (1985). Hysteria. *International Journal of Psycho-Analysis*, 66: 423–432.

Briggs, J. (1992). *Fractals: The Patterns of Chaos*. New York: Touchstone.

Brown, L. J. (1987). Borderline personality organization and the transition to the depressive position. In: J. S. Grotstein, J. F. Solomon, & J. A. Lang (Eds.), *The Borderline Patient: Emerging Concepts in Diagnosis, Psychodynamics, and Treatment, Vol. 1* (pp. 147–180). Hillsdale, NJ: Analytic Press.

Butler, J. (1990). *Gender Trouble: Feminism and the Subversion of Identity*. New York & London: Routledge.

Campbell, J. (1990). *The Hero with a Thousand Faces* (second edition). Princeton, NJ: Princeton University Press.

Chasseguet-Smirgel, J. (1986). *Sexuality and Mind: The Role of the Father and the Mother in the Psyche*. New York: New York University Press.

Chasseguet-Smirgel, J. (1989). *Éthique et esthétique de la perversion*. Seyssel, Champ Vallon: L'or d'Atalante.

Clarkin, J., Yeomans, F., & Kernberg, O. (1999). *Psychotherapy for Borderline Personality*. New York: John Wiley.

Conford, P. (1972). John Macmurray: a neglected philosopher. *Radical Philosophy* (Parts 2 & 3): 16–20.

Cooper, D. A. (1997). *God Is a Verb: The Practice of Mystical Judaism*. New York: Riverhead Books.

Cosnier, J., Grosjean, M., & Lacoste, M. (1994). *Soins et communication, approches interactionnistes des relations de soin*, Lyon: Presses Universitaires de Lyon.

Damasio, A. (1994). *Descartes's Error: Emotion, Reason and the Human Brain*. New York: Grosset/Putnam.

Deleuze, G., & Guatarry, F. (1980). *Mille Plateaux*. Paris: Ed. de Minuit.

Dicks, H. V. (1967). *Marital Tensions*. New York: Basic Books.

Dostoevsky, F. (1864). *Notes from Underground* (trans. Jessie Cousson). Harmondsworth, U.K., & New York: Penguin Books, 1972.

Einstein, A. (1933). On the method of theoretical physics. In: Coley, N. C., & Hall, V. M. (Eds.), *Darwin to Einstein: Primary Sources on Science & Belief* (pp. 143–148). Harlow, U.K., & New York: Longman & The Open University, 1980.

Eisold, K. (1994). The intolerance of diversity in pschoanalytic institutes. *International Journal of Psycho-Analysis, 75*: 785–800.

Ellenberger, H. F. (1970). *The Discovery of the Unconscious. The History and Evolution of Dynamic Psychiatry*. New York: Basic Books.

Erikson, E. H. (1959). *Identity and the Life Cycle Psychological Issues*. New York: International Universities Press.

Fairbairn, W. R. D. (1929a). Dissociation and repression. In: E. F. Birtles & D. E. Scharff (Eds.), *From Instinct to Self: Selected Papers of W. R. D. Fairbairn, Vol. 2. Applications and Early Contributions* (pp. 13–79). Northvale, NJ: Jason Aronson, 1994.

Fairbairn, W. R. D. (1929b). The superego. In: E. F. Birtles & D. E. Scharff (Eds.), *From Instinct to Self: Selected Papers of W. R. D. Fairbairn, Vol. 2. Applications and Early Contributions*. Northvale, NJ: Jason Aronson, 1994.

Fairbairn, W. R. D. (1930). Libido theory re-examined. In: E. F. Birtles & D. E. Scharff (Eds.), *From Instinct to Self: Selected Papers of W. R. D. Fairbairn, Vol. 2. Applications and Early Contributions* (pp. 115–156). Northvale, NJ: Jason Aronson, 1994.

Fairbairn, W. R. D. (1931a). Features in the analysis of a patient with a physical genital abnormality. In: *Psychoanalytic Studies of the Personality* (pp. 197–222). London: Tavistock, 1952.

Fairbairn, W. R. D. (1931b). Psychoanalysis and the teacher. In: E. F. Birtles & D. E. Scharff (Eds.), *From Instinct to Self: Selected Papers of W. R. D. Fairbairn, Vol. 2. Applications and Early Contributions* (pp. 350–362). Northvale, NJ: Jason Aronson, 1994.

Fairbairn, W. R. D. (1937). Arms and the child. In: E. F. Birtles & D. E. Scharff (Eds.), *From Instinct to Self: Selected Papers of W. R. D. Fairbairn, Vol. 2. Applications and Early Contributions* (pp. 327–332). Northvale, NJ: Jason Aronson, 1994.

Fairbairn, W. R. D. (1938a). Prolegomena to a psychology of art. In: E.

F. Birtles & D. E. Scharff (Eds.), *From Instinct to Self: Selected Papers of W. R. D. Fairbairn*. London: Jason Aronson, 1994.

Fairbairn, W. R. D. (1938b). The ultimate basis of aesthetic experience. In: E. F. Birtles & D. E. Scharff (Eds.), *From Instinct to Self: Selected Papers of W. R. D. Fairbairn*. London: Jason Aronson, 1994.

Fairbairn, W. R. D. (1940). Schizoid factors in the personality. In *Psychoanalytic Studies of the Personality* (pp. 3–27). London: Tavistock, 1952. Also in: *An Object-Relations Theory of the Personality* (pp. 3–27). New York: Basic Books, 1954.

Fairbairn, W. R. D. (1941). A revised psychopathology of the psychoses and psychoneuroses. *International Journal of Psycho-Analysis*, 22 (2 & 3): 250–279. Reprinted in: *Psychoanalytic Studies of the Personality* (pp. 28–58). London: Tavistock, 1952.

Fairbairn, W. R. D. (1942). Letter undated 1942 to Dr Marjorie Brierley. In: E. F. Birtles & D. E. Scharff (Eds.), *From Instinct to Self: Selected Papers of W. R. D. Fairbairn, Vol. 2. Applications and Early Contributions* (pp. 443–447). Northvale, NJ: Jason Aronson, 1994.

Fairbairn, W. R. D. (1943). The repression and return of bad objects (with special reference to war neuroses). *British Journal of Medical Psychology, 19*: 327–341. Reprinted in: *Psychoanalytic Studies of the Personality* (pp. 59–81). London: Tavistock, Routledge & Kegan Paul, 1952.

Fairbairn, W. R. D. (1944). Endopsychic structure considered in terms of object-relationships. In: *Psychoanalytic Studies of the Personality* (pp. 82–136). London: Tavistock, 1952.

Fairbairn, W. R. D. (1946). Object-relationships in dynamic structure. *International Journal of Psycho-Analysis, 27*: 30–37. Also in: *Psychoanalytic Studies of the Personality* (pp. 137–151). London: Tavistock, 1952.

Fairbairn, W. R. D. (1949). Steps in the development of an object-relations theory of the personality. *British Journal of Psychology, 28* (1 & 2). Also in: *Psychoanalytic Studies of the Personality* (pp. 152–161). London & Boston: Routledge & Kegan Paul, 1952.

Fairbairn, W. R. D. (1951). A synopsis of the development of the authors views regarding the structure of the personality. In: *Psychoanalytic Studies of the Personality* (pp. 162–182). London: Tavistock, 1952.

Fairbairn, W. R. D. (1952a). *Psychoanalytic Studies of the Personality* (Intro. D. E. Scharff & E. F. Birtles). London: Tavistock Publications.

Fairbairn, W. R. D. (1952b). Theoretical and experimental aspects of psychoanalysis. In: D. Scharff & E. F. Birtles (Eds.), *From Instinct to*

Self: Selected Papers of W. R. D. Fairbairn, Vol. 1: Clinical and Theoretical Papers (pp. 103–110). Northvale, NJ: Jason Aronson, 1994.

Fairbairn, W. R. D. (1954a). The nature of hysterical states. In: D. Scharff & E. F. Birtles (Eds.), *From Instinct to Self: Selected Papers of W. R. D. Fairbairn, Vol. 1: Clinical and Theoretical Papers* (pp. 13–40). Northvale, NJ: Jason Aronson, 1994.

Fairbairn, W. R. D. (1954b). *An Object Relations Theory of the Personality.* New York: Basic Books.

Fairbairn, W. R. D. (1954c). Observations of the nature of hysterical states. *British Journal of Medical Psychology, 27*, 105–125.

Fairbairn, W. R. D. (1955). Observations in defence of the object relations of the personality. In: D. Scharff & E. F. Birtles (Eds.), *From Instinct to Self: Selected Papers of W. R. D. Fairbairn, Vol. 1: Clinical and Theoretical Papers* (pp. 111–128). Northvale, NJ: Jason Aronson, 1994.

Fairbairn, W. R. D. (1956). Reevaluating some basic concepts. In D. Scharff & E. F. Birtles (Eds.), *From Instinct to Self: Selected Papers of W. R. D. Fairbairn, Vol. 1: Clinical and Theoretical Papers.* London: Jason Aronson, 1994.

Fairbairn, W. R. D. (1957). Freud, the psycho-analytical method and mental health. *British Journal of Medical Psychology, 30*: 53–62.

Fairbairn, W. R. D. (1958). On the nature and aims of psychoanalytical treatment. *International Journal of Psycho-Analysis, 39*: 374–383. Reprinted in: D. Scharff & E. F. Birtles (Eds.), *From Instinct to Self: Selected Papers of W. R. D. Fairbairn, Vol. 1: Clinical and Theoretical Papers* (pp. 74–92). Northvale, NJ: Jason Aronson, 1994.

Fairbairn, W. R. D. (1963). An object relations theory of the personality. In: D. Scharff & E. F. Birtles (Eds.), *From Instinct to Self: Selected Papers of W. R. D. Fairbairn, Vol. 1: Clinical and Theoretical Papers* (pp. 155–156). Northvale, NJ: Jason Aronson, 1994.

Fairbairn, W. R. D. (1981). *Estudos psicanalíticos da personalidade.* Lisbon: Editorial Vega [Portuguese translation of *Psychoanalytic Studies of Personality.* London: Tavistock Publications, 1952].

Fairbairn, W. R. D. (1994a). *From Instinct to Self: Selected Papers of W. R. D. Fairbairn, Vol. 1: Clinical and Theoretical Papers,* ed. by D. E. Scharff & E. F. Birtles. Northvale, NJ: Jason Aronson.

Fairbairn, W. R. D. (1994b). *From Instinct to Self: Selected Papers of W. R. D. Fairbairn, Vol. 2: Applications and Early Contributions,* ed. by E. F. Birtles & D. E. Scharff. Northvale, NJ: Jason Aronson.

Fairbairn, W. R. D. (1998). *Études psychoanalytique de la personalité.* Paris: Ed Dre monde inteme. [French translation of *Psychoanalytic Studies of the Personality.* London: Tavistock Publications, 1952].

Farber, L. (1976). *Lying, Despair, Jealousy, Envy, Sex, Suicide, Drugs, and the Good Life*. New York: Basic Books.

Ferenczi, S. (1909). Transfert et introjection. In: *Psychanalyse I, Œuvres complètes Tome I : 1908–1912*. Paris: Payot, 1982.

Ferenczi, S. (1933). Confusion of tongues between adults and the child. In: *Final Contributions of the Problems and Methods of Psychoanalysis* (pp. 156–167). London: Hogarth Press, 1955.

Foucault, M. (1969). *L'Archéologie du Savoir*. Paris: Gallimard. [English translation: *The Archeology of Knowledge*. Washington, D.C.: Irvington, 1972.

Freud, S. (1892–93). A case of successful treatment by hypnotism. *SE*, 1.

Freud, S. (1895d) (with Breuer, J.). *Studies on Hysteria. S.E., 2*.

Freud, S. (1900a). *The Interpretation of Dreams. S.E., 5*.

Freud, S. (1905e [1901]). Fragment of an analysis of a case of hysteria. *S.E., 7*.

Freud, S. (1908a). Hysterical phantasies and their relation to bisexuality. *S.E., 7*.

Freud, S. (1910c). *Leonardo da Vinci and a Memory of His Childhood. S.E., 11*.

Freud, S. (1911c [1910]). Psycho-analytic notes upon an autobiographical account of a case of paranoia (Dementia Paranoides). *S.E., 12*.

Freud, S. (1914c). On narcissism: an introduction. *S.E., 14*.

Freud, S. (1914g). Remembering, repeating, and working-through. (Further recommendations on the technique of psycho-analysis, II). *S.E., 12* (pp. 145–156).

Freud, S. (1915). Letter to Abraham, 4 May 1915. In: *The Complete Correspondence of Sigmund Freud and Karl Abraham 1907–1925*, ed. by E. Falzeder. London: Karnac, 2002.

Freud, S. (1915d). Repression. *S.E., 14* (pp 143–158).

Freud, S. (1917e [1915]). Mourning and melancholia. *S.E., 14* (pp 237–260).

Freud, S. (1921c). *Group Psychology and the Analysis of the Ego. S.E., 18*.

Freud, S. (1923b). *The Ego and The Id. S.E., 19* (pp. 13–66).

Freud, S. (1926e). *The Question of Lay Analysis. S.E., 20* (pp. 183–258).

Freud, S. (1927e). Fetishism. *S.E., 21* (pp 149–158).

Freud, S. (1931b). Female sexuality. *S.E., 21*.

Freud, S. (1936a). Letter to Romain Rolland: a disturbance of memory on the Acropolis. *S.E., 22*.

Freud, S. (1937c). Analysis terminable and interminable. *S.E., 23* (pp. 209–253).

Freud, S. (1940a [1938]). *An Outline of Psycho-Analysis. S.E., 23*.

Freud, S. (1940e [1938]). Splitting of the ego in the process of defense. *S.E., 23* (pp. 271–278). London: Hogarth Press, 1964.

Freud, S. (1950a [1887–1902]). *The Origins of Psycho-Analysis. S.E., 1.*

Freud, S. (1950 [1892–1899]). Extracts from the Fliess Papers (letter to Fliess, 27 October 1897). *S.E., 1.*

Freud, S. (1966/1920). Lettre du 19 octobre 1920 à Stefan Zweig. *Correspondance 1873–1939*, trans. A. Berman & J.-P. Grossein. Paris: NRF Gallimard, Connaissance de l'inconscient.

Freud, S., & Abraham, K. (2002). *The Complete Correspondence of Sigmund Freud and Karl Abraham, 1907–1925.* London: Karnac.

Galatzer-Levy, R. (1995). Psychoanalysis and chaos theory. *Journal of the American Psychoanalytic Association, 43*: 1095–1113.

Genet, J. (1988). *O estúdio de Alberto Giacometti.* Lisbon: Assirio e Alvim.

Gleick J. (1987). *Chaos: Making a New Science.* New York: Viking Penguin.

Green, A. (1983). The dead mother. In: *On Private Madness* (pp. 142–173). London: Karnac, 1986.

Green, A. (1993). *The Work of the Negative*, trans. A Weller. London: Free Association Books, 1999.

Green, A. (1999). *The Work of the Negative.* London & New York: Free Association Books.

Greenberg, C. (1965). Modernist painting. In: *Modern Art and Modernism: A Critical Anthology*, ed. by F. Franscina & C. Harrison. London: Harper Row & Open University.

Groddeck, G. (1923). *The Book of the It.* New York: International Universities Press, 1976.

Grotstein, J. (1977a). The psychoanalytic concept of schizophrenia: I: The dilemma. *International Journal of Psycho-Analysis, 58*: 403–425.

Grotstein, J. (1977b). The psychoanalytic concept of schizophrenia: II: Reconciliation. *International Journal of Psycho-Analysis, 58*: 427–452.

Grotstein, J. (1981). *Splitting and Projective Identification.* New York: Jason Aronson.

Grotstein, J. (1990a). The "black hole" as the basic psychotic experience: Some newer psychoanalytic and neuroscience perspectives on psychosis. *Journal of the American Academy of Psychoanalysis, 18* (1): 29–46.

Grotstein, J. (1990b). Nothingness, meaninglessness, chaos and the "black hole": 1. The importance of nothingness, meaninglessness, and chaos in psychoanalysis. *Contemporary Psychoanalysis, 26* (2): 257–290.

Grotstein, J. (1990c). Nothingness, meaninglessness, chaos, and the "black hole": 2. The black hole. *Contemporary Psychoanalysis, 26* (3): 377–407.

Grotstein, J. (1991). Nothingness, meaninglessness, chaos, and the "black hole". 3. Self regulation and the background presence of primary identification. *Contemporary Psychoanalysis, 27* (1): 1–33.

Grotstein, J. (1993). A reappraisal of W. R. D. Fairbairn. *The Journal of the Menninger Clinic, 57* (4): 421–449.

Grotstein, J. (1994a). Notes on Fairbairn's metapsychology. In: J. Grotstein & D. Rinsley (Eds.), *Fairbairn and the Origins of Object Relations* (pp. 112–148). New York: Guilford Publications.

Grotstein, J. (1994b). Endopsychic structures and the cartography of the internal world: Six endopsychic characters in search of an author. In: J. Grotstein & D. Rinsley (Eds.), *Fairbairn and the Origins of Object Relations* (pp. 174–194). New York: Guilford Publications.

Grotstein, J. (1995a). Orphans of the "real": I. Some modern and post-modern perspectives on the neurobiological and psychosocial dimensions of psychosis and primitive mental disorders. *Bulletin of the Menninger Clinic, 59*: 287–311.

Grotstein, J. (1995b). Orphans of the "real": II. The future of object relations theory in the treatment of psychoses and other primitive mental disorders. *Bulletin of the Menninger Clinic, 59*: 312–332.

Grotstein, J. (1995c). Object relations theory. In: E. Nersessian & F. Kopff (Eds.), *Textbook of Psychoanalysis* (pp. 89–126). Washington D.C.: American Psychiatric Press.

Grotstein, J. (1996a). Why Oedipus and not Christ? The importance of "innocence", "original sin", and human sacrifice in psychoanalytic theory and practice. 1. The crucifixion and the Pietà, and the trans-ference/counter-transference neurosis/psychosis. *American Journal of Psychoanalysis, 57* (3): 193–219.

Grotstein, J. (1996b). Why Oedipus and not Christ? The importance of "innocence", "original sin", and human sacrifice in psychoanalytic theory and practice. 2. A selective re-reading of the myth of Oedipus and of the synoptic gospels. *American Journal of Psychoanalysis, 57* (4): 317–335.

Grotstein, J. (1997a). "The sins of the fathers" . . .: Human sacrifice and the inter- and trans-generational neurosis/psychosis. *International Journal of Psychotherapy, 2* (1).

Grotstein, J. (1997b). Integrating one-person and two-person psychologies: Autochthony and alterity in counterpoint. *Psychoanalytic Quarterly, 66*: 403–430.

Grotstein, J. (1997c). "Internal objects" or "chimerical monsters?": The demonic "third forms" of the internal world. *Journal of Analytical Psychology, 42:* 47–80.

Grotstein, J. (1997d). Klein's archaic Oedipus complex and its possible relationship to the myth of the labyrinth notes on the origin of courage. *Journal of Analytical Psychology, 42:* 585–611.

Grotstein, J. (1998). A comparison of Fairbairn's endopsychic structure and Klein's internal world. In: N. Skolnick & D. Scharff (Eds.), *Fairbairn's Contribution* (pp. 71–97). Hillsdale, NJ: Analytic Press.

Grotstein, J. (2000). *Who Is The Dreamer Who Dreams the Dream?: A Study of Psychic Presences.* Hillsdale, NJ: Analytic Press.

Grotstein, J., & Rinsley, D. R. (Eds). (1994). *Fairbairn and the Origins of Object Relations.* New York: Guilford.

Guntrip, H. S. J. (1969). *Schizoid Phenomena, Object Relations and the Self.* New York: International Universities Press.

Guntrip, H. S. J. (1975). Analysis with Fairbairn and Winnicott (How complete a result does psychoanalytic therapy achieve?). *International Journal of Psychoanalysis, 2.*

Hamilton, V. (1996). *The Analyst's Preconscious.* Hillsdale, NJ: Analytic Press.

Hartmann, H. (1939). *Ego Psychology and the Problem of Adaptation* (tr. by David Rapoport). New York: International Universities Press, 1958.

Heard, D., & Lake, B. (1997). *The Challenge of Attachment for Caregiving.* London: Routledge.

Hegel, G. W. F. (1817). *The Logic of Hegel* (trans. from *The Encyclopaedia of the Philosophical Sciences* by William Wallace). Oxford: Clarendon Press, 1874.

Heidegger, M. (1927). *Being and Time* (trans. by J. Macquarrie & E. Robinson). San Francisco: Harper San Francisco/HarperCollins, 1962.

Henley, W. E. (1903). "Invictus". In: L. Untemeyer (Ed.), *Modern British Poetry, Vol. 3.* New York: New Bartleby Library, 1999.

Hollande, C. (1973). A propos de l'identification hystérique, *Revue Française de Psychanalyse, 37:* 323–330.

Isaacs, S. (1948). The nature and function of phantasy. *International Journal of Psycho-Analysis, 29:* 73–97. Reprinted in: M. Klein, P. Heimann, S. Isaacs, & J. Riviere (Eds.), *Developments in Psychoanalysis.* London: Hogarth Press, 1952.

Jacobson, E. (1954). The self and the object world. *Psychoanalytic Study of the Child, 9:* 75–127. New York: International Universities Press.

Jacobson, E. (1964). *The Self and the Object World.* New York: International Universities Press.

Jouvet, M. (1992). *Le sommeil et le rêve*. Paris: Odile Jacob.

Kanzer, M. (1969). Sigmund and Alexander Freud on the Acropolis, *American Imago*, 26: 324–354.

Kaufmann, W. (1975). *Existentialism: From Dostoevsky to Sartre*. New York & Scarborough Ontario: New American Library, Times Mirror.

Kernberg, O. (1980). *Internal World and External Reality*. Nortvale, NY: Jason Aronson.

Kernberg, O. F. (1984). *Severe Personality Disorders: Psychotherapeutic Strategies*. New Haven, CT: Yale University Press.

Kernberg, O. F. (1992). *Aggression in Personality Disorders and Perversions*. New Haven, CT: Yale University Press.

Kernberg, O. F. (1994). Aggression, trauma, and hatred in the treatment of borderline patients. In: I. Share (Ed.), *Borderline Personality Disorder: The Psychiatric Clinics of North America, 17*, (4): 701–714). Philadelphia: Saunders.

Kernberg, O. F. (2000). *Object Relations, Affects, and Drives: Toward A New Synthesis*. Unpublished manuscript.

Kernberg, O., & D. Scharff (1998). Fairbairn's contribution: An interview with Otto Kernberg. In N. J. Skolnick and D. Scharff (Eds.), *Fairbairn Then and Now*. Hillsdale, NJ: Analytic Press, 1998.

Khan, M. (1981). *The Privacy of the Self*. London: Hogarth Press & Institute of Psychoanalysis.

Klein, M. (1928). Early stages of the oedipus conflict. In *Contributions to Psycho-Analysis, 1921–1945* (pp. 202–214). London: Hogarth Press, 1950.

Klein, M. (1929). Infantile anxiety situations reflected in a work of art and in the creative impulse. In *International Journal of Psycho-Analysis, 10*. Reprinted in: *Contributions to Psychoanalysis*. London: Hogarth Press, 1948.

Klein, M. (1929). Situations of infant anxiety in a work of art. In: *Contributions to Psychoanalysis*. London: Hogarth Press, 1948.

Klein, M. (1935). A contribution to the psychogenesis of manic-depressive states. In: *Contributions to Psycho-Analysis, 1921–1945* (pp. 282–310). London: Hogarth Press, 1948.

Klein, M. (1940). Mourning and its relation to manic-depressive states. In: *Contributions to Psycho-Analysis, 1921–1945* (pp. 311–338). London: Hogarth Press, 1948.

Klein, M. (1946). Notes on some schizoid mechanisms. In: J. Riviere, P. Heimann, S. Isaacs, & J. Riviere (Eds.), *Developments of Psycho-Analysis* (pp. 292–320). M. Klein, Ed. J. Riviere. London: Hogarth Press, 1952.

Klein, M. (1950). On the criteria for the termination of a psychoanalysis. *International Journal of Psycho-Analysis, 31*: 78–80.

Klein, M. (1952a). Discussion of the mutual influences in the development of ego and id. *Psychoanalytic Study of the Child, 7*: 51–68. New York: International Universities Press.

Klein, M. (1952b). Some theoretical conclusions regarding the emotional life of the infant. In: J. Riviere (Ed.), *Developments in Psycho-Analysis* (pp. 198–236). London: Hogarth Press, 1952.

Klein, M. (1957). *Envy and Gratitude*. New York: Basic Books.

Kuhn, T. S. (1970). *The Structure of Scientific Revolutions* (second edition). *International Encyclopedia of Unified Science*. Chicago, IL: Chicago University Press.

Laplanche, J. (1984a). La pulsion de mort dans la théorie de la pulsion sexuelle. In: *La révolution copernicienne inachevée, Travaux 1967–1992*. Paris: Aubier, 1992.

Laplanche, J. (1984b). La pulsion et son objet—source in *La révolution copernicienne inachevée*. In: *La révolution copernicienne inachevée, Travaux 1967–1992*. Paris: Aubier, 1992.

Laplanche, J. (1987). *Nouveaux fondements pour la psychanalyse*. Paris: Presses Universitaires de France.

Laplanche, J. (1989). *New Foundations for Psychoanalysis*. Oxford & New York: Basil Blackwell.

Laplanche, J. (1992). *Seduction, Translation and the Drives*. London: Institute of Contemporary Arts.

Laplanche, J. (1993). *Le fourvoiement biologisant de la sexualité chez Freud*, Paris: Collection Les empêcheurs de penser en rond, Paris Ed. Synthélabo.

Lechte, J. (1994). *Fifty Key Contemporary Thinkers: From Structuralism to Postmodernism*. London & New York: Routledge.

Levine, S. Z. (1998). Alter egos—Close encounters of the paranoid kind, W. R. D. Fairbairn, Salvador Dali and Me. In: N. Skolnick & D. Scharff (Eds.), *Fairbairn Then and Now*. London: Analytic Press.

Lewin, B. D. (1946). Sleep, the mouth and the dream screen. *Psychoanalytical Quarterly, 15*: 419.

Lichtenstein, H. (1977). *The Dilemma of Human Identity*. New York. Jason Aronson.

Loewald, H. W. (1980). *Papers on Psychoanalysis*. New Haven, CT: Yale University Press.

Lubtchansky, J. (1973). Le point de vue économique dans l'hystérie à partir de la théorie du traumatisme dans l'œuvre de Freud. *Revue Française de Psychanalyse, 37*, 373–405.

MacIntyre, A. (1985). *After Virtue*. London: Duckworth, 1999.

Mack Brunswick, R. (1940). The pre-oedipal phase in the development of the libido. *Psychoanalytic Quarterly*, 9: 293–319.

Macmurray, J. (1935). *Reason and Emotion* (Intro. by John Costello). London: Faber & Faber, 1992.

Macmurray, J. (1957). *The Self as Agent*. London: Faber & Faber, 1995.

Macmurray, J. (1961). *Science, Art and Religion*. Liverpool: Liverpool University Press.

Mahler, M. (1968). *On Human Symbiosis and the Vicissitudes of Individuation*. New York: International Universities Press.

Marty, P., & de M'Uzan, M. (1963). La pensée opératoire. *Revue Française de Psychanalyse*, 27, 345–356.

Marty, P., Fain, M., de M'Uzan, M., & David, C. (1967). Le cas Dora et le point de vue psychosomatique. *Revue Française de Psychanalyse*, 32, 679–714.

Marx, K. (1844). Economic and philosophical manuscripts (trans. R. Livingston & G. Benton). In: *Early Writings* (pp. 279–400). Harmondsworth, U.K., & New York: Penguin Books, 1975. (latest edition 1984).

Masson, J. M. (1984). *The Assault on Truth: Freud's Suppression of the Seduction Theory*. New York: Farrar Straus & Giroux.

Matos, A. Coimbra de (1980). A extensão da identidade. *Jornal do Médico*, 1879.

Matos, A. Coimbra de (1982). Esquema do núcleo depressivo da personalidade. *O Médico*, 1597.

Matos, A. Coimbra de (1985a). Depressão, depressividade e depressibilidade. *Revista Portuguesa de Psicanálise*, 1: 41–47.

Matos, A. Coimbra de (1985b). De l'hystérie à la dépression. *Revue Française de Psychanalyse* (special issue, 52): 374–379.

Matos, A. Coimbra de (1996). Percursos da identidade. Processos transformadores. *Revista Portuguesa de Pedopsiquiatria*, 11: 23–33.

Matos, A. Coimbra de (1997a). Narcisismo e depressão. *Revista Portuguesa de Psicanálise*, 16: 19–25.

Matos, A. Coimbra de (1997b). Progressos no tratamento psicanalítico. *Acta Médica Portuguesa*, 12: 871–874.

Matte Blanco, I. (1975). *The Unconscious as Infinite Sets*. London: Duckworth Press.

Matte Blanco, I. (1988). *Thinking, Feeling and Being. Clinical Reflections on the Fundamental Antinomy of Human Beings*. London & New York: Tavistock and Routledge.

McGuire, W. (Ed.) (1994). *The Freud–Jung Letters*. Princeton, NJ: Princeton University Press.

Meltzer, D. (1973). *Sexual States of Mind*. Perthshire: Clunie Press.

Meltzer, D. (1980). *Explorations in Autism*. Perthshire: Clunie Press.

Meltzer, D., & Williams, M. (1988). *The Apprehension of Beauty: The Role of Aesthetic Conflict in Development, Violence and Art*. Perthshire: Clunie Press.

Merleau-Ponty, M. (1964a). *L'Oeil et l'esprit*. Paris: Gallimard.

Merleau-Ponty, M. (1964b). *Le visible et l'invisible*. Paris: Gallimard.

Mitchell, S. (1991). Contemporary perspectives on self: Toward an integration. *Psychoanalytic Dialogues 1* (2): 121–147.

Mitchell, S. (1998). Fairbairn's object seeking: Between paradigms. In: *Fairbairn Then and Now*, ed. by N. J. Skolnick & D. E. Scharff (pp. 115–135). Hillsdale, NJ, & London: Analytic Press.

Nietzsche, F. (1882–83). *Thus Spake Zarathustra*, trans. R. J. Hollingdale. London & New York: Penguin Books, 1961 (latest edition 1969).

Nietzsche, F. (1887). *The Gay Science*, trans. Walter Kaufmann. New York: Random House & Vintage Books, 1974.

Ogden, T. (1983). The concept of internal object relations. *International Journal of Psycho-Analysis, 64*: 227–241.

Ogden, T. (1994). *Subjects of Analysis*. Northvale, NJ: Jason Aronson.

Ortega y Gasset, J. (1941). Man has no nature. In: *Towards a Philosophy of History*, trans H. Weyl, E. Clark, & W. Atkinson. Reprinted as: *History as a System*. New York: W. W. Norton, 1961. In: W. Kaufmann (Ed.), *Existentialism: From Dostoevsky to Sartre* (pp. 153–157). New York & Scarborough, Ontario: New American Library, Times Mirror, 1975.

Padel, J. (1995). Review of *The Autonomous Self: The work of J. D. Sutherland*, ed. by Jill Savage Scharff. *International Journal of Psycho-Analysis, 76*: 177.

Pasche, F. (1964). L'anti-narcissisme. In: *A Partir de Freud*. Paris: Payot, 1969.

Pasche, F. (1969). *A Partir de Freud*. Paris: Payot.

Peirce, C. S. (1931). *Collected Papers Vols. I–VIII*, ed. by C. Hartshore & P. Weiss. Cambridge, MA: Harvard University Press.

Pereira, F. (1997a). "A Dupla Face do Símbolo." Paper presented at the Twelfth Colloquium of the Psychoanalytic Portuguese Society.

Pereira, F. (1997b). "The Symbol as Presence". Invited address to the International Conference on Literature and Psychoanalysis, Avila, Spain.

Pereira, F. (1999a). "Fairbairn et l'Esthétique". Paper presented at the International Conference on Literature and Psychoanalysis, Urbino, Italy.

Pereira, F. (1999b). *Sonhar Ainda: do Sonho-desejo-realizado ao Sonho Emblemático*. Lisbon: ISPA.

Pirandello, L. (1921). *Six Personnages en quête d'auteur*. In: *Thétre Complet* (pp. 993–1081). Paris: Gallimard, 1977. [English translation: *Six Characters in Search of an Author*. Harmondsworth: Penguin Books].

Pirandello, L. (1977). *Théatre complet*. Paris: Gallimard.

Racamier, P.-C. (1989). *Antoedipe et ses destins*. Paris: Apsygée Editions.

Racamier, P.-C. (1992). *Le génie des origines*. Paris: Payot.

Racamier, P.-C. (1995). *L'inceste et l'incestuel*. Paris: Apsygée Editions.

Read, H. (1951). Psychoanalysis and the problem of aesthetic value. In *International Journal of Psycho-Analysis, 32* (2).

Reich, W. (1928). On character analysis. In: *The Psycho-Analytic Reader, Vol. 1*, ed. R. Fleiss (pp. 129–147). New York: International Universities Press, 1948.

Reich, W. (1949). *Character Analysis*. New York: Noonday.

Ricoeur, P. (1965). *De l'Interprétation*. Paris: Ed. du Seuil.

Ricoeur, P., 1969: *Le Conflit des Interprétations*. Paris: Seuil [English translation: *The Conflict of Interpretations*. Evanston, IL: Northwestern University Press, 1974].

Ricoeur, P. (1970). *Freud and Philosophy: An Essay on Interpretation*, trans. D. Savage. New Haven, CT: Yale University Press.

Rosenberg, B. (1991). Masochisme mortifère et masochisme gardien de la vie. *Monographies de la Revue française de psychanalyse*, Paris: Presses Universitaires de France.

Rosenfeld, H. (1971). Contribution to the psychopathology of psychotic states: The importance of projective identification in the ego structure and the object relations of the psychotic patient. In: P. Doucet & C. Laurin (Eds.), *Problems of Psychosis* (pp. 115–128). Amsterdam: Excerpta Medica.

Rosenfeld, H. (1987). *Impasse and Interpretation: Therapeutic and Anti-Therapeutic Factors in the Psychoanalytic Treatment of Psychotic, Borderline, and Neurotic Patients*. London: Tavistock.

Rubens, R. (1994). Fairbairn's structural theory. In: J. S. Grotstein & D. B. Rinsley (Eds.), *Fairbairn and the Origin of Object Relations* (pp. 151–173). London: Free Association Books.

Rubens, R. (1998). Fairbairn's theory of depression. In: N. Skolnick & D. Scharff (Eds.), *Fairbairn Then and Now* (pp. 215–234). Hillsdale, NJ, & London: Analytic Press.

Rupprecht-Schampera, U. (1995). The concept of early triangulation as a key to a unified model of hysteria, *International Journal of Psycho-Analysis, 76*, 457–473.

Rycroft, C. (1968a). The function of words. In: *Imagination and Reality*. London: Hogarth Press and Institute of Psycho-Analysis.

Rycroft, C. (1968b). Symbolism and its relationship to the primary and secondary processes. In: *Imagination and Reality*. London: Hogarth Press and Institute of Psycho-Analysis.

Sá-Carneiro, M. (1913). Quasi. In: *Poemas Completos*. Lisbon: Ed. Assírio & Alvim, 1996.

Sami-Ali, M. (1985). La poétique de Hallaj. In *Hallaj—Poèmes Mystiques*. Paris: Sinbad.

Sami-Ali, M. (1989). Poésie et espace chez Ibn' Arabi. In: *Ibn' Arabi: Le Chant de l'Ardent Désir*. Paris: Sinbad.

Sartre, J. P. (1953). *Existential Psychoanalysis*. Chicago, IL: Gateway.

Sartre, J. P. (1956). *Being and Nothingness: An Essay on Phenomenological Ontology [Être et le néanat]*, trans. with an introduction by H. E. Baines. New York: Philosophical Library.

Schafer, R. (1976). *A New Language for Psychoanalysis*. New Haven, CT: Yale University Press.

Scharff, D. E. (1982). *The Sexual Relationship: An Object Relations View of Sex and the Family*. London: Routledge; Northvale, NJ: Jason Aronson.

Scharff, D. E. (1994). *Refinding the Object and Reclaiming the Self*. Northvale, NJ: Jason Aronson.

Scharff, D. E., & Birtles, E. F. (1994). Editors' introduction. In: *From Instinct to Self: Selected Papers of W. R. D. Fairbairn, Vol. 1: Clinical and Theoretical Papers*, ed. by D. Scharff & E. F. Birtles (pp. xi–xxi). Northvale, NJ: Jason Aronson.

Scharff, D. E., & Birtles, E. F. (1997). From instinct to self: the evolution and implications of W. R. D. Fairbairn's theory of object relations. *International Journal of Psychoanalysis, 78* (6): 1085–1103.

Scharff, J. S. (1994). *The Autonomous Self: The Work of J. D. Sutherland*. Northvale, NJ: Jason Aronson.

Scharff, J. S. (1998). Fairbairn and the self: an extension of Fairbairn's theory by Sutherland. In: *Fairbairn Then and Now*, ed. by N. J. Skolnick & D. E. Scharff (pp. 161–175). Hillsdale, NJ, & London: Analytic Press.

Schore, A. N. (1994). *Affect Regulation and the Origin of the Self*. Hillsdale, NJ: Lawrence Erlbaum.

Schore, A. N. (2000). The right brain as the neurobiological substratum of Freud's dynamic unconscious. In D. E. Scharff (Ed.), *The Psychoanalytic Century: The Evolution of Psychoanalysis*. New York & London: Karnac Books.

Segal, H. (1952). A psychoanalytical approach to aesthetics. *International Journal of Psycho-Analysis*. In: *Delusion and Artistic Creativity and Other Psychoanalytic Essays.* London: Free Association Books & Maresfield Library, 1986.

Skolnick, N. J., & Scharff, D. E. (Eds.) (1998). *Fairbairn Then and Now.* Hillsdale, NJ: Analytic Press.

Spezzano, C. (1993). *Affect in Psychoanalysis.* Hillsdale, NJ: Analytic Press.

Steiner, J. (1979). The border between the paranoid-schizoid and the depressive positions in the borderline patient. *British Journal of Medical Psychology, 52*: 385–391.

Steiner, J. (1987). The interplay between pathological organizations and the paranoid-schizoid and depressive positions. *International Journal of Psycho-Analysis, 68*: 69–80.

Steiner, J. (1990a). The defensive function of pathological organizations. In: L. Bryce Boyer & P. Giovacchini (Eds.), *Master Clinicians: On Treating the Regressed Patient.* (pp. 97–116). Northvale, NJ, & London: Jason Aronson.

Steiner, J. (1990b). Pathological organizations, as obstacles to mourning: the role of unbearable guilt. *International Journal of Psycho-Analysis, 71*: 87–94.

Steiner, J. (1992). The equilibrium between the paranoid-schizoid and depressive positions. In: Robin Anderson (Ed.), *Clinical Lectures on Klein and Bion* (pp. 46–58). London & New York: Tavistock/Routledge.

Steiner, J. (1993). *Psychic Retreats: Pathological Organizations in Psychotic, Neurotic and Borderline Patients.* London: Routledge.

Sterba, R. (1934). The fate of the ego in analytic therapy. *International Journal of Psycho-Analysis, 15*: 117–126.

Stern, Daniel (1985). *The Interpersonal World of the Infant.* New York: Basic Books.

Stern, Donnel (1997). *Unformulated Experience: From Dissociation to Imagination.* Hillsdale, NJ: Analytic Press.

Stirner, M. (1845). *The Ego and His Own* [*Der Einzige und Sein Eigentum*], trans. by S. T. Byington. London: Jonathan Cape, 1921.

Styron, W. (1979). *Sophie's Choice.* New York: Random House.

Sutherland, J. D. (1963). Object-relations theory and the conceptual model of psychoanalysis. *British Journal of Medical Psychology 36*: 109–124.

Sutherland, J. D. (1965). Obituary: W. R. D. Fairbairn. *International Journal of Psycho-Analysis, 46*: 245–247.

Sutherland, J. D. (1969). Psychoanalysis in the post industrial society. *International Journal of Psycho-Analysis, 50*: 675–679.

Sutherland, J. D. (1979). "The British object relation theorists: Balint, Winnicott, Fairbairn, and Guntrip". Presented at a scientific meeting of the Association for Psychoanalytic Medicine, May. Unpublished.

Sutherland, J. D. (1983). The self and object relations: a challenge to psychoanalysis. *Bulletin of the Menninger Clinic, 47*: 525–541.

Sutherland, J. D. (1989). *Fairbairn's Journey into the Interior*. Free Association Books, London.

Sutherland, J. D. (1994a). The autonomous self. In: J. S. Scharff (Ed.), *The Autonomous Self: The Work of J. D. Sutherland* (pp. 304–330). Northvale, NJ, & London: Jason Aronson.

Sutherland, J. D. (1994b). Fairbairn and the self. In: J. S. Scharff (Ed.), *The Autonomous Self: The Work of J. D. Sutherland* (pp. 332–349). Northvale, NJ, & London: Jason Aronson.

Sutherland, J. D. (1994c). The self and object relations. In: J. S. Scharff (Ed.), *The Autonomous Self: The Work of J. D. Sutherland* (pp. 285–302). Northvale, NJ, & London: Jason Aronson.

Tausk, V. (1919). On the origin of the influencing machine in schizophrenia. *Psychoanalytic Quarterly, 2*: 519–556.

Thurber, J. (1932). The secret life of Walter Mitty. In: D. Madden (Ed.), *The World of Fiction* (pp. 977–981). Fort Worth, TX: Holt, Rinehart and Winston, 1990.

Todorov, T. (1981). *Mikhaïl Bakhtine: Le Principle Dialogique. Ecrits du Cercle de Bakhtine*. Paris: Ed. du Seuil.

Turquet, P. (1975). Threats to identity in the large group. In: L. Kreeger (Ed.), *The Large Group: Dynamics and Therapy* (pp. 87–144). London: Constable.

Tustin, F. (1981). *Autistic States in Children*. London: Routledge & Kegan Paul.

Van der Kolk, B. (1987). *Psychological Trauma*. Washington, D.C.: American Psychiatric Press.

Vargish, T., & Mook, D. M. (1999). *Inside Modernism: Relativity Theory, Cubism, and Narrative*. New Haven, CT, & London: Yale University Press.

Vermorel, H., & Vermorel, M. (1993). *Sigmund Freud et Romain Rolland, Correspondance 1932–1936. Coll. Histoire de la psychanalyse*, ed. by A. de Mijolla. Paris: Presses Universitaires de France.

Vermorel, H., Clancier, A., & Vermorel, M. (1995). *Freud, judéité, lumières et romantisme. Champs psychanalytiques*. Lausanne: Delachaux et Niestlé.

Whitman, W. (1855). *Song of Myself. Complete Poetry and Selected Prose and Letters,* ed. by E. Holloway (pp. 26–85). London: Nonesuch Press.

Winnicott, D. W. (1951). Transitional objects and transitional phenomena. In: *Collected Papers: Through Paediatrics to Psychoanalysis* (pp. 229–242). London: Tavistock, 1958.

Winnicott, D. W. (1960). Ego distortion in terms of the true and false self. In: *The Maturational Processes and the Facilitating Environment: Studies in the Theory of Emotional Development* (pp. 140–152). London: Hogarth Press & Institute of Psychoanalysis, 1965.

Winnicott, D. W. (1962). Ego integration in child development. In: *The Maturational Processes and the Facilitating Environment* (pp. 56–63). London: Hogarth Press & Institute of Psychoanalysis, 1965.

Winnicott, D. M. (1965). The capacity to be alone. In: *The Maturational Processes and the Facilitating Environment* (pp. 29–36). London: Hogarth Press & Institute of Psychoanalysis.

Winnicott, D. M. (1966). Psycho-somatic illness in its positive and negative aspects. In: *Psycho-Analytic Explorations,* ed. by C. Winnicott, R. Shepherd, & M. Davis (pp. 103–118). London: Karnac, 1989.

Winnicott, D. M. (1971a). Dreaming, fantasying, and living. In: *Playing and Reality* (pp. 26–37). London: Tavistock.

Winnicott, D. M. (1971b). *Playing and Reality.* London: Tavistock.

Winnicott, D. M. (1989). *Psycho-Analytic Explorations,* ed. by C. Winnicott, R. Shepherd, & M. Davis. London: Karnac.

Wisdom, J. O. (1961). A methodological approach to the problem of hysteria. *International Journal of Psycho-Analysis, 42,* 224–237.

INDEX

251